CHILD SEXUAL ABUSE

Child sexual abuse is a major public policy challenge. Many child protection measures were beginning to reduce its occurrence. However, that progress was impeded by online grooming, the downloading of indecent images of children and even their abuse online in real time. This now places major demands on national and international policing. The book brings together groundbreaking case studies from a wide range of settings. As well as family members and those near the home, offenders can also be found in religious, sporting and childcare settings.

This extensive picture is drawn deliberately in order to highlight a split in the academic analysis of child sexual abuse. The mainstream or orthodox view, defended by the author, is that child sexual abuse is an under-reported crime. However, a minority view, presented but criticised, is that it is a moral panic created by public hysteria, child protection experts and campaigning politicians. By the end of the book, this division of academic opinion and its implications for public policy are explored in detail.

The book is essential reading for anyone interested in preventing child sexual abuse and the dilemmas of responding to both victims and perpetrators. It will be of particular use to practitioners in social work, the police and in the mental health professions.

David Pilgrim has spent his career divided between working as a clinical psychologist in the British NHS and researching mental health policy. Now semi-retired, he is Honorary Professor of Health and Social Policy at the University of Liverpool and Visiting Professor of Clinical Psychology at the University of Southampton, UK.

'This book is a vital primer on the contemporary state of child sexual abuse. Pilgrim illuminates how the recent history of the normalisation and trivialisation of child sexual abuse underlies proliferating contemporary scandals. He is an uncompromising witness to the multiple dimensions of the sexual exploitation of children, and attendant cover-up efforts by perpetrators, allies and collusive bystanders. His book establishes that child sexual abuse is a practice that is parasitic on social denial, and only possible when authorities, academics and the community prefer to look the other way. This book is a must-read for students and scholars of child abuse, and for readers looking for a comprehensive understanding of the relationship between trauma and social denial.'

– *Dr Michael Salter, Senior Lecturer, Western Sydney University, Australia, and Associate Editor of* Child Abuse Review

'Survivors of childhood sexual abuse and a wealth of research provide a knowledge base about the impact and extent of abuse in institutional and family settings. Pilgrim presents the facts alongside case examples enabling analysis of theories, investigations and media reports. The book provides a unique, immensely important and timely contribution to the theory and practice of child sexual abuse. Pilgrim introduces concepts of "moral stupor" and "webs of complicity" whereby non-offenders do not challenge offending behaviour. In this courageous, measured and accessible book, Pilgrim interrogates the multiple barriers to challenging child sexual abuse and effective collective responsibility for the protection of children.'

– *Dr Liz Davies, Reader in Child Protection (Emeritus), London Metropolitan University, UK*

CHILD SEXUAL ABUSE

Moral Panic or State of Denial?

David Pilgrim

LONDON AND NEW YORK

First published 2018
by Routledge
2 Park Square, Milton Park, Abingdon, Oxon OX14 4RN

and by Routledge
711 Third Avenue, New York, NY 10017

Routledge is an imprint of the Taylor & Francis Group, an informa business

British Library Cataloguing-in-Publication Data
A catalogue record for this book is available from the British Library

Library of Congress Cataloging-in-Publication Data
A catalog record for this book has been requested

ISBN: 978-1-138-57836-4 (hbk)
ISBN: 978-1-138-57837-1 (pbk)
ISBN: 978-1-351-26456-3 (ebk)

Typeset in Bembo
by Out of House Publishing

CONTENTS

ACKNOWLEDGEMENTS

The idea for the book came out of conversations with an old friend and NHS colleague, Pat Harvey, about the mental health impact of child sexual abuse on its victims and the range of forces in society that operate to suppress knowledge of that link. Further conversations with my friends Cas Schneider and Paul O'Reilly helped me clarify my thoughts on the connection between the clinical world and its wider social context.

Members of my family have tolerated my hobby horse about child sexual abuse in the past few years. They have also given me helpful feedback on aspects of its content and the rationale of the chapters. My special thanks go then to Anne Rogers, Nigel Rogers, Steve Pilgrim, Jack Pilgrim, Maria Andrews and John Raynor.

The chapter on Australia was helped by feedback from colleagues attending workshops on child sexual abuse I conducted in Sydney and Melbourne in 2016 for the Australian Psychological Society. I am also grateful to staff at the Sydney Jones Library, University of Liverpool, for facilitating my access to the restricted Fairbridge Society collection of documents on the 'forgotten children'. I am particularly grateful to Michael Salter (Western Sydney University) for his helpful comments on a number of chapters. From Dublin, I have been helped by Niall Meehan and Marie Keenan to make a start on understanding the peculiarities of clerical abuse in Ireland and the generalities they might illuminate.

Some valued UK colleagues have included Andrew Kendrick, Sarah Nelson, Liz Davies, Helen Williams and Sarah Goode, whose personal support has been very useful, along with the insights of their own writings on our shared topic. I am particularly grateful to Sarah for her patience in reading the draft chapters at the end of the book, which turn to the obstacles within academia itself to exploring the grim reality of child sexual abuse, and what, if anything, we can do about it.

During the production of the book I tested the deep, and sometimes dark, water of academic opinion in social science by putting aspects of my ideas into journal submissions. That exercise was salutary. After a number of rejections, eventually I managed to get some papers into peer-reviewed journals about the serious short-comings of a moral panic position. But *en route* to these successes I met a number of hostile anonymous reviewers, who were clearly outraged by my attack upon the sacred cow of social constructionism, that has in my view at times undermined social justice since the modish 'postmodern turn'.

Mervyn Hartwig, the editor of the *Journal of Critical Realism*, supported me in the face of attempts to impede the appearance of one paper about that sacred cow. Mervyn's recent replacement at the journal, Leigh Price, has also been very helpful in supplying me with papers on the social science of conspiracies, which helped me to kick-start the second chapter of the book. Thanks too to all the hostile reviewers and objectors; they confirmed that I needed to push on with my critique of strong social constructionism and loose libertarian special pleading, when they are applied to child sexual abuse.

Over the past few years I have worked with a group of like-minded colleagues who are interested in what has *happened* to people with mental health problems (rather than only what is wrong with them). Child sexual abuse has been one aspect of this work in the group, so my final thanks go to Lucy Johnstone, Mary Boyle, Eleanor Longden, John Read, Dave Harper, Richard Bentall, Peter Kinderman, John Cromby and Jacqui Dillon. Jacqui's knowledge of child sexual abuse is impor-tant, as is her work with the Hearing Voices Network. All royalties from this book are being donated to the latter organisation.

INTRODUCTION

In the past few years, the sexual abuse of children has been reported on most days in the mass media, often being headline news. News of predators from the world of politics, light entertainment and sport has jostled for attention with report after report of recent organised child sexual exploitation on the streets of England. This book will explore this complex picture.

I will be addressing an unresolved crisis about child sexual abuse (CSA), which has two aspects. The first is that people disagree about whether it is an overstated or understated public policy challenge. Second, people disagree about what to do about it, especially in the face of an increase in online offending in the wake of the mass availability of the Internet.

Although it may not always seem to be the case from reporting in the mass media, most of the sexual abuse of children actually occurs at home. However, the scenario of those outside the family grooming and assaulting children, male and female, is not a scarcity, as will become evident in the coming pages. Moreover, the explosion of interest in this trend has become a frequently reported public policy matter, implicating 'the great and the good', as well as those who our society traditionally has trusted to care for children. The chapters ahead examine this widespread political concern through a series of case studies from Anglophone countries in which perpetrators of CSA have come from ordinary families, light entertainment, politics, academic life, religious organisations, nurseries, schools, sports coaching, youth work and urban street life.

For most lay people, the term 'paedophilia' refers to all adult sexual interest in children and the abusive acts it stimulates in its wake. The professional literature is more nuanced. Recent medical definitions separate such a sexual interest in pre-pubescent children ('true' paedophilia) from that orientated towards post-pubescent young people, who are designated legally to be still children. In current psychiatric terminology, the term 'hebephilia' is used in relation to an adult who has a sexual interest in the latter group. (Another technical term, 'ephebophilia', is used to describe adults with a sexual interest in older adolescents, who are typically above the age of legal consent.) In line with its everyday use, the term paedophilia will be used to cover both of the first two groups unless there is a pointed reason to do otherwise. I will also keep reminding the reader that paedophilia is only a crime when the desire and orientation are put into practical form. Genuinely celibate paedophiles do not abuse children or masturbate to indecent images of them. Other distinctions in the literature to note for clarity include sexual abuse in childhood committed by other children and it can be at the hands of adults, who more typically have sexual relationships with adults. The fact sheet below summarises this complexity for the reader.

Child sexual abuse fact sheet

Over 90% of the perpetrators of CSA are already well known to victims (in their home or immediate network). Thus, less than 10% of children sexually assaulted are victims of true 'stranger danger', even though this receives more mass media attention. Victims are exposed to sexual infections and pregnancy and may show immediate signs of psychological distress. The long-term impacts of CSA include repeatedly proven raised levels of mental health problems, suicide, relationship difficulties and substance misuse.

Between 1 and 2% of the male population have a persistent and exclusive sexual interest in children, but up to 20% of men report some degree of sexual attraction to children, whether or not that is ever acted upon. For this reason, paedophiles and hebephiles (the first group), who act on their desires, are not the only adults who might sexually assault children. The second group may have regular sexual relationships with adults and additionally may offend against children rarely, routinely or episodically. There is a distinction between a sexual *orientation* towards children and CSA. Some may use indecent images of children alone and not assault children directly. We have few precise estimates about the frequency of activity linked to these sub-groups. The perpetrators of CSA are from very diverse backgrounds: only male gender defines the trend.

Not all sexual abuse of children is by adult males. A minority of perpetrators are women (estimates vary from 1–40% but the consensus is 5%) and some are other children (estimates vary from 25–33%). The latter group includes those already victimised, who re-enact sexual acts with peers and who might at times sexually approach adults they encounter. Sexual activity between teenagers is common and legally ambiguous (when one is just over the age of legal consent and the other not). This 'Romeo and Juliet' scenario is a legal and ethical grey area in developed societies and dealt with variably.

While in common everyday terminology all adults sexually offending against children might be dubbed 'paedophiles' or 'paedos', in the professional literature, a sexual orientation towards children is divided into three groups. True paedophiles are those noted above who have an exclusive and persistent interest in pre-pubescent children. Adults with a persistent interest in young teenagers are called 'hebephiles'. 'Ephebophiles' are those with a persistent interest in older teenagers (typically over the age of legal consent). These are not fixed categories – some adults offend against those in a wide age range but many do become fixated in a persistent way about a particular age group. This means that those offending against children who come to the recurrent attention of the criminal justice system will tend, as they age, still to retain an interest in one age profile of potential victims. These are the 'hard core' recidivists who may accumulate many victims across the life span.

Gay and straight adults may have a sexual interest in children. However, because heterosexuality predominates in society more generally and most perpetrators are male, then there is a higher rate of girl victims (especially in home settings). Where gender segregation occurs (for example, in residential institutions) then same-sex offending *ipso facto* is more likely. Explanations for perpetrator motivation have included biological, psychological and social factors and there is no 'magic bullet' to either prevent sexual offending against children or to reduce the probability of reoffending in particular individuals. Recidivism rates vary with a range from those with a single offence in a lifetime to incorrigible offenders, seemingly untouched by repeated periods in prison and treatment programmes.

Because adult–child sexual contact is a taboo, and today typically criminal globally, it is difficult to estimate both the number of first cases (incidence) and cumulative or aggregating cases (prevalence) in a particular population. The consensus in the literature is that only around one in three cases of sexual assault on children is formally reported to the police in developed societies. Of those, only some proceed to successful prosecution. Accordingly, recorded sexual crimes against children only reflect a fraction of actual cases.

Debates are common in the social science literature about CSA. For some, it is a 'moral panic', but others emphasise its underestimation and the real physical and psychological harm done to victims and its social costs, especially for the budgets of the police, mental health, and drug and alcohol services. In the first camp are those who emphasise that it is a 'socially constructed' problem that arises from particular rules in particular times and places ('mores').

Recent historical context

This book is concerned with CSA in recent times and one of its aims is to put its topic into historical context. However, the time frame is not a look back at Ancient Greece (a period favoured conveniently by pederasts and their apologists). Instead, I am concerned only with modern history because our views about adult–child sexual contact have changed so quickly and dramatically over the past 50 years.

One legacy of the 1960s and 1970s has been that sexual minorities have been included, not excluded, from citizenship. Beginning with the civil rights campaigns in the early 1960s led by Martin Luther King and ending in the late 1970s with assertive 'second wave' feminism, a whole range of people previously disvalued and even criminalised were brought into mainstream society and their human rights recognised. Some of this was about the simple recognition of human equality as a moral matter and some was about legal rights, such as the equal treatment of homosexuals in relation to marriage or age of sexual consent.

Those 'New Social Movements' reflected very honourable struggles; they were aimed at establishing and enlarging the rights of people, who were female, homosexual, young, 'of colour', disabled or old. Arguments about 'speciesism' even at times extended human compassion and rights-based claims to animals. The work of these 'liberation' movements is not complete globally today and some groups remain debarred, in whole or part, from the rights of individual autonomy and full citizenship. For example, in some parts of the world homosexuality remains criminalised and this can culminate in the state execution of gay men.

Another aspect of the move towards respecting rights of autonomy for all is that some groups, even in the most progressive socially reformed societies are consistently exempted. J. S. Mill made a case that children, idiots and lunatics were justifiably excluded from citizenship, on grounds of their absent or lost reason. And it remains the case today, following Mill's strictures, that the question of 'mental capacity' justifies not citizenship and full human personal autonomy but instead a preferred policy option of official and celebrated state paternalism or, in formal legal terms, *parens patriae*.

Whether we endorse or query state paternalism, children are for now deemed to be in need of protection or 'safeguarding'. Their status as rational and reflective adults has yet to be established, even if all concerned recognise that this is a gradual developmental process, not a black-and-white matter of present or absent human agency. We can all agree that an average eight-year-old is more reflective and morally autonomous than an average two-year-old. But we all agree as well that they are both children. State paternalism tends to be enshrined in law and becomes itself a right of sorts. The right to be protected from economic or sexual exploitation is a core defining feature offered to us about good child protection policies by the United Nations.

We can see that for those *with* mental capacity, political successes are all around us in legislation to protect citizenship for all and to safeguard people from hate crimes. It is also seen in shifts in cultural attitudes towards several social groups, who previously were the focus of hostility, disgust, derision and arbitrary and unwarranted physical violence. However, the notion of 'liberation' also had an ambiguous edge. In particular, the 'sexual revolution of the 1960s' tended to be a permissive cue for some men to act licentiously. Feminists might note that the sexual exploitation of women and children may have been encouraged not reduced by the 'sexual revolution'.

During the 1970s, those who wanted to enjoy sexual contact with children attempted to special plead that they too were an oppressed minority, who deserved tolerance by those without the same proclivities. The great majority of that special pleading came from men, reflecting the gender bias in paedophilia. However, women at times, albeit rarely, can sexually offend against children and they too may want to justify their sexual interest.

This book then, in part, is about a 'liberation movement' that was left behind or which never properly got off the ground. If that assumption is in any doubt at the outset, let us compare and contrast events in the 1970s with those in the past ten years. Following the Stonewall Riots of 1969, Gay Liberation Activists globally were emboldened to campaign for their rights. A small offshoot of that was the formation in Britain of the Paedophile Information Exchange (PIE).

Alongside the PIE activity, other events of the 1970s illustrate how much has changed over time. At the start of the 1970s, Gary Glitter had innumerable hits with his Glitter Band. In 1974, he appeared on BBC Television's *Clunk Click* (the pilot for the famous *Jim'll Fix It*) with Jimmy Savile, snuggled up with two girls of around 12 or 13. Glitter, gripping them tightly, says excitedly, 'I get two'. Savile chuckles in response, 'You get two. I should be giving girls away'. By the end of the 1970s, Pope John Paul II embarked on a long succession of international visits, spreading peace and love and confirming the benign authority and dominium of the credo about 'One Holy, Catholic and Apostolic Church'.

Wind forward to the present. Gary Glitter (real name Paul Gadd) is now an imprisoned child rapist and Jimmy Savile has been declared posthumously as the most prolific predatory sex offender known to British criminal history. Moreover, the Catholic Church for now remains mired in a seemingly unending damage limitation exercise about paedophiles in its midst.

And yet, justifications and rationalisations for adult–child contact did not die with the closure of PIE in 1984. One thing that has not changed since the 1970s is that some people have been willing to offer elaborate justifications about adult–child sexual contact. At the centre of those justifications is the notion that the public reaction to paedophilia has simply been a 'moral panic'.

Moral panic?

The 'moral panic' position basically argues that there is an unwarranted or disproportionate public reaction of disgust, anger or anxiety about some form of transgression linked to a minority social group. Here I will simply note that part of the current debate about paedophilia is whether its public policy aspects (especially in relation to claims about its prevalence and harmful impact) are exaggerated or even an irrelevant diversion from more important and pressing matters.

A related argument from libertarians is anti-Statism: the *parens patriae* trend I noted above is viewed as being inherently oppressive or wrong-headed or both. For this reason, some libertarians can be found queuing up to deflect public hostility from paedophiles, even today. One group of apologists has been those arising from a defunct ultra-left group, the 'Revolutionary Communist Party' (RCP). This morphed into the 'Institute for Ideas' and drives the online debating forum *Spiked*, and it has adopted this second wave of moral panic reasoning, with the first being from PIE members and their supporters.

A leading publicist for the ex-RCP Group is Frank Furedi, a sociologist. On March 3, 2015, David Cameron announced that it would be a criminal offence for public-sector workers to fail to report causes for concern about the sexual exploitation of children, on grounds of their wilful neglect. For Cameron, child sexual exploitation was now a 'national threat'. Mandatory reporting could of course be required but does not itself entail criminalising non-reporters, as Cameron's critics immediately noted. Furedi was interviewed that evening on BBC Radio 4 about this move to mandatory reporting. He argued that it weakens the capacity of social workers to act effectively and that they should take risks about their ways of working. He argued his points with no evidence but ideologically (even though another interviewee on the programme offered evidence from international policy comparisons that have demonstrated improved child protection). Indeed, one reason that child abuse has declined in frequency in the past 20 years is *because* the safeguarding of children is now taken more seriously than it used to be. As we will see when looking at the norms of the 1970s, children were exposed to sexual predation in ways that would now shock many of us.

The day of the interview with Furedi was the one in which the report on a child sexual exploitation gang in Oxford was released. As will become clear from the description of Rotherham and its aftermath, the counter-argument to libertarians is that standing by and not reporting and acting was part of the pattern of complicity that led to hundreds of children being sexually violated in British towns. Rather than there being a moral panic, the problem is that for years agents of the state and adults in a range of roles have not been concerned and responsible *enough* about their duties to protect children. Hence, the opposite view from that of Frank Furedi was offered earlier in the day when BBC Radio 4 interviewed Alexis Jay, the chair of the report on sexual exploitation in Rotherham. She completely endorsed David Cameron's view that CSA was indeed a 'national threat' and that current recorded levels of abuse were underestimates. She argued that this under-reporting was particularly the case in relation to ethnic minorities and boys.

A critical realist analysis

At present, an ideological struggle is taking place in academic circles between those who have studied child sexual victimisation as a harmful and wrongful process and outcome and those who focus on it as a social construction. These reflect quite distinct philosophical positions in social science. On the one hand, a naïve realist or positivist stance in the first grouping may simply be taking social norms for granted and assume that adult–child sexual contact is self-evidently wrong and harmful. On the other hand, in the second group are those who take it for granted that CSA is largely or wholly a moral panic, conjured up collusively by child protection experts, sensationalist mass media and politicians gaining from being 'moral entrepreneurs'.

As this book is guided by the philosophy of critical realism, here at the outset I will note its main premises. This may help the reader to understand why I have written each chapter in the particular way I have. Critical realism is a philosophy (not a theory) that offers itself to both social and natural science to clarify what can and what cannot be said confidently in any branch of academic inquiry. It stands in a middle position philosophically between naïve realism (positivism) on one side and idealism (versions of social constructionism) on the other. Naïve realists tend to reduce reality only to what is empirically proven already (empiricism). They also assume that the same lawful causal relationships operate in all times and places. By contrast, critical realists distinguish between empirical knowledge and what actually happens in the world (the former is only part of the latter). Also, a wider and deeper domain of the real contains past events and those still to occur. Moreover, not all actual events are empirically recorded or known. Thus, reality is complex and exists beyond the empirical alone.

Thus, this commitment is to a view of layered or laminated reality, some aspects of which are known and some not, some in the past and some still in potential. Some forms of reality entail a very slow-moving and relatively stable process (such as rock formations) whereas other aspects of reality are unstable and often changeable across time and place, sometimes very quickly (such as the downturn in 2008 of international capitalism or the abrupt rise of ISIS). Social systems in particular are in constant flux and are open systems, which makes predictions very difficult. A final way that critical realists are different from naïve realists is that they deny that we can separate facts from values. Facts and theories are value-laden: we ask questions for particular reasons and we interpret our findings in particular ways.

For those readers accustomed now to social constructionist arguments, this might all sound reasonably agreeable, because it sees knowledge as being context-driven and values, not just facts, are examined sceptically. However, critical realists also reject the premise of social constructionism that *everything* is about knowledge or language fluxing from one situation to another. This (true enough) *aspect* of human activity is called 'epistemological relativism' but it is only *one part* of a complex picture. Social constructionists tend to rest on their laurels with this insight and then set about producing 'narratives' and 'discourses' (and even the unending spiral of 'discourses on discourse'). This reduces our complex existence to the matter of language: linguistic reductionism.

By contrast, critical realists are committed to the premise above about complex and layered reality, which exists *independently* of our thoughts, speech and ideology. Thus, critical realism accepts the need to consider epistemological relativism but we must first prioritise 'ontological realism'. The first (way of construing the world) is called the 'transitive' aspect of reality and the second the 'intransitive' aspect of reality. In other words, reality is not merely socially constructed; it is mind-independent. It will be there when you and I are dead and even when and if the human species disappears. Basically, one of the clichés of social constructionism that you might hear ('everything is socially constructed') is simply wrong. We construe the world; we do not construct it. Those construals can lead to *actions* (real events) on our part as human agents to reinforce our external *status quo* or in some way or other transform it. Thus, critical realism also emphasises the role of human agency in the world we all inhabit and are constrained and shaped by.

The final point that differentiates social constructionism from critical realism is that the former, by singularly emphasising differences across time and place (i.e. historical and geographical relativism), can lead us with no benchmarks about the truth or any sense of right and wrong. In other words, epistemological relativism can morph quickly into judgemental relativism, offering us no sense of which view of reality is more likely to be true. What critical realists argue instead is that although we should approach reality very cautiously (for reasons that include the time–space flux question) we still can take our best shot about truth statements (and what is morally correct for the survival and advancement of the human species). In their own terminology, critical realists favour 'judgemental rationalism' over 'judgemental relativism'. The implications of these distinctions for the investigations described in this book are two-fold.

First, we should do our best to investigate CSA in an honest and systematic way, albeit sceptically: we must adopt ontological realism about the topic. Children really are sexually abused in their families and elsewhere and we should measure this process in the best ways we can and think about the conditions that led to its emergence. Victims really do suffer its consequences and we should be honest about the reality of that suffering and its scale. Some adults really are sexually preoccupied with children and many will act on those desires regularly and hide their incorrigible intentions and actions from those around them. Some of those really do conspire criminally to sexually exploit children. Some of those conspirators really have used their political and intellectual influence to promote a liberalisation of policy about enacted paedophilia and to hide its consequences from social accountability. Adults with a sexual interest in children really will use both soft power ('grooming') to achieve their ends and some will also resort to hard power (coercive intrusions, including rape) if that fails. The trade in indecent images of children really is overwhelming the best efforts of the police. Each image downloaded by the masturbating 'non-contact' offender has entailed real sexual violence against a child. The existence of child brides in developing countries today really does constitute an international scandal.

Second, because CSA is both a moral and legal concern globally today, what we say and do not say about it matters. We can seek to clarify its scale, define its features and uncover wrongdoing or we can choose to dismiss it all as a socially constructed moral panic; a storm in a teacup driven by mass media hyperbole and the irrationality and repressive and puritanical impulses of the moral majority.

That broad separation of two positions is what I come to discuss by the end of the book. That separation reflects a serious and significant ideological division in academia at present between the moral panic claimers on the one hand and orthodox child protection workers and researchers on the other. In this book I will do my best to persuade the reader that they should remain in, or join, the second camp of argument. Once there, they should defend children not only against the sexual advances of adults but also against the misguided, or even wilfully deceitful, arguments of some in academia, which trivialise the scale, harmfulness and wrongfulness of adult–child sexual contact.

The subtitle of the book takes its lead from a doyen of moral panic theory, Stanley Cohen, who studied both moral panics and what he called 'states of denial'. The latter refer to the various ways in society in which we might suppress our awareness of oppression and human suffering. That transition from one interest to another created a tension for Cohen. By the end of his career, he made frank statements about the pitfalls of his own social scientific tradition of social constructionism (or constructivism). He made particular reference to both torture and child abuse when expressing this *angst*. I think that Cohen's honest ambivalence was useful in illuminating why we should now adopt a critical realist approach to CSA, rather than adhere to a moral panic understanding. For this reason, in the final chapters of the book I spend some time unpicking Cohen's confessed regrets about his own work. His honesty was invaluable.

1

SLEAZY POLITICIANS AND CELEBRITIES

Introduction

In July 2015, the British Home Secretary, Theresa May, seemed to have at last acquired a trustworthy lawyer, Justice Lowell Goddard, to head up a public inquiry into claims of extensive CSA from the past.[1] The start of the inquiry had been delayed for over a year because May's first and second suggestions for the leadership of the inquiry (Baroness Butler-Sloss and Lady Fiona Woolf) failed because of claims of their personal bias as part of the British Establishment.[2] Goddard is from New Zealand and so May literally had to go to the other side of the world to find a credible leader for the task. And even her term in the role was short and controversial. More on this below, but first I trace the political history of the ongoing Independent Inquiry into Child Sexual Abuse in England and Wales.

The British Establishment

In 2012, the Metropolitan Police launched Operation Fairbank to investigate historical accusations about CSA at the hands of those in the 'British Establishment'.[3] By March 2015, the Independent Police Complaints Commission (IPCC) was asked by 'the Met' to examine serious allegations not only about politicians, but also a police cover-up during a period between the 1970s and 2005.[4]

The following main allegations were to be examined by the IPCC in relation to what the BBC in its news reports called 'serious high-level corruption' in relation to children being supplied to paedophiles in Westminster:

1. That there had been 'failures to properly investigate child sex abuse offences in South London and further information about criminal allegations against a politician being dropped'.

2. That investigations into 'sex parties' with young male victims in South West London were halted because the police officers involved were 'too near prominent people'.

3. That a document with an identifier from the Houses of Parliament was found at the address of a known paedophile, which showed a link with 'highly prominent individuals'. The latter named were MPs and senior police officers. Despite this primary evidence, the Met had taken no further action.

4. That a witness statement of a victim was altered in order to remove the name of a senior politician.

5. That details of child sex abuse at the hands of senior politicians were covered up by the police.

6. That a surveillance operation of a child abuse ring was closed down because of 'high-profile people being involved'.

7. That some police officers themselves sexually abused a boy and then carried out surveillance upon him.

The very idea that politicians might sexually abuse children may be shocking. However, in the light of the points I explore later in the book about abusers being spread across the whole of society, we should not be surprised at all. We would *expect* a certain quota of any adult group to be paedophiles. Politicians are no exception to the rule of the dispersed character of CSA in modern societies. The importance of this first chapter then is not to shed a light on our political class, for containing abusers uniquely or exceptionally, but on the special privileges it tends to enjoy, once that activity emerges. In particular, this relates to the episodic collusive role of the police and the secret services in order to cover up active paedophiles within the political elite.

As a powerful wing of the state, the police are in a unique position to either amplify pre-existing privileges or challenge them. George Orwell noted in his diaries that although the political left are understandably suspicious of the police and its hard state power to defend capitalism, police officers are often highly aware of social injustice because of the very work they do. Because so much of criminality they encounter is linked to the economic powerlessness of the 'underclass',[5] they may be insecure when, much more rarely, they have to deal with the rich and the powerful and are expected to confront them about serious crimes.

The case of Sir Jeremy Thorpe MP

The early investigation of the Leader of the Liberal Party, Jeremy Thorpe, about his lover Norman Scott (for whose murder Thorpe was later tried as a co-conspirator) was slowed down because police visiting him were embarrassed and instinctively deferential. They could not bring themselves to confront such a suave man of 'high breeding', with the claims of homosexual contact.[6]

The relationship with Scott, a stable lad and later male model, began in 1961 when homosexuality was illegal in Britain and the police were instructed to inquire by their Special Branch colleagues. Under the canopy of 'national security', the latter force can issue directives at whim. As will become clear below, when we think of 'the police' we need to extend the concept to Special Branch and from that onto deeper security services such as MI5 and MI6.

The Thorpe case was also an example of Establishment bias and bonds in the judiciary. The hostile summing up by the judge against the prosecution in the conspiracy to murder trial, when Thorpe was acquitted, is now notorious and became the focus of satirical attack.[7] That ambivalence and bias about those charged with investigating and prosecuting those 'in high places' comes through too in the topic of this chapter.

A key figure and counter-example in this story was the Metropolitan Police officer who tried to hold a line about the pursuit of truth and blow the whistle on what he suspected. Clive Driscoll, a retired chief inspector from the force, was investigating politicians and a paedophile ring in 1988. When he began to name names in case conferences, he encountered resistance from his managers and was moved to other duties. He has now become a key informant for BBC investigations about child sex abuse in the past in London.[8]

Driscoll embodied and exemplified our hopes for decency in our police. The fact that he was a failed whistle-blower highlights that the British police still have much to learn about upholding the law 'without fear or favour'. This involves not just the problem of the police investigating itself, (even the 2015 inquiry triggered by the IPCC was handed over to the police to action) but also the police acting as the guardian of other parts of the state. The tendency of those in power to protect their own is not peculiar to Britain as the Belgian case study in Box 1.1 indicates.

BOX 1.1 THE BELGIAN PARALLEL

In 2004 in Belgium, a sadistic paedophile, Marc Dutroux, who had imprisoned, tortured and eventually killed girls, with the complicity of his wife, was put on trial and found guilty. He was arrested in 1996 and when the story first broke a mass demonstration of over 300,000 people took to the streets of Brussels in protest. The time lapse between arrest and successful conviction is one of many unnerving aspects of this case. Another was that two girls he kept in a dungeon, actually starved to death during a period when he received a short sentence for thieving. Despite being found guilty in the 1980s for child rape, Dutroux only served 4 years of his 12-year sentence. In the 8-year interim after 1996 it emerged that, as with the British case, there was police complicity and that senior politicians and other members of the Belgian 'Establishment' were implicated in a paedophile network. A link to that network was the Brussels businessman Jean Michel Nihoul. In 2002, the investigative journalist Olenka Frenkiel pieced together the story for *The Observer* newspaper, showing how Dutroux was part of a criminal network that had been shaped and 'played' by Nihoul.[9] Although arrested and tried, he was released after only a short sentence, raising suspicions that the criminal justice system protected Nihoul in order that he in turn would protect other paedophiles, including police officers, judges and politicians.

Frenkiel presented her findings on the Belgian case study in a BBC documentary and it contained an interview with a police officer who, like Driscoll in the 1980s, had been blocked from further investigations. His managers too realised that senior Establishment figures were emerging as part of the paedophile network that was supplied with victims by Dutroux and other criminals. Children abused at those paedophile parties gave accounts in Frenkiel's documentary of Nihoul being a sadistic participant. However, when brought to trial he was not convicted as a co-defendant in relation to the Dutroux murders but instead only for criminal conspiracy and drugs charges. Nihoul received a 5-year sentence, Dutroux life with no release and his wife received 30 years.

Thus, the 'end point' perpetrators eventually got their just desserts but the brains behind the crime, Nihoul, who arrogantly dubbed himself 'The Beast of Brussels', was barely punished by the state. He was part of the exploitation of children in what was simply another criminal 'racket'. In Belgium, hitmen tracked and threatened investigating magistrates. State lawyers were being driven around in bulletproof cars in Brussels at the turn of this century: an extraordinary scenario in Northern Europe. The Belgian case reminds us that paedophilia is multi-faceted. The selfish need of some adults to use children for personal sexual satisfaction may be at its centre but there are other pertinent layers to consider of commercial exploitation, involvement of agents of the state and organised violence against those trying to protect victims or seek justice for them.

The challenge of challenging state power

If we think then of an axis of power between politicians and the police, which might be closed and corrupt rather than open and benign in its workings, then the 'VIP paedophile ring' is a good case study. Paedophiles from any part of society who want to act on their desires conspire, of necessity, in order to avoid detection. Paedophiles 'in high places' have more to lose but they also have more resources (cultural, political and financial) at their disposal to avoid shame and prosecution. Moreover, the inner dynamics of Establishment power take on a particular life of their own, even before there is a risk of scrutiny from without.

Tim Fortescue MP, who died in 2008, was Ted Heath's Chief Whip between 1970 and 1973. In a BBC documentary about the role of the Whip in party politics in 1998, he revealed that when MPs had problems, then he would do all that he could to help them. In this pastoral role, as he put it in the particular language of the British public-school system, he would do his best to 'get a chap out of trouble'. But this was in exchange for voting loyalty when required. He gave two examples casually in passing: problems of debt and problems with 'small boys'.[10]

To confirm this pact of mutual backscratching, Ted Heath kept a 'dirt book' of these personal difficulties revealed to the Whip, in order to keep his troops in line. Thus, there is an inner working of power, where 'a nod is as good as a wink' to colleagues to keep a group secret. Complicity with wrongdoing and strong group loyalty within the power elites then become opposite sides of the same coin. Nothing has to be said explicitly in the subtle but powerful bonds of trust between 'gentlemen'.

The case of Sir Cyril Smith MP

As well as that inner dynamic of party political loyalty, the 'Westminster village' has relied on the police to keep its secrets about CSA hidden from public view. On the day that the IPCC announced its concerns about historical abuse and the Met cover-up (March 16, 2015) BBC *Newsnight* began with a piece on Cyril Smith MP. It reported for the first time on a three-month investigation in the early 1980s in South London. Detectives had kept six addresses in South London under surveillance, where they believed that paedophiles were holding sex parties. They raided one of these venues in Lambeth and, amongst others, found Smith. He was arrested and taken to a nearby police station.[11]

During the detention period when Smith was interviewed and paperwork prepared, a senior officer, till then unknown to those working on the case, appeared and ordered them to release him and destroy all records of the arrest. The latter included notebooks, photographs and video recordings. Defiance of his order, the senior officer insisted, would lead to the arresting detectives being prosecuted under the Official Secrets Act (OSA). This was a dedicated operation involving the crime squad from the Met as well as specialist detectives seconded from the Yorkshire force.

Clearly until 2015, when the story eventually came out, those officers were intimidated into silence by the threat of the OSA. Although the latter was, and still is, intended in spirit to be limited in use to protect matters of grave national security, in Britain it has been used in a wider manner at times to keep public servants in quiet compliance. The Act at that time was from 1911 and its Section 2 did provide for the possibility of the prosecution of any public servant who disclosed entrusted information. However, even then a public interest argument had to be made for the prosecution and approved by the Attorney General. In this case, it is inconceivable in practice that the officers would have actually been prosecuted but the threat of it carried the day.

In 1989, the Act was revised and in that modernised form even the tiny theoretical risk of a police officer, in the course of their legitimate duties, being prosecuted completely disappeared. The remaining reticence of officers now coming forward after 30 years of silence may be more psychological than about legal threats to their careers or pensions. After such a time lapse, they might be accused of early original complicity and so they may now be tempted to let 'sleeping dogs lie', in order to save face.

Back in the early 1980s, in exchange for responding to the OSA threat, the detectives were assured that Smith would no longer take any further part in public life. This was not true: he continued as a Liberal MP for Rochdale until 1992. He died a free man in 2010 and the extent of his criminality in relation to the abuse of boys (he enjoyed spanking his entrapped victims) only came to light posthumously.

At least one of the arresting officers provided an account of the chicanery over 30 years later to the BBC. He was still so cautious about his disclosure and the threat of the OSA that he would only relay his account to BBC journalists via an intermediary. That account noted how, working in shifts, the detective team had gathered evidence of men abusing boys of around 14 years of age. Using a co-operative caretaker, they had installed a hidden camera at the venue where Smith was arrested. Thus, this was a planned and systematic inquiry with a strong evidence base, which was on the cusp of successful completion.

Significantly, not only was Smith caught on camera but so was a senior member of Britain's intelligence service and two serving police officers.[12] For such a strong and expensive operation to be shut down in that way then political intervention was highly likely, mediated by Special Branch officers.[13] With evidence before them, arrests made and a successful prosecution in the offing about abused children, the stakes must have been high for both those invoking the OSA and those intimidated by it.

Soon, the conspiracy of silence within the police spread elsewhere, for example to the Lancashire force when local detectives began to take an initial interest in the crimes and misdemeanours of Cyril Smith in Rochdale.[14] Back in London, according to the informant for this BBC piece, Smith was subsequently arrested on a second occasion at a different sex party in Streatham and taken to a different police station. The night desk sergeant there, who wanted to book him in for custody, was reprimanded by his commanding officer. But the 1980s was not the first period when the police had become aware of Smith as a sadistic pederast.

In the 1960s, Smith helped to set up a residential home for troubled boys in Rochdale: Cambridge House. By the end of that decade, eight residents gave witness statements to Lancashire police, in which they said that Smith molested and enjoyed spanking them. The local Criminal Investigation Department prepared an 80-page summary of the evidence, which seemed to give credibility to the boys and pointed the finger at Smith. But a friend of Smith, the local Labour MP at the time, Jack McCann, spoke to the Director of Public Prosecutions advocating Smith's innocence. (Smith had previously been the Labour mayor of Rochdale before switching parties.) Local Liberals harassed police officers to drop the case. This political lobbying prevailed and the file was marked 'NFA' (no further action). The file was sent to be locked in a safe at Special Branch in Lancashire.[15]

In 1977, MI5 took an interest in the file and requested that it was sent to them from Special Branch by courier. In Rochdale at the time, the local press was still printing concerns about Smith. The leader of the Liberals at the time David (now Lord) Steel was asked to take action about the accusations against Smith by journalists. His office replied dismissively, 'it's not a very friendly gesture publishing that. All he seems to have done is spank a few bare bottoms'.[16]

During the same period, Smith helped to set up a second establishment for boys in Rochdale: Knowl View School. Further accusations from victims then emerged. Again, no police action was taken. In 1988, Smith was given a knighthood. The scrutiny committee for this process briefed Margaret Thatcher and informed her of the accusations against Smith but she did not veto the proposal and he died a knight of the realm.

Returning to the arrest of Smith in the 1980s, the investigating team had come to the view that boys were being supplied 'to order' from care homes. This implied the active co-operation of those outside of the police in Lambeth council. In response to the *Newsnight* piece, two Labour MPs were interviewed. The first was Simon Danczuk who said:

> It is my view that Smith was being protected and being protected by some fairly powerful people [...] He was protected because he knew of other pae-dophiles in the networks in which he operated and had he been prosecuted, then I think those other people would have been named by Smith and that's why they ensured that he was never put before the courts.[17]

Danczuk (until May 2017 the Labour MP in Rochdale) knew details of Smith's life and crimes and was in constant touch with local men who were surviving victims. An elaborate account of the story of Cyril Smith can be found in Danczuk's 2014 book *Smile for the Camera: The Double Life of Cyril Smith*, written with researcher Matthew Baker.[18]

The local story about Smith was well known to Don Hale who was editor of the *Bury Messenger* (Bury is close to Rochdale) and was given a dossier by Barbara Castle MP in the 1980s. It contained evidence of 16 well-known political figures, including Smith, with details of their paedophile activities.

Hale tried to use the dossier as the start of his investigations. He was visited by Smith who tried to convince him that the claims were fanciful 'poppycock'. Presently, Hale received another visit but now from Special Branch, who demanded the dossier, threatening him with prosecution. But, between the two visits, Hale had called the Home Office to discuss the names he had in his possession. Civil servants there dismissed the information and told him to stop asking 'daft' questions because nothing untoward was happening in Parliament. Under threat of imprisonment, Hale agreed to keep quiet about the accusations. However, in 2014, Hale recounted this story to his colleagues in the press and it was then widely reported.[19]

Also in March 2015, another twist from the past about the Smith story was revealed: there had been an attempt by the South African Secret Services (BOSS) to discredit Liberal politicians because of their opposition to apartheid. Special Branch became aware of this threat, after police during the 1970s had charged and interviewed a man about an art theft. He claimed that he had film footage of Smith sexually abusing boys. The police established that the man had been working as a BOSS agent.[20]

Smith's role as an influential politician abusing children in local residential facilities, in this case in Lancashire, was not unique. An organised lobby of survivors of abuse were to make claims that in Lambeth in South London, physical and sexual abuse took place on an 'industrial scale'.[21]

The tipping point: Tom Watson's parliamentary question

In the wake of the expanding case against Cyril Smith, Danczuk, with his parliamentary Labour colleagues Tom Watson MP and John Mann MP, kept up the pressure inside the House of Commons. Their focus was on increasing transparency about the role of the Home Office in the 1980s in suppressing knowledge of CSA at the hands of the 'great and the good'. And with that transparency, it was hoped that the public would at long last find out what was happening in a murky period in the 1970s and 1980s, when some lobbyists were arguing for the decriminalisation of paedophilia and some in the British elite were acting upon those criminal desires in well-protected secrecy.

When interviewed about the *Newsnight* piece about Smith, Watson noted the ambivalence of victims still in touch with him. On the one hand, he pointed out that they had a real sense that the full story about 'VIP paedophiles' was at last about to break. On the other hand, given the false dawns from the past, when victims' accounts had been dismissed by the police over many years, some were still taking the 'I will believe it when I see it' approach to their unresolved grievance.

Watson's role as a campaigning MP is important because of the tipping point he created in Westminster with his parliamentary question in 2012, which alludes to the pivotal role of the national child protection expert Peter Righton I will explore further in Chapter 9:

> The evidence file used to convict paedophile Peter Righton, if it still exists, contains clear intelligence of a widespread paedophile ring. One of its members boasts of his links to a senior aide of a former prime minister, who says he could smuggle indecent images of children from abroad. The leads were not followed up.[22]

That question set in chain a series of investigations ongoing at the time of writing. Now I provide an account of the flurry of investigatory activity from the British State after 2012. Caught between the instinctive tendency to protect the secrets of the 'Westminster village' and the wider apparatus of the state on one side and the need to provide democratic transparency on the other, Theresa May, the Home Secretary of the time, issued a set of orders. Not only were new police investigations initiated but also a public inquiry about historical cases of sexual abuse in public life more generally was announced by May.

From the start, cynics made their views evident on social media and May did herself no favours in the tactics she used when putting her overall strategy into practice. But this was less about her personal competence and more about the stresses involved in *being* a Home Secretary. Politicians and agents of the British State have been caught between telling the whole truth, and nothing but the truth, and 'damage limitation'. The need of Home Office civil servants to protect the role and reputation of their colleagues began to become part of the story of the inquiry, claimed to be independent by Theresa May.

Operations (and knights and lords) galore

Even before the recent phase of British democracy, when the personal integrity of agents of the state has been summarily thrown into doubt, we had a role model for how the truth can be blocked: 'Operation Countryman'. It was so dubbed because the investigators were from a rural squad (Dorset) and hence the sarcastic nickname given by the Cockney cops under scrutiny. 'The Sweedy' involved an inquiry into corruption in both the Metropolitan force and the London City Police in the early 1980s. But this was about money, not sex.[23]

The investigation looked at the bribe system from the criminal world and its corruption of law enforcement. The 'bent' police of the metropolis ignored or destroyed evidence on a grand scale. Although eight officers were eventually prosecuted, not a single conviction was secured. The report, presented to the Home Office after six years and at a cost of £4 million to the taxpayer, was immediately protected by placing a secret and classified status upon it for 50 years.

Those parts leaked to the press made it clear that corruption in 'the Met' went from top to bottom and was not reducible to a few bad apples. Here we can see one challenge in how to analyse policy problems about criminality. For example, the clerical abuse scandal I examine in Chapter 4 was contained for a while by pointing to the existence of a few deviant paedophile priests. In truth, they could not have continued in their ways without a more general culture of complicity; so too with police corruption.

With the precedent of Operation Countryman in mind to temper our optimism, this is a summary of what happened in the months following Watson's parliamentary question. The second item relates to the Jimmy Savile case (see Box 1.2) but is included for completeness and a starting context of understanding.

1. Operation Fairbank was set up by the Met after the Watson parliamentary question as a scoping exercise to test the evidence for a larger formal inquiry about 'VIP paedophiles' at Westminster. The other criminal investigations below flowed from its conclusions.
2. Operation Yewtree was set up in October 2012 specifically to examine the wrongdoing surrounding Jimmy Savile. The inquiry team of 30 officers reported rapidly (early 2013) and it elicited nearly 600 informants claiming to be victims

of Savile. Most were female and most of the reported abuse occurred with children. I cautiously use 'claiming' here because those opposed to posthumous inquiries argue that no trial is logically possible and the presumption of innocence has disappeared by pre-emptively calling informants, or witnesses, 'victims'. However, the legal presumption of innocence in any case is not logically the same as the absence of actual guilt, a point I pick up again in the next chapter.

3. Operation Fernbridge was then launched in February 2013 to extend the rationale of Fairbank specifically to look at Grafton Close Children's Home. A Catholic priest from Norwich, Tony McSweeney, was arrested and tried for abusing boys, and a second defendant, John Stingemore, was found dead while awaiting trial. The operation was closed down in March 2015 but its findings fed into nearby operations.

4. Operation Cayacos was directed to one line of inquiry about Peter Righton and his associated paedophile network, but implicating politicians. The full scale of the enmeshment of the Paedophile Information Exchange with the sexual offending of high-status politicians will be considered further in Chapter 9.

5. Operation Midland focused on allegations of three murders of children and other illegal activity in connection with initial intelligence gathered by Operation Fairbank. These events were suspected of occurring at the Dolphin Square Development in Pimlico. Press reports indicated that there was an overlap of the presence of both victims and perpetrators at Dolphin Square and Elm Guest House (see next), but Operation Midland limited its focus to its homicide inquiries.

6. Operation Ahabasca examined the evidence of wrongdoing at Elm Guest House in Barnes, South London. Press leaks about those attending the gay brothel with underage victims included unnamed politicians from Sinn Fein, the Labour Party and the Conservative Party. Others were named specifically. These were Sir Cyril Smith MP, Sir Nicholas Fairbairn MP, the Soviet spy Sir Anthony Blunt and the former British diplomat Sir Peter Hayman. Former Conservative Party chairman Sir Peter Morrison also was a visitor. Morrison was Margaret Thatcher's parliamentary private secretary. Another attendee was Colin Peters, a Foreign Office barrister. In 1989, Operation Hedgerow gained evidence of 650 offences by him against 150 boys, some as young as ten; this led to Peters' conviction, with an eight-year jail sentence. The witnesses reported being drugged at Elm House with some of them being trafficked to Amsterdam for further exploitation.[24] Although Operation Hedgerow opened up the specific prosecution of Colin Peters, when John Mann MP offered further evidence to the police about Elm House in 1998, no action was taken.

7. Operation Enamel was set up as a joint investigation in 2014 between London and Leicester police to examine criminal charges against Lord Greville Janner dating back over 20 years; more on this in the next chapter.

The above are the main London-focused police investigations at the time of writing but they need to be put into a UK-wide context. For example, the investigation of claims of historical CSA in Scotland, Northern Ireland, North Wales and Jersey are also ongoing. The first two of these overlap with a focus on Catholic abuse I discuss in Chapter 4. The Elm House investigation (Operation Ahabasca) involved inquiries from Greater Manchester Police about the offending of Cyril Smith.

By May 2015, another overarching sweep of the whole range of historical investigations by the police was announced: Operation Hydrant. Chief Constable Simon Bailey heading the operation announced that out of 1,433 alleged offenders, 76 were politicians, 43 were from the music industry and 135 were from TV, film or radio. Notably, 216 of the alleged perpetrators were dead but this meant well over 1,000 suspects were probably still at large.

Commenting on the announcement in news reports (May 20, 2015) Peter Saunders, from the National Association of People Abused in Childhood, pointed out that the scale of the police challenge was not surprising but also noted that most of the calls his organisations received from survivors referred to abuse in their own homes. I return to this point in Chapter 3. The context of political concern about CSA in recent years in Britain was also reinforced by scandals in light entertainment, especially at the BBC (see Box 1.2).

BOX 1.2 CELEBRITY OFFENDING AND THE BBC

Jimmy Savile is now renowned, posthumously, as the most prolific sexual offender against children in British history. He was an eccentric and garish DJ who had been employed at the BBC since the 1960s on its flagship programme *Top of the Pops*. Prior to his death in 2011, he was seen as 'a national treasure' for his charity fundraising for the NHS and other causes. By 2012, ten women had reported abuse by Savile from their childhood years in the 1960s and 1970s. The police operation Yewtree triggered 400 witness reports with *prima facie* evidence of 200 crimes, including 31 rapes. Around 80% of the reports referred to female victims and 80% had been children or young people. Most were teenagers but the youngest victim was ten years of age. Savile mainly had a penchant for girls between 13 and 17, suggesting that in the main his orientation was that of a hebephile but the claims against him included pre-pubescent children of both sexes, as well as of adult women.

With the shock of the scale of Savile's offending generally, the BBC came under particular scrutiny. Police interest in Savile was known to the BBC in the 1970s and in 2007 but neither party took any further action. Shortly after his death (October 29, 2011) BBC's *Newsnight* interviewed women who had been children in the care of Duncroft Approved School and at Stoke Mandeville Hospital and who were reporting sexual offences against them by Savile. Controversially, the material known to journalists for months was not broadcast until after Savile's death, when the BBC at first only showed fawning tributes to him.

Savile was not alone in his offending in British light entertainment. Chris Denning was a DJ on BBC Radio 1. Within the first decade of this century he was convicted and jailed in both Slovakia and the Czech Republic for sexual offences against children and for producing and distributing indecent images of children. He was arrested by police on his return to the UK for past offences. At his trial in Britain in 2014 he admitted over 40 counts of indecency against 28 boys, aged between 10 and 14, stretching over a 20-year period. He was given a 13-year prison sentence.

In December 2014, Ray Teret, who was a Radio Caroline and club DJ from Manchester during the 1960s and 1970s, and friend of Savile's, was sentenced to 25 years in prison. He was convicted of 7 counts of rape and 11 counts of indecent assault involving girls during his early career. The fun-loving general entertainer Rolf Harris was jailed for five years and nine months in 2014 for historical cases of abuse against young girls. While serving his sentence, he was brought back before the courts to face further charges of sexual assaults in the past on women and girls between the ages of 12 and 42. Others making their careers at the BBC were also convicted of sexual offences against children, including Gary Glitter, Stuart Hall and Jonathan King.[25] Apart from the lessons about unchecked criminality at the Corporation, we also now have come to understand the complicity of those who knew of the offending of Savile and others (colleagues, managers and the police).

A final notorious case to note in the 'pop business' was that of Ian Watkins, the lead singer of the group Lostprophets. In December 2013, he received a 29-year prison sentence for sexual offences against children, with an additional 6 years on licence. He had eventually pleaded guilty to a charge of attempted rape and sexual assault of a child under 13. He pleaded guilty to a further three counts of sexual assault involving children and six involving taking, making or possessing indecent images of children. His youngest victim was a baby. He also admitted an extra charge of possessing an extreme pornographic image of bestiality. His female co-defendants, named only in press releases as 'Woman A' and 'Woman B', were given 14- and 17-year sentences respectively. These were female fans who were mothers to Watkins' victims.

Relevant factors to note across this pattern of offending include: the complicit third parties turning a blind eye to events they witnessed; co-offenders; managers protecting their jobs and the reputation of their employer; police inaction; and naïve public confidence in celebrities they came to adore. This web of complicity impeded justice for children who were sexually victimised by those in the public eye. All of the factors were evident when the full stories of the offending were eventually reported in the mass media. They mirror a theme of this whole book, which is that CSA is sustained by multiple acts, small and large, of collective denial across the whole of society. The perpetrators are at the centre and the easiest to identify and understand. It is the complicity of others which warrants our particular scrutiny and analysis.

How high did it go?

Although it is already evident that VIP paedophiles were present at Westminster and the *prima facie* evidence is that there was both security service interference and general police collusion (mixed with integrity) in the suppression of evidence, there is a common question asked in the mass media on behalf of a curious general public. Who exactly knew about this in the British government? This question was posed well before Tom Watson's 2012 triggering parliamentary question by the 'maverick' Conservative MP Geoffrey Dickens.[26]

On November 29, 1985, Dickens made a statement in Parliament claiming that a paedophile ring operated at Westminster. Earlier, in 1981, he had used parliamentary privilege (a British point of law that prevents MPs from being sued for slander when making any statement in the debating chamber) to name Sir Peter Hayman as a paedophile. Hayman had been the British High Commissioner to Canada. Dickens, in his 1985 statement, complained of harassment since his 1981 claim about Hayman. He still wanted to know why Hayman had evaded prosecution since 1978.

That year, Hayman had left a package containing accounts of CSA on a London bus. In their investigations of the material, the police traced it to Hayman's address and found that he had been using a pseudonym of 'Peter Henderson'. There they found diaries containing his fantasies about children and prostitutes. It transpired that Hayman was a member of the Paedophile Information Exchange (PIE) (which I discuss in Chapter 9). The police cautioned Hayman but took no further action. In Parliament in 1981, Sir Michael Havers, the Attorney General, argued that a combination of the lack of extremity of the material, the lack of any evidence of commercial gain and the fact that Hayman had no executive or leadership role in PIE, justified his continued freedom from prosecution. Havers also attacked Dickens for abusing parliamentary privilege in his statements. And yet hindsight tells us that he was on the scent of an important story.

By 1984, Hayman was back in trouble, being convicted of an act of gross indecency in a public toilet, with a lorry driver. Although homosexuality was no longer illegal, some gay men continued to be turned on by 'cottaging'. Hayman was obviously one of them. (In the UK under the 2003 Sexual Offences Act, today 'cottaging' remains illegal; it is not that it is gay sex but that it is public sex. The same law applies, for example, to the heterosexual liking for 'dogging'.)

By 2015, with National Archive files being released, it transpired that the security services were aware of the risks attached to Hayman of blackmail. One of the files about Hayman's sexual fantasy material was used to brief the prime minister, Margaret Thatcher. The latter, therefore, would have been very mindful of active paedophiles in her circle, the most important of whom was Peter Morrison, noted above, but Dickens never received a satisfactory answer about his concerns.

To this day, some depict him as a buffoon or slightly unhinged renegade to the Conservative cause. For example, in an exchange for the *The Spectator* between an academic child protection expert (Liz Davies),[27] with years investigating organised CSA in London, and Matthew Parris an ex-Conservative MP, the latter described Dickens thus:

> All we know is that Geoffrey Dickens, who was a delightful man – we all liked Geoffrey very much – but he was pretty nuts. He had lots of conspiracy theories. And he did believe Britain was in the grip of a huge paedophile ring involving very senior people in government. I think it highly unlikely that the Home Office would have wilfully destroyed the documents that he gave to the Home Secretary.[28]

However, Dickens had high-status Tories who supported his line of reasoning about active paedophiles in Thatcher's inner circle. For example, in 2002, Edwina Currie, who was Health Minister in the 1980s, described Peter Morrison as a 'notable pederast' in her published diaries.[29] Moreover, beyond rumour and hearsay accounts, there were publicly recorded prosecutions. In 1986, *The People* newspaper reported that the Conservative MP Harvey Proctor had paid 'rent boys' for spanking sessions in his flat. They were under the age of consent (which at that time for gay sex was 21). He pleaded guilty and was convicted of gross indecency in 1987. He was fined, not imprisoned, and he resigned his post.[30]

More recently, it may appear to be significant that apart from Theresa May, who had to be the Home Office backstop for the whole CSA controversy across the piece and for the whole nation, the critics of the VIP scandal were Labour politicians (Danczuk, Watson and Mann). In 2014, Mann handed information of 12 ex-ministers to the police, who he believed had been involved in child sex abuse.

However, these Labour critics were fully aware that the rumoured crimes of the past implicated parliamentarians of all political hues. Some of the biggest fallen idols may well turn out to be senior Labour figures, rather than Conservatives or Liberals. Also, Cyril Smith was originally a Labour Party member, not a Liberal. The case of Lord Janner (see next chapter) reinforces this point that it is not about party loyalty. The Labour Party has produced champions for justice for victims but also it has been implicated strongly at times in local government complicity with offending as well (see Chapter 6). From the points I develop next, it is the case that none of us should expect evidence of clandestine CSA to follow party political lines. This nefarious scheming in Parliament is explored further in the next chapter.

Notes

1   IICSA Independent Inquiry Into Child Sexual Abuse. www.iicsa.org.uk. In August 2016, Judge Goddard resigned and returned to her native New Zealand. She was replaced by Professor Alexis Jay, a social worker who conducted the inquiry into the sexual exploitation of children on the streets of Rotherham I discuss in some detail in Chapter 6. After her resignation, Goddard offered the view that the scope of the inquiry was too large and

unwieldy and advised that only recent cases should be investigated. This view was rejected by the incoming chair, Jay. On September 29, 2016, the senior lawyer in the inquiry team, Ben Emmerson, was suspended following accusations about his poor leadership style. The next day he resigned. Some survivors who were angry about slow progress immediately claimed that the British government knew of his tough style at his appointment and also knew of Goddard's ambivalence at the outset about the overly broad scope of the inquiry. With Jay being now the fourth chair appointed in two years, this led to the cynical hypothesis that the British government was setting up the inquiry to fail (see note 19 as well below). The role of the Home Office in the inquiry and its conflict of interest was central to this hypothesis. See www.bbc.co.uk/programmes/b07wgkz2 (no longer available), September 29, 2016, BBC Radio 4. Thus, the fears of a conspiracy at the heart of the British State even now extended to the very process of (mis)managing the inquiry; more on conspiracies and theories about them in the next chapter.

2 Abuse Enquiry: Fiona Woolf steps down as chairwoman. October 31, 2014. BBC News UK, Politics. Available at www.bbc.co.uk/news/uk-politics-29855265.

3 The idea that every nation has its own self-serving, intimately connected, elite group is traceable to Ralph Waldo Emerson in the USA. In the UK, the notion of the 'British Establishment' has been considered in several populist accounts including Jeremy Paxman's *Friends in High Places*, Peter Hennessy's *The Great and the Good: An Inquiry Into the British Establishment* and Owen Jones' *The Establishment – And How They Get Away With It*.

4 IPCC to investigate allegations of historic corruption relating to child sexual abuse in the Metropolitan Police. March 16, 2015. Independent Police Complaints Commission. www.ipcc.gov.uk/news/ipcc-investigate-allegations-historic-corruption-relating-child-sexual-abuse-metropolitan.

5 This term is common now in the vernacular but Marx used 'lumpenproletariat' and more recently the British Sociological Association prefers 'precariat'. They all describe the unemployed, retired, low waged and insecurely employed. Herbert Marcuse describes the 'unemployed and unemployable' to signal a potential radical set of elements outside of able-bodied, well-paid stable employment. Another term, 'Jams' (just about managing), can now be added to the list.

6 Jeremy Thorpe: The Silent Conspiracy. Available at www.youtube.com/watch?v=6j4X-I21xBc.

7 Peter Cook Biased Judge. Available at www.youtube.com/watch?v=6xi-agPf95M.

8 Kuenssberg, L. (2014). Metropolitan Police officer was moved 'from child abuse inquiry'. July 15. BBC *Newsnight*. Available at www.bbc.co.uk/news/uk-28316874.

9 Frienkel, O. (2002). Belgium's silent heart of darkness. May 5. *The Observer*. Available at www.theguardian.com/world/2002/may/05/dutroux.featuresreview.

10 Hope, C. & Swinford, S. (2014). Member of Edward Heath's government boasted he could cover up a 'scandal involving small boys'. July 7. *The Telegraph*. Available at www.telegraph.co.uk/news/politics/10952138/Member-of-Edward-Heaths-government-boasted-he-could-cover-up-a-scandal-involving-small-boys.html.

11 Narain, J. & Robinson, M. (2015). Cyril Smith was spared court because he would have exposed other high-profile child abusers says former police detective. March 15. *Mail Online*. Available at www.dailymail.co.uk/news/article-2997971/Cyril-Smith-held-paedophile-sex-party-police-told-cover-face-prosecution-Official-Secrets-Act.html.

12 In another case reminiscent of Lord Janner visiting children's homes (see next chapter), a senior police officer in North Wales sexually abused boys at Bryn Estyn and other locations in the 1970s and 1980s. Gordon Anglesea was then a police superintendent. He was confronted by the press in 1991 and he (successfully) sued for libel, when claims

about him were first made, gaining £375,000. He boasted then that the pay-out vindicated him completely. However, he was brought to justice and found guilty of his crimes and received a sentence of 12 years' imprisonment in November 2016. See Bagnall, S. (2016). How Gordon Anglesea went from respected police chief to disgraced paedophile. October 21. *Daily Post*. Available at www.dailypost.co.uk/news/north-wales-news/how-gordon-anglesea-went-respected-12054885; Gordon Anglesea: Paedophile ex-police boss gets 12 years. (2016). November 4. BBC News, North East Wales. Available at www.bbc.co.uk/news/uk-wales-north-east-wales-37861254.

13 Most British police forces have a 'Special Branch', which focuses on matters of national security and those of political sensitivity. The one in the Metropolitan force has now been subsumed by its Counter-Terrorism Unit.

14 Syal, R. (2014). Cyril Smith: 'evidence of sex abuse' was overruled CPS report shows. July 16. *The Guardian*. Available at www.theguardian.com/politics/2014/jul/16/cyril-smith-sex-abuse-cps-1970-report-lancashire-dpp.

15 In October 2017, the Independent Inquiry into Child Sexual Abuse was told of how the 1970 report from the police about Smith abusing boys in Rochdale was not acted upon by the Director of Public Prosecutions. Moreover, in 1979, the office of the latter also denied the existence of that earlier report, according to documentation supplied to the inquiry by the security services (MI5). See Rochdale inquiry: MI5 'told of Cyril Smith abuse case lie'. (2017). October 9. BBC News, Manchester. Available at www.bbc.co.uk/news/uk-41547471.

16 Watt, N. (2014). Serious Cyril Smith allegations were not known to us at the time, says Lord Steel. April 29. *The Guardian*. Available at www.theguardian.com/politics/2014/apr/29/serious-cyril-smith-allegations-not-known-lord-steel.

17 Travis, A., Syal, R. & Weaver, M. (2015). Home secretary: Cyril Smith cover-up claims 'could lead to prosecutions'. March 17. *The Guardian*. Available at www.theguardian.com/politics/2015/mar/17/home-secretary-theresa-may-cyril-smith-cover-up-claims-shocking-prosecutions.

18 Danczuk, S. & Baker, M. (2012). *Smile for the Camera: The Double Life of Cyril Smith*. London: Biteback.

19 Adams, G. (2014). Chilling day Special Branch swooped to seize ANOTHER dossier on VIP abusers: 16 MPs' names mentioned in 1984 report on paedophile lobby's influence in Westminster. July 19. *Mail Online*. Available at www.dailymail.co.uk/news/article-2697947/Chilling-day-Special-Branch-swooped-seize-ANOTHER-dossier-VIP-abusers-16-MPs-names-mentioned-1984-report-paedophile-lobby-s-influence-Westminster.html.

20 Hanning, J. & Owen, J. (2015). Child abuse scandal: Did a botched blackmail attempt by South African intelligence help Cyril Smith escape justice? March 22. *The Independent*. Available at www.independent.co.uk/news/uk/crime/child-abuse-scandal-did-a-botched-blackmail-attempt-by-south-african-intelligence-help-cyril-smith-escape-justice-10125355.html.

21 www.shirleyoakssurvivorsassociation.co.uk/news. The Shirley Oaks Survivors Association (SOSA) made their case about the scale of the abuse in Lambeth in a report issued in October 2016, in advance of their evidence being considered by the wider inquiry about England and Wales. They expressed a concern that the inquiry was not able to be truly impartial. This indicated that there remains now a persistent suspicion that the British Establishment will be prone to interfere with justice, when and if its own members are under scrutiny. That suspicion from this particular survivors' group was in the wake of local investigations in Lambeth considered by the group to be a series of 'whitewashes'. In December 2016, Lambeth Council

decided to make compensation payments to all those who were resident in its care at Shirley Oaks between 1965 and 1994 (see Chapter 6). See also Proctor, K. (2016). Revealed: London council to pay tens of millions to child abuse scandal victims. December 15. *Evening Standard*. Available at www.standard.co.uk/news/education/revealed-london-council-to-pay-tens-of-millions-to-child-abuse-scandal-victims.

22 Hansard, October 24, 2012, Column 923 (Hansard is the official record of business in the British Parliament).

23 Operation Countryman. https://en.wikipedia.org/wiki/Operation_Countryman.

24 Cahalan, P. & Hanning, J. (2013). Paedophile ring leader, Colin Peters, linked to Barnes scandal. March 3. *The Independent*. Available at www.independent.co.uk/news/uk/crime/paedophile-ring-leader-colin-peters-linked-to-barnes-scandal-8518078.html.

25 Relevant prison sentences imposed were: Hall, 30 months, July 2013; King, seven years, September, 2001; and Glitter, 15 years, February 2015. In the latter case, Glitter was found guilty of attempted rape and four counts of indecent assault, and one of having sex with a girl under the age of 13. From jail, he continues to appeal against the sentences. Glitter had narrowly escaped the death penalty for a conviction for sexual assaults on girls in Vietnam. He was given a three-year sentence with immediate deportation and was arrested by British police on his return to the UK, having tried unsuccessfully to seek asylum in other countries. A motif of all the BBC-related offenders is that they flatly denied the charges at the time and then continued to either deny their wrongdoing (and appealing against their sentences) or blame the victims for fortune seeking. As with many ordinary sex offenders, this group of celebrities seems to show neither guilt nor shame about their actions. The notion of a claimed 'compensation culture' to explain away false accusations has been put forward by some libertarian critics of the prosecution of historic cases. I pick this up again in Chapter 10.

26 Tory MP warned of powerful paedophile ring 30 years ago. (2013). February 22. *The Independent*. Available at www.independent.co.uk/news/uk/crime/tory-mp-warned-of-powerful-paedophile-ring-30-years-ago-8507780.html.

27 Liz Davies was a whistle-blower during the early 1990s about child sexual abuse in homes run by Islington Council and continues to clarify the extent of the abuse and the complicity of non-perpetrators.

28 Cited on blog of *The Spectator*, July 11, 2014.

29 Owen, G. (2012). Former Minister says Thatcher aide was paedophile who preyed on boys' home - and Hague should have known. October 27. *Mail Online*. Available at www.dailymail.co.uk/news/article-2224167/Former-Minister-says-Thatcher-aide-paedophile-preyed-boys-home-Hague-known.html.

30 Pierce, A. (2015). Spanking parties and the Enoch fan too right wing for Maggie: Shamed Tory MP Harvey Proctor revelled in notoriety, writes ANDREW PIERCE. March 6. *Mail Online*. Available at www.dailymail.co.uk/news/article-2981983/Spanking-parties-Enoch-fan-right-wing-Maggie-Shamed-Tory-MP-Harvey-Proctor-revelled-notoriety.

2
CONSPIRACIES AND CONSPIRACY THEORIES

Introduction

A problem with the notion of 'conspiracy theories', in this case favoured by those like Matthew Parris (see previous chapter) and David Cameron (see this one below),[1] is that it closes down cool analytical reasoning.[2] The label acts as a self-validating confirmation of a delusion (e.g. Dickens was 'pretty nuts') simply by appending it to a claim that is discomforting. The central point which the throw-away dismissal misses, is that when and if wrongdoing requires *group* communication and practical organisation then there *is* a conspiracy. Those robbing banks and abusing children *have to* conspire to achieve their ends. That is a fact, not a delusion. What remains in doubt is the scale of the conspiracy, the named persons within it and the roles they adopted and for what motives.

For intelligent people in positions of power to reach all too readily for general-ist dismissals of conspiracy theories raises our legitimate suspicion of their motives for doing so. To dismiss legitimate questions about VIP paedophile rings as being a ridiculous 'conspiracy theory' is a tactic of denial on offer to some more than others in society. The more powerful people are, the more effective this type of denial is likely to be. We can make a distinction between fanciful speculation and the grim facts. When and if the latter are investigated properly and in good faith, we can operate our own judgemental rationality about probabilities and motives for wrongdoing. To dismiss factual claims, with contempt, as 'conspiracy theories', can be a coded way of denying the need for serious and proper investigation.[3]

This important distinction between logical and illogical analysis of claimed conspiracies is warranted in our case because British political culture has been very secretive about sex until very recently. At the centre of this coy tradition has been the high rate of gay and bisexual politicians in Westminster. This was prob-lematic before homosexuality was decriminalised in 1967. But even after that, the career-threatening stigma of being gay meant politicians would generally opt to stay 'in the closet'; the complications, which this homophobic tradition has created for political transparency, have been documented at length in Michael Bloch's *Closet Queens*.[4] Bloch's examination of political culture is not about a moral judgement about homosexuality as a sexual orientation, but the *norm of secrecy it required* when it was considered to be wrong in Britain. This meant politicians, for reasons of public respectability, pretending to be 'normal': in the jargon of sociology, it was about 'heteronormativity' and 'passing'. A wife and children was the preferred career option for MPs of all hues.

Coyness about sex in British politics

As Bloch spells out, the habit of secrecy has been a boon to individual politicians. Personal ambition can require secret plotting and factional cliques. In Britain, many MPs have come from all-male boarding schools, where their first sexual excitement may have been with other boys, requiring trysts and subterfuge. 'Impression management'[5] (finding the credible appearance to fit the role) from the 'closet' brings a certain personal adroitness, under conditions of risk, valuable for success in politics.

Leading Liberal politicians at the turn of the twentieth century who hid their homosexual lives included a prime minister, the Earl of Rosebery, and his cousin Earl Beauchamp, a government minister. Both outwardly appeared to be straight. They were married and they had children. Beauchamp's secret recurrent gay life was eventually exposed and he had to flee to the Continent. (The character of Lord Marchmain in the novel *Brideshead Revisited* by Evelyn Waugh is probably based on this event.) During the twentieth century, Conservative MPs 'in the closet' included Lord 'Bob' Boothby, Viscount 'Hinch' Hinchingbrooke, Henry 'Chips' Channon, Alan Lennox-Boyd, Sir Philip Sassoon and Sir Paul Latham. The latter was jailed for homosexual activity during the Second World War.

By the 1950s, when the decriminalisation of homosexuality was being considered by Parliament, leading Conservative MPs who took part in the deliberations included government ministers in the closet: Derick Heathcoat-Amory and Selwyn Lloyd. As the 1960s progressed, casualties included those having to resign their ministerial posts when their gay life was exposed, including Ian Harvey, Charles Fletcher-Cooke and Denzil Freeth.

The secret gay and bisexual world of Labour in the mid-twentieth century included MPs Hugh Dalton, Tom Driberg, Harold Nicolson, Hugh Gaitskell, Leo Abse, Roy Jenkins, Tony Crosland, Richard Crossman and George Thomas. In more recent times, since decriminalisation, leading Labour politicians still wanting to stay in the closet have included Peter Mandelson and Ron Davies. The former was 'outed' inadvertently on TV by the Conservative Matthew Parris, and the latter in 1998 was mugged at knifepoint on Clapham Common, when 'cruising' for casual sex with men. Mandelson, the great schemer and survivor, retained his power during the Blair years but Davies lost his credibility in Labour circles and left the party before eventually joining Plaid Cymru (the Welsh Nationalist Party) in 2010.

So, from the late nineteenth century onwards, a parliamentary culture prevailed that was secretive about the sex lives of politicians and persisted even *after* homosexuality was decriminalised, suggesting a cultural time lag. It is worth noting that the covert dealings that transgressed heterosexual norms in Parliament were *necessarily* between men because men dominated that institution. Mendacity arose ultimately from patriarchy in this case. With more women politicians now and a post-feminist expectation or sensibility, the culture has changed since the 1970s. Concurrent with that change about women has been the formal acceptability now of gay (and lesbian) politicians.

The pressure to stay 'in the closet' for career reasons has diminished in political life, though today we still see examples of duplicity about 'men who have sex with men', reflecting the cultural time lag. In 2016, the Labour MP Keith Vaz, who was chair of the influential parliamentary Home Affairs Select Committee, resigned. He had been exposed by journalists, who pointed out that he was married with two children, for his use of male prostitutes and recreational drugs.[6] It seems that heteronormativity was still largely the name of the game in political life and a wife and children were a standard symbol of that normality, even in 2016.

The uncertain role of Lord Brittan

In the previous chapter, I discussed the claims of Geoffrey Dickens in 1985. He complained of being under threat from the paedophile ring he wanted investigating. He mentioned abusive phone calls and his house being burgled twice. Of more gravity, he said that he was now on the hit list of a killer. The allusion to the burglaries was in relation to a dossier he had prepared for the Home Secretary about paedophiles. The break-ins did not involve any thefts and so Dickens assumed that the intruders were looking for information instead.

These claims brought another senior Conservative minister under scrutiny. The Home Secretary of the time was Leon Brittan. He was the youngest of Thatcher's cabinet to be appointed in 1981 but he was 41 and had never married. Just before his appointment, he married a divorcee who already had two children. Until his death and beyond, this meant speculation about Brittan's sexuality. The metropolitan Conservative inner circle had its fair share of gay men, though homosexuality remained problematic for the party for reasons described above.

Thatcher had it both ways; she relied on close advisers who were gay and yet she passed legislation ('Clause 28') that made it a punishable offence to 'promote' homosexuality in schools (the word was taken to mean 'discuss' by fearful teachers). Although homosexuality was no longer illegal, its very existence was still offensive to the puritanical wing of the Conservative Party. In more recent times, David Cameron had to absorb the heat from the latter, including a petition to 10 Downing Street from hostile Tory local councillors, when he defended gay marriage.

Attitudes in the Conservative Party to homosexuality have been mixed, and hypocrisy (for example about Thatcher's 'Clause 28') par for the course within the Westminster right. Not only had Peter Morrison, Thatcher's close aide, been a visitor to the gay brothel Elm Guest House but also, by early 2015, press reports had begun to appear about Leon Brittan. The reports suggested that he had not only made decisions as Home Secretary to cover up the scandal Dickens was attempting to expose in the 1980s, but that he too was a visitor to Elm Guest House. Brittan had just died and this meant that the claims from two Elm House victims implicating him were never going to be tested in a court of law.

Their accounts proved to be controversial in the wake of an unwise statement by the Metropolitan Police that the account of one of the witnesses was 'credible and true (sic)'. In response, the BBC *Panorama* programme (October 6, 2015) showed that one anonymised witness may have been encouraged to recall the presence of Leon Brittan at Elm Guest House by a campaigner for survivors.

The programme posed more questions than offered answers. The scale of abuse was emphasised and the credibility of cases already proven in the public's mind (such as those of Sir Jimmy Savile and Sir Cyril Smith) were re-emphasised. What the programme did usefully was to make investigators (be they journalists or the police) aware of the obvious need to check facts and proceed with due caution, case by case. For their part, the police were angry that journalists might compromise ongoing investigations and might deter new witnesses coming forward. These points are not mutually exclusive: the programme did highlight the risk of the police pre-judging the truth of allegations but it might also undermine the confidence of new witnesses to speak out.

A pendulum swing was becoming evident about the police's attitude to alleged victims. Having been attacked with good cause for being tardy and even complicit in CSA in the late twentieth century, by 2015 they were making amends by at times offering the notion of proof in advance of legal due process (the witness account was deemed to be 'credible and true').[7] But, of course, tactical errors from the police in public statements, or doubts about particular witnesses (the focus of this *Panorama* episode), tell us nothing about the substantive and aggregate picture of CSA. At the end of it, Brittan's family and friends remained outraged about the posthumous trashing of his reputation.[8] And yet we were still none the wiser about whether he was or was not a paedophile.

The relevance of Brittan's death, beyond the absence of a criminal prosecution, was that the attempt by Theresa May to appoint a chair of her public inquiry into historical CSA ran into the buffers. May's preferred candidates became suspect. Lady Butler-Sloss[9] was the sister of Sir Michael Havers. Remember that the latter had rebuked Geoffrey Dickens for abusing parliamentary privilege. And May's next effort fared little better. Fiona Woolf was a neighbour of Lord Brittan and a friend of his wife. May was discovering, if she had not already done so, that members of the metropolitan elite living in expensive localities tend to be neighbours, friends, relatives or some combination of the above. Elite networks, like any other, learn to look after their own. They are not always a conspiracy but they *are* always a network. And an elite network, *ipso facto*, is saturated with power and privilege: some explicit and some covert. That power and privilege can be self-interested in intent and action. It can at certain moments become conspiratorial.

A very private man: the case of Sir Edward Heath

In early August 2015, a story broke suddenly about an ex-British prime minister being an alleged paedophile. The IPCC's remit, noted in the previous chapter, and the emerging evidence from the swathe of police operations, meant that transparency became a priority for police forces harbouring any suspicions about the past. The immediate media storm about Ted Heath began when Wiltshire police referred themselves to the IPCC. This was a full decade after his death.[10]

An ex-senior officer from the Wiltshire force had come forward to claim that, during the 1990s, a case of prosecution against a brothel owner, Myra Ling-Ling Forde, prepared for court was dropped. The alleged reason was that she was about to claim at the time that she supplied underage clients to Ted Heath. Forde subsequently served two prison sentences for organising illegal sexual activity from premises in Salisbury, near to Heath's home.

Within hours of the Wiltshire statement about their self-referral to the IPCC, other forces in London, Kent and Jersey reported that Heath was of interest to them in their own inquiries about alleged CSA. It transpired that Heath had been the subject of lines of police inquiry for two years. Tom Watson told the press that he had referred evidence he had about allegations against Heath to the police in 2013.

With the cat well and truly out of the bag about allegations and inquiries, and a string of quick press statements from other police forces (the Met, Hampshire, Kent, Gloucestershire, North Yorkshire and Jersey) about Heath, Myra Forde's solicitor told the press that his client did not threaten to expose Heath at her collapsed trial, nor did she supply him with clients. The statement went on to say that Forde had no dealings with Heath.[11]

And then a day later, the prosecutor in the dropped case (now a judge), disputed this account in a particular way. Nigel Seed QC said that it was a lack of evidence-giving that stopped the case against Myra Forde. Judge Seed, in a letter to *The Times* (August 6), insisted that problems with other witnesses giving evidence against Forde was the impediment to the case continuing. Seed asserted that two prosecution witnesses failed to appear and that another in custody refused to leave her cell to give evidence. However, Judge Seed recalled that journalists were indeed keen to attend in order to confirm Forde's account that she had supplied clients to Heath. She hinted in advance of the court hearing about Heath's use of her brothel; hence the waiting, but disappointed, journalists when the case did not proceed.

Two days after Seed's clarification, Matthew Parris, the man who dismissed Geoffrey Dickens as being 'pretty nuts', offered the view in his column in *The Times* that, 'If Heath was a child abuser, I'm an aardvark'. A similarly incredulous letter then appeared in the same newspaper. It was from Lord Armstrong, a long-standing friend and colleague of Heath, who argued that he had no sexual life at all and that given the constant police presence around him as a prime minister, any illegal activity was out of the question.[12] His allusion to the police presence and Heath's lack of opportunity to offend had some substance. But Heath was an MP for over 40 years. He was only prime minister for a tenth of that period. Logically, he had the opportunity away from police scrutiny to act in ways alleged by his accusers for most of his political life. The police scrutiny realistically had little bearing on our sense making about competing claims.

A final twist in the tail in the immediate aftermath of the story breaking was that Myra Forde told Channel 4 News on August 10 that she *did* indeed supply male clients to Heath, but they were not minors. She said that he was not a paedophile, just an 'old sad gay man'. Whatever the truth of the matter, Forde's account seemed to be inconsistent and even at odds with the statement of her own lawyer a few days earlier.

Heath's supportive friends and biographers came out immediately the police interest increased and rejected the idea that he had a sexual life of any sort. A documentary clip from Michael Cockerell's interview with Heath in 1998[13] was played on news programmes. It showed a subdued and at times monosyllabic Heath admitting that in his younger days he had had one female suitor. That was it, so far as any public confession of sexual desire went. The interview exemplified Heath's taciturn and irritable response to 'human interest' journalism.

Prior to these claims and counter-claims about Heath, the standard image from the mass media and his biographers was of a very private man. He was consistently reticent about his private life. But, logically, this wariness about *talking about* his intimate relationships did not of course necessarily mean that he was a sort of 'neuter' with no sexual needs, expressed or unexpressed. Logically, a person who was 'private' might also have been 'secretive'. The word 'private' was saturated with ambiguity. His taciturnity about his intimate life could either have indicated that he had nothing to report and it was his basic right to privacy, or that what there was to report would be unpalatable or incriminating. All are possible; we simply do not know.

A few of us are genuinely asexual (about 1% of the population[14]) and this might have applied to Heath. Lord Armstrong argued that there was not a 'whiff of sexuality' from the ex-prime minister. However, this is at odds with Heath's allusion (above) to his unrequited love and to one of the versions of the facts provided by Ms Forde, that she supplied him with gay prostitutes.

Heath's image of lonely and discreet celibacy, sublimated into hard work in his political career, yachting and performing classical music, was queried strongly by a barrister, Michael Shrimpton, who wrote the book *Spyhunter*. This focused on the alleged residual role of German intelligence services operating in Britain since the Second World War. Shrimpton claimed that Heath was supplied with boys, to his yacht in the waters around Jersey, by Jimmy Savile. He also claimed that some of these boys were murdered and then thrown overboard.[15] The alleged link Shrimpton makes with security services relates to their traditional tactic of setting up compromising sexual scenarios in order to gain political leverage.

Shrimpton's wilder speculations remind us that we have to weigh each case to distinguish between unproven assertion and the real mutual protectiveness of power elites and takes us back to the introduction above and its distinction between generalist and particularist objections to conspiracy theories. Political networks provide *opportunities* for deals and common causes. Logically, that does not mean that at all times they are in conspiratorial mode.

Those like Shrimpton seek to impose order on a multi-layered web of complex and shifting connections. They *presume* hidden conspiracies. However, although the connections may be there, order and meaning have to be teased out and secured cautiously and persuasively by evidence, case by case and claimed event by claimed event. The Internet now offers a giant playground for wild and evidence-free monologues from those like Shrimpton, unchecked by legitimate empirical challenge from fair-minded or doubting critics.

Shrimpton provides those like David Cameron and Matthew Parris with ready evidence that *their* preferred denial of VIP paedophile rings is clearly correct and that they are indeed dealing with adversaries who are 'pretty nuts'. However, as C. Wright Mills notes in his classic book *The Power Elites*, knee-jerk speculation and a naïve conservative acceptance of conventional wisdom can *both* be errors of reasoning.[16] Whether we prefer 'cock up' or 'conspiracy' explanations, either have to be carefully demonstrated; neither is automatically true or false. Also, much of the time we must tolerate uncertainty and often we may never get to the bottom of allegations or suspicions.

The consequence of the gap between speculation and evidence was Shrimpton's recent undoing. He was convicted in February 2015 for telephoning the Defence Secretary, Philip Hammond, just prior to the 2012 London Olympics, claiming that its ceremony was about to be attacked by Nazi spies, using a stolen Russian nuclear device.[17] Shrimpton received a 12-month prison sentence. He was also put on the Sex Offenders Register after police found 40 indecent images of children on his computer during the investigation. He claimed, unsuccessfully, that they had been planted there by security services.

Thus, we have various alternative versions of Ted Heath: gentle, harmless, celibate and asexual from his friends and hagiographers, or a scheming serial offender against children implicated in murder from Shrimpton, or a sad old gay man from a local brothel-keeper. The list remains a head-scratcher. At the time of writing, the various police inquiries into Heath are taking their course and, eventually, maybe we will all be able to draw our own conclusions. We shall see.[18]

Back to the future: the case of Lord Greville Janner

The Conservatives and their links to all-male boarding schools and the sexual habits learned there is a factor to consider, as I noted above. However, privileged educational backgrounds are also evident in other political parties, including the Labour Party. In the case of Greville Janner, he was educated at St Paul's in London and Bishop's College School, Quebec (he was evacuated to Canada during the Second World War). He was no working-class hero of the Labour movement. All political parties have been career paths for those in the British Establishment. Janner is a good example of this point.

By early 2015, the reporting of CSA at the hands of powerful political figures contained mixed messages about the British Establishment. The Home Secretary, Theresa May, was still pursuing a credible formula for an inquiry into historical sexual abuse in public bodies. This had not been easy for her. May's continuing efforts may have reflected her leadership ambitions[19] within the Conservative Party, which had been trailed subtly over a number of months. David Cameron had alluded to 'conspiracy theories' about VIP abuse in the run-up to the General Election of May 2015,[20] suggesting his interest was more in denying the past than in visible justice hereafter. Instead, strategically, and clearly at odds with Cameron, May was looking to the future.[21]

But leaving aside these differences of approach inside the Conservative Party, the workings of the criminal justice system threw up a new controversy involving the ageing Labour peer, Greville Janner, who was diagnosed with dementia. In 2014, Alison Saunders, the Director of Public Prosecutions (DPP), had said that she was intent on pursuing prosecutions against child sex offenders, whoever they were and whether the evidence gathered was about recent events or from years gone by.[22] The case of Janner was to stress-test this pronouncement and the outcome was not good for Saunders; it was one of widespread public anger and disbelief.

In April 2015, Saunders announced that despite substantial evidence on offer against Janner, which would warrant it being tested legitimately in a criminal court, a prosecution would not proceed because of age and ill health. Simon Danczuk, the Labour MP who had exposed the offending of Cyril Smith, went on record immediately (on Radio 4's PM programme on April 16) to say this was an Establishment cover-up. In the wake of a recent parliamentary scandal, which found MPs 'fiddling' their living expenses, some like Danczuk, Watson and Mann were mindful that the very credibility of elected politicians was fundamentally at stake. Their view was that sunlight was the best disinfectant, but the old ways of self-protection were still evident and this soon became very apparent in relation to Lord Janner.

The case had three main elements: first, although Janner had been named as a suspect in a criminal case in 1991 about the sexual abuse of boys in a residential facility, he was not arrested at the time and the police investigation petered out. Further police inquiries in 2002 and 2007 still led to no action against him. Evidence put to the local Crown Prosecution Service (CPS) in Leicester was not passed on to London central office. At the time of writing, we do not know the reason for that inaction.[23]

Second, in his work into the pursuit of Nazi war criminals (he was a Zionist), Janner had emphasised indignantly that suspects should be brought to justice whatever their age or state of health.[24] Although some of the press reporting of the Janner case smacked of barely veiled anti-Semitism,[25] the central relevance of this aspect of the concern was his self-righteous rhetoric about the pursuit of justice for victims of persecution. That concern did not seem to extend to allegations affecting victims of CSA, especially when he was the one being accused.

Third, the dementia diagnosis was problematic. Janner claimed to have been diagnosed as early as 2009 and yet, until 2013, he had regularly attended the House of Lords. In the months before his house was raided for evidence by the police in 2013, he had attended the House of Lords on 15 occasions and was paid over £2,000 in expenses for the effort.[26] Moreover, there was some public cynicism about a previous case.

In the early 1990s, a businessman, Ernest Saunders, was sentenced with others for fraud ('the Guinness Affair'). He was serving a five-year sentence in an open prison when his lawyers made a successful appeal for his early release (after ten months) because of a diagnosis of early dementia. Despite dementia being an incurable and deteriorating brain disorder, Ernest Saunders went back to lucrative work. After his release, he went on to be a consultant for many companies including Carphone Warehouse, Harpur-Gelcon and Seed International, a Cayman Islands-based company.

This sort of story played into the cynicism about Janner (who, by the way, may have genuinely had more substantial symptoms of dementia than Saunders). But of greatest concern was the sense of a miscarriage of natural justice for the victims, who had come forward to the police to allege evidence of Janner's peder-asty between 1969 and 1988. Simon Danczuk was speaking on their behalf when alluding to an Establishment 'cover-up'. This conclusion was reinforced by other contrasting cases.

In December 2014, 84-year-old John Hayford was found guilty of molesting a seven-year-old girl, over 20 years previously. Hayford came to the attention of the police when his daughter saw him assaulting a girl in a supermarket in 2012, from footage shown on the BBC show *Crimewatch*. She persuaded her father to give himself in to the police. Hayford did not speak during the trial. He was found guilty but not sent to prison. But the issue here was that he was *put* on trial, despite his dementia being agreed by all parties.[27]

There was also a case in May 2010 when an Exeter man, Michael Collingwood, was found guilty of 23 sexual offences against 6 children, including 1 of rape. He was tried in his absence because he was currently in hospital with severe dementia. The judge instructed the jury forewoman to use the words 'did the act charged' rather than being 'guilty'. His subsequent disposal by the court was under the Mental Health Act but the facts of the case had been put plainly into the public domain and the person originally responsible for them was clearly identified.[28]

A third analogous case suggests strongly that the DPP decision about Janner was unfair and perverse. In June 2014, the case of David Massingham was heard at Teesside Crown Court. Massingham was 77 years of age and was suffering from dementia, but the judge and jury heard evidence against him for sexually abus-ing two boys, even though the accused was not fit to stand trial. His victims, now adults, were central witnesses to the case; when confronted by the police with their accounts, Massingham simply denied wrongdoing. In the absence of Massingham, the jurors decided that he had committed the acts alleged (ten indecent assaults and two other serious sexual offences). He was ordered to be detained under the Mental Health Act, as he was still judged to be a risk to children.[29]

These cases are an example of how discretion exists in judicial processes. Hayford, Collingwood and Massingham, as offenders from ordinary backgrounds, were brought to justice but Janner, the lord and long-standing member of the political elite, was not. And these contrasting cases illuminate another way in which Janner was dealt with, not only in a lenient way, but also in a way in which, procedurally, other 'offender patients' or 'mentally disordered offenders' are not. When considering this difference, a critical distinction is between the estimated state of mind of an offender at the time of the offences and his current state of mind.

Current and past states of mind

In the case of Janner, it was his current state of mind that drove the decision. No one in the investigation was linking his putative mental disorder to the *offending itself* (from 1969 to 1988 when he was in his political prime). Had it gone to trial and a claim been made *retrospectively* of a mental disorder applying to the time of his offending, he could have been deemed to be not guilty due to insanity or even guilty but with diminished responsibility. But none of these matters were at issue, only why his *current* mental state had a bearing.

In British law, a defendant may be considered unfit to plead because of their impaired mental capacity. However, if the person is an accused sex offender, that should then lead to them being sent to a secure psychiatric facility at the discretion of the court or placed on a community order and put on the Sex Offenders Register. They might even be sent back home, if now judged to be genuinely harmless and to not have contact with children. But by that time the facts of the case would have been heard and the evidence ruled upon by a judge and jury. In the case of Janner, this 'determination of the facts' option was pre-empted by the decision of the DPP, Alison Saunders. Remember, a year earlier she had taken the stance that no one was above the law and how it mattered not to her whether the allegations involved were 30 days or 30 years old. Her decision left Janner's family asserting his complete innocence both notionally (because he had not yet been tried) and actually.[30] However, logically, how could they know that for certain and why not opt instead for a trial in order to clear his name?

With this assertion of Janner's innocence by his family, came anger from the police, who had by now extensive evidence of Janner's alleged offending. And, obviously, his alleged victims and their families were incredulous. The witnesses against him were now in limbo and, from their perspective, without justice. The only consequence for Janner was that (eventually) he was suspended from the Labour Party, though the leaders of the latter made no public statement about him.

Some of those involved in the original investigation in 1991 were still alive and some were willing to speak out. One was the Chief Constable of Derbyshire, Mick Creedon, who, in 2014, reported to the press that when he was an investigating officer in 1991, he and his colleagues wanted to arrest Janner but were prevented from doing so by 'more senior officers' (resonances here of the Cyril Smith case). Creedon and colleagues wanted to search Janner's home and offices but were prevented from doing so by those more senior officers.[31]

The allegations from that period surrounded the trial of Frank Beck who ran one of the children's homes visited by Janner in his Leicester constituency. Beck was jailed for five life sentences for abusing boys in his care. Part of his defence was that he was being targeted as a diversion from more important political figures. One of the key trial witnesses was Paul Winston who, during Beck's trial, reported under oath that Janner had repeatedly had sex with him when he was between 13 and 15. Two others giving sworn testimony against Beck also recalled the involvement of Janner.[32]

Further evidence of Janner's alleged offending was passed to the Labour MP Andrew Faulds in 1992 and 1995 from a group of victims and their supporters. This evidence was relayed to the police but no further action was taken. However, this material was revisited by the Leicestershire police in the wake of the Jimmy Savile inquiries.[33]

By 2015, the police in Leicester from Operation Enamel had presented the CPS with the evidence to prosecute Janner on 22 counts of sexually abusing 9 boys – 6 of buggery and 16 of indecent assault. On the day of Alison Saunders' decision not to proceed, strong disquiet about the decision was expressed by Sir Clive Loader, the Police and Crime Commissioner for Leicestershire. He said that the decision was 'not just wrong' but 'wholly perverse' and 'contrary to any notion of natural justice', a sentiment echoed by Peter Saunders speaking on behalf of The National Association for People Abused in Childhood.[34]

Moreover, Loader noted that the DPP had admitted that the case had passed the 'evidential test' for prosecution on the 22 counts noted above. So, Alison Saunders' decision was tenuously based upon the current health status of the accused. On that alone, and so wilfully ignoring the compelling evidence, Alison Saunders had decided that it was not in the 'public interest' to proceed with the prosecution against Janner.

The immediate reaction from both the public and the police suggests that she was simply wrong. What she was not doing was protecting children in the present, leaving aside the lack of justice for past victims. With Janner not going to trial, there was no risk management in place to protect children who might still have contact with him. In a later statement, Saunders argued that part of her 'lack of public interest' judgement included the assertion that Janner was not an immediate risk to children. This confirmed that his state of mind and adjudged risk was at the centre of her decision-making, not justice for the alleged victims awaiting their day in court to give testimony.

With all this in mind, concern about an actual or perceived cover-up was reflected in the decision of a group of 11 MPs from all parties to write a letter to *The Times* (April 22, 2015). The signatories, headed by Simon Danczuk, complained of the injustice inherent in the DPP decision and asked that it be reversed. In the meantime, the police in Leicester and the lawyers acting on behalf of the witnesses were exploring other options of legal redress. Within weeks, the absurdity of Janner's protection from prosecution on grounds of his recent mental incapacity became even more evident. Up to five days before being told by the DPP that she would not prosecute him, Janner had been a company director.[35]

Hostility to the decision of the DPP about Janner prompted a review and, by the end of June 2015, it was reversed and a court trial was now agreed. In August however, when Janner was about to go for trial, his lawyers argued that he was now without language and that it would be 'barbaric, inhumane and uncivilised' to let the trial proceed.[36] But this cut no ice. The court officials argued that there *was* a strong public interest in the case (contra the earlier view of the DPP) and that Janner must attend or risk arrest for contempt.

In a day of high drama (August 14) when Janner failed in the morning to appear for his initial magistrates' hearing, he was threatened with arrest and so, reluctantly, his lawyers ensured that he was in court that afternoon. If he was indeed too demented to stand in the dock accused, then there would now be a 'trial of the facts'. At last, the case law I noted above from lower-status offenders was starting to impinge on a slow-moving legal system focusing on the political elites. Alison Saunders could have ensured that consistency at a much earlier date, but she did not.

But what then ensued within weeks was a common pattern: Janner died (in December 2015) and so even a trial of the facts about him while he was still alive was denied to those alleging his wrongdoing.[37] Like other frustrated complainants about historical abuse, they discovered that slow justice is ultimately no justice.

Given the public cynicism that was abroad about the Janner case, it is not surprising that, when eventually the government inquiry began its business in earnest in March 2016, it prioritised hearing evidence about him. So, within weeks of his death preventing the original and intended trial of the facts, the latter were being weighed up in very public view and with the press reporting them immediately (but obviously not the inquiry's judgement about them). Two main disclosures of public interest were obvious.

First, very quickly the broad picture that the stalled trial of the facts would have revealed became manifest. Ben Emmerson QC and counsel to the inquiry stated that:

> it is alleged that Janner abused his position as an MP by arranging for children in whom he had a sexual interest to be brought to the Houses of Parliament. The offences are alleged to have taken place in children's homes and hotels between 1955 and 1988.[38]

This summary emerged from the statements of 17 complainants available to the inquiry but more than that (30 accusers) were subsequently reported in the mass media after Janner's death. Janner's relatives refused to co-operate with the inquiry on the grounds that there was no presumption of innocence for the accused and that they would not be allowed to cross-examine the complainants[39] (this was an inquiry, not a trial, and so it played by different rules). Outside of the inquiry, some 20 of the complainants took out compensation claims against Janner's estate, which were then contested in court by his family.

Second, the inquiry heard of the alleged failure to act on warnings about Janner in the early 1990s. This allegation implicated the then Home Secretary, Kenneth

Clarke. At the start of the Goddard proceedings, a representative of the survivors' organisation 'White Flowers', Nigel O'Mara, sent a statement to the inquiry, which claimed that as a result of allegations made by young men on their helpline the Home Secretary was made aware of Janner's wrongdoing in principle. Clarke did not act upon that information, according to O'Mara.[40]

The 'public interest' and the public's verdict

The cases of Janner, Smith, Thorpe, Hayman and Brittan formed a pattern that reflected the process of collective or cultural denial similar to that at the BBC about Jimmy Savile.[41] With hindsight, we can identify: widespread but ignored rumours; police and CPS laxness and inaction; suppression of evidence, political threats and interference from Special Branch; lost dossiers at the Home Office; futile victim protests in the press; and inconsistent DPP judgements. Together, these deferred transparency about CSA until the accused perpetrators were too sick to be tried properly or, simply, dead. By that time, defenders of the accused understandably could protest that the dead cannot defend themselves and the legal presumption of innocence is being violated. For their part, those actually and genuinely victimised were denied justice. Everyone was unhappy and the dead accused (guilty or not of past crimes being claimed) was oblivious to it all.

Wrong-headed decisions by the DPP are just the end point in a series of events that might be random working against the interests of justice, but might also reflect a planned cover-up.[42] The latter can signal the corruption of power in democratic societies. In relation to CSA, many people have already concluded that such corruption was self-evident. In the case of Alison Saunders, her seeming bias in favour of the rich and powerful may not have been conscious. We are left with the fact that there was already case law (cited above) involving dementing patients of ordinary backgrounds, who were brought to court regardless of their condition. Why did she not compare and contrast those cases with the Janner case? We may never know.

Although the judicial process may require a presumption of innocence, the public verdict over time may reach the opposite conclusion. In these cases, the absence of criminal proof tested in a court of law is not necessarily proof of the absence of criminal behaviour; the scientific mantra is 'absence of evidence is not evidence of absence'. The cases of Cyril Smith, Greville Janner and Jimmy Savile all exemplify this point. Death or dementia may put those suspected strongly of CSA beyond the practical possibility of a full and fair trial. But they also deny those accusing them their 'day in court', seeking justice for crimes against them when they were children.

True and false positives; true and false negatives

A central problem we have in making judgements about CSA is not peculiar to that crime. However, it takes on a particularly emotive salience given the moral revulsion typically associated with it; this is the problem of true and false positives.

The complementary problem relates to true and false negatives. This produces four possible scenarios for our topic:

1. A person committed a crime of CSA and is validly found guilty (true positive)
2. A person did not commit a crime of CSA but is found guilty in error (false positive)
3. A person did not commit a crime of CSA and is validly found not guilty (true negative)
4. A person is found not guilty of CSA in error: they really did commit the crime (false negative).

Hallowed though the presumption of innocence may be, where a suspect is *not* brought to trial then the risk of a 'false negative' (scenario 4) is bound to increase. An unquantifiable number of actual perpetrators of CSA are not put on trial and the complaints of their victims not heard. In legal terms, they are regarded formally as being 'innocent', but in reality they are guilty of a crime.

Logically, those suspected or accused but not brought to trial (in the cases above because of dementing or being dead) could potentially be cases in any of the scenarios from 1–4. However, they are *all* afforded the privilege of being in scenario 3: they are regarded as innocent of the crime. Cases left too late, where alleged perpetrators die or where the case cannot proceed to trial for health reasons, mean that when any crimes that *really were* committed are being considered, then the real-enough victims will remain on record as simply being 'alleged victims', adding insult to their existing injury.

When confidence is lost in the judicial process because of public suspicion of incompetence or cover-ups and suppression of evidence, then the honourable liberal tradition of presumption of innocence itself becomes suspect. Our typical concern with miscarriages of justice relates to scenario 2, where someone is found guilty, when they are not guilty. However, once cover-ups and investigatory incompetence come into play, then the inverse of this concern emerges: people worry that the guilty are getting away with serious crimes that they actually committed. In the case of 'VIP CSA', we are now encountering this loss of public confidence and for good reason. There is a higher-order suspicion, beyond the guilt or innocence of particular individuals: wittingly or unwittingly, elites may be protecting their own and 'power' is not being brought to book.

In later chapters, I return to the link between various forms of power structure and CSA. First though, it is important to put the latter into context by examining its occurrence inside ordinary settings, away from the rarified world of high politics. This does not imply that one form of CSA is more important than another, but the next chapter reminds us that the risk to children does not only exist away from their homes in other surroundings (the ecology of risk of 'stranger danger'). When taken in the round, it is evident that there is no fail-safe place in society where children are free from sexual predation. As we now see, the most prevalent risk begins at home.

Notes

1 Slack, J. & Gayle, D. (2014). Cameron attacked by sexual abuse victims after calling claims of Home Office cover-up a 'conspiracy theory'. November 12. *Mail Online*. Available at www.dailymail.co.uk/news/article-2831025/Cameron-attacked-sexual-abuse-victims-calling-claims-Home-Office-cover-conspiracy-theory.html.

2 The academic literature on conspiracy theories makes a distinction between generalist rejections (as, for example, suggested by Matthew Parris) of all conspiracy theories and particularist approaches. The latter are wiser because they rely on evidential testing. Generalist rejections are actually irrational because they are blind and *a priori*; they do not proceed to evidence testing but rely instead on an axiom. See Pigden, C. (2007). Conspiracy theories and the conventional wisdom. *Episteme: A Journal of Social Epistemology* 4(2), 219–232.

3 Bale, J. (2007). Political paranoia v. political realism: on distinguishing between bogus conspiracy theories and genuine conspiratorial politics. *Patterns of Prejudice* 41, 45–60. This particularist, case-by-case caution should also apply to the futile debate between those who are credulous about all retrospective reports of child sexual abuse and those who dismiss them all as fanciful. That false dichotomy has been created by those either accepting the veracity of *all* 'recovered memories' during psychotherapy, and those dismissing them as being simple products of suggestion, with no historical basis. Academic debates about this false dichotomy can be found at www.psyctc.org/archive/upaukcp.htm.

4 Bloch, M. (2015). *Closet Queens*. London: Little Brown Book Group.

5 This technical term was introduced by the social psychologist and sociologist Erving Goffman in 1959. See his *The Presentation of Self in Everyday Life*. New York: Doubleday.

6 Syaland, R. & Asthana, A. (2016). Keith Vaz resigns as chair of home affairs select committee. September 6. *The Guardian*. Available at www.theguardian.com/politics/2016/sep/06/keith-vaz-resigns-as-chair-of-home-affairs-select-committee.

7 In 2016, in the wake of this debacle about poor police procedures, an inquiry led by Sir Richard Henriques drew out lessons for future investigations. These included the suggestions that the word 'complainant' should be used, not 'victim', and that complainants should be listened to carefully. They should be neither disbelieved nor believed automatically but their account dealt with objectively. The culture of disbelief and suppression since the days of cover-ups in the 1980s had certainly created confusion in police circles about how to approach investigations impartially and with an eye on justice for both the accused and the complainant.

8 In the wake of the *Panorama* programme, Brittan's brother called for the resignation of Tom Watson for referring the matter to the police. David Cameron also was pleased that Watson's action was to be the subject of scrutiny by the Home Affairs Parliamentary Select Committee. The Murdoch press in particular set upon Watson (see *Sunday Times*, October 11, 2015). Old scores were being settled, given Watson's earlier role in exposing the hacking scandal linked to the British wing of Rupert Murdoch's media empire. For his part, Watson went into Parliament a day later unabashed, saying:

> Earlier, the prime minister has said that I should examine my conscience. Well, I think we should all examine our consciences in this house. We have presided over a state of affairs where children have been abused and then ignored, dismissed and then disdained. If anyone deserves an apology, it's them.

9 After resigning from Theresa May's appointment, Butler-Sloss hardly sustained an impartial reputation about her stance on child sexual abuse, given the strange scenario in 2015 of her

being a character witness for a man who was convicted for raping a 13-year-old girl. See Morris, S. and agency (2015). Man convicted of raping 13-year-old despite testimony by Lady Butler-Sloss. August 18. *The Guardian*. Available at www.theguardian.com/uk-news/2015/aug/18/man-convicted-raping-13-year-old-despite-testimony-lady-butler-sloss.

10 Wiltshire Police. Statement from Wiltshire Police following the IPCC announcement re. Sir Edward Heath. (2017). October 26. Available at www.wiltshire.police.uk/news/1816-statement-from-wiltshire-police-following-the-ipcc-announcement-re-sir-edward-heath-investigation1.

11 Laville, S. & Syal, R. (2015). Investigation into Edward Heath child abuse claims to go national. August 5. *The Guardian*. Available at www.theguardian.com/politics/2015/aug/05/investigation-edward-heath-child-abuse-claims-go-national.

12 Hamilton, F. (2015). Heath was no abuser, says Lord Armstrong. August 11. *The Times*. Available at www.thetimes.co.uk/tto/news/politics/article4523466.ece.

13 Cockerell, M. (1998). A Very Singular Man: A Film Portrait of Edward Heath. BBC 2 documentary, September. Producer: Matthew Barrett. Available at https://youtu.be/fozuOsUxy7o.

14 Bogaert, A. (2004). Asexuality: prevalence and associated factors in a national probability sample. *Journal of Sex Research* 41(3), 279–287.

15 Michael Shrimpton Interview – Bristol Community Radio. (2012). January 19. Available at http://missingmadeleine.forumotion.net/t22572-michael-shrimpton-interview-bristol-community-radio.

16 Wright Mills, C. (1956). *Power Elites*. Oxford: Oxford University Press.

17 O'Keeffe, H. (2015). Jail for pervert barrister who said nuclear bomb would blow up the Queen at the London Olympics. February 6. *The Bucks Herald*. Available at www.bucksherald.co.uk/news/more-news/jail-for-pervert-barrister-who-said-nuclear-bomb-would-blow-up-the-queen-at-the-london-olympics-1-6566127.

18 In early October 2017, Wiltshire Police released a report on their investigation of claims about Ted Heath. Many of these were dismissed as unsafe or mendacious, but seven key allegations would, according to the report, have warranted formal police investigation were Heath still alive. The seven victim disclosures for which Sir Edward would have been interviewed under caution are as follows: London, 1961 – Sir Edward allegedly raped and indecently assaulted an 11-year-old boy during a paid sexual encounter in a private dwelling; Kent, 1962 – Sir Edward allegedly indecently assaulted a ten-year-old boy during a chance encounter in a public place; Sussex and London, 1964 – Sir Edward allegedly indecently assaulted a 15-year-old boy in three paid sexual encounters; Guernsey, 1967 – Sir Edward allegedly indecently assaulted a 15-year-old boy in a public building; Jersey, 1976 – Sir Edward allegedly indecently assaulted, over clothing, an adult male at a public event; Wiltshire, 1992 – Sir Edward allegedly assaulted an adult male after consent was withdrawn in a hotel; Wiltshire, 1990–1992 – Sir Edward allegedly indecently assaulted a male, aged between 12 and 14 years, in private gardens. The police statement did not extend to claim these implied his guilt, only that they would have warranted him being interviewed under caution.

19 In the aftermath of the Brexit referendum, David Cameron resigned as prime minister and Theresa May replaced him.

20 Slack, J. & Gayle, D. (2014). Cameron attacked by sexual abuse victims.

21 On July 11, 2016, Theresa May replaced David Cameron as the British prime minister, though her poor performance in the general election she called in 2017, without need, was to be her undoing as party leader.

22 Topping, A. (2014). Historic sex case prosecutions will continue, vows chief prosecutor. February 20. *The Guardian*. Available at www.theguardian.com/law/2014/feb/20/historic-sex-case-prosecutions-continue-cps.

23 Adams, G. (2014). Child sex claims, a police 'cover-up' and troubling questions for a Labour peer: This special report reveals the full extent of the deeply disturbing allegations against ex-MP Greville Janner. October 3. *Mail Online*. Available at www.dailymail.co.uk/news/article-2779973/Report-reveals-extent-allegations-against-ex-MP-Greville-Janner.html.

24 Sabin, L. (2015). Lord Janner criticised justice system for excusing alleged Nazi war criminal who had dementia. April 17. *The Independent*. Available at www.independent.co.uk/news/uk/crime/lord-janner-criticised-justice-system-for-excusing-alleged-nazi-war-criminal-who-had-dementia-but-now-hes-in-the-same-position-10183717.html.

25 The most explicit anti-Semitic blog is http://aanirfan.blogspot.co.uk/2014/07/leon-brittan-bigger-picture.html.

26 Pearson, A. (2015). Forgive my cynicism at the timely onset of Lord Janner's 'dementia'. April 22. *The Telegraph*. Available at www.telegraph.co.uk/news/health/elder/11554636/Forgive-my-cynicism-at-the-timely-onset-of-Lord-Janners-dementia.html.

27 Shammas, J. (2014). Paedophile found guilty of assaulting seven-year-old girl over 20 years ago. December 7. *The Mirror*. Available at www.mirror.co.uk/news/uk-news/paedophile-found-guilty-assaulting-seven-year-old-4764630.

28 Glover, S. (2015). STEPHEN GLOVER: After Lord Janner I now believe the Establishment DOES shamelessly twist justice to protect its own. April 22. *Mail Online*. Available at www.dailymail.co.uk/debate/article-3049762/STEPHEN-GLOVER-believe-Establishment-DOES-shamelessly-twist-justice-protect-own.html.

29 Lightfoot, G. (2014). Sex offender who abused two boys over 30 years ago detained indefinitely under hospital order. June 11. *GazetteLive*. Available at www.gazettelive.co.uk/news/teesside-news/david-massingham-sex-offender-detained-7247319.

30 This reaction of the family to a dead politician investigated for child sexual abuse can be contrasted with that of the widow of Clement Freud (accused by two women separately after his death). Jill Freud said on the very day the BBC announced the allegations (June 15, 2016) that she was 'deeply saddened and profoundly sorry for what has happened to these women'. See Sir Clement Freud accused of abusing two girls. (2016). June 15. BBC News. Available at www.bbc.co.uk/news/uk-36535263.

31 Greenwood, C. (2014). Police 'told to limit abuse probe into MP': Derbyshire Chief Constable claims he was forbidden to arrest Labour man or search his home when he worked as a detective. September 26. *Mail Online*. Available at www.dailymail.co.uk/news/article-2770235/Police-told-limit-abuse-probe-MP.html.

32 Bracchi, P. (2015). Vile abuse, 3 bungled probes and a 45-year 'cover up', PAUL BRACCHI reviews decision not to charge Labour peer over child abuse claims because he has Alzheimer's. April 17. *Mail Online*. Available at www.dailymail.co.uk/news/article-3042821/Vile-abuse-3-bungled-probes-45-year-cover-PAUL-BRACCHI-reviews-decision-not-charge-Labour-peer-child-abuse-claims-Alzheimer-s.html.

33 Adams, G. (2014). Child sex claims, a police 'cover-up' and troubling questions for a Labour peer.

34 www.leics.pcc.police.uk/News-and-Events/Latest-News/2015/Sir-Clive-condemns-decision-not-to-prosecute-suspected-serial-sex-offender.aspx (no longer available).

35 Gore, A. (2015). Greville Janner was still company's director days before dementia saw him spared child abuse charges. May 2. *The Mirror*. Available at www.mirror.co.uk/news/uk-news/greville-janner-still-companys-director-5625877.

36 Halliday, J. (2015). Lord Janner makes first court appearance over child sex abuse claims. August 14. *The Guardian*. Available at www.theguardian.com/uk-news/2015/aug/14/lord-janner-makes-first-court-appearance-over-child-sex-abuse-claims?CMP=share_btn_fb.

37 Hall, J. (2016). Lord Janner sex abuse 'trial of the facts' dropped one month after Labour peer's death as 12 victims speak out. January 15. *The Independent*. Available at www. independent.co.uk/news/uk/crime/lord-janner-sex-abuse-trial-of-the-facts-formally-dropped-one-month-after-the-labour-peers-death-a6813631.html.

38 Janner sexually abused children for 33 years, public inquiry hears. (2016). March 9. BBC News. Available at www.bbc.co.uk/news/uk-35765395.

39 O'Neill, S. (2016). Janner family snub 'unfair' abuse inquiry. July 26. *The Times*. Available at www.thetimes.co.uk/article/janner-family-refuse-to-take-part-in-inquiry-z5vxhvb2j.

40 Barrett, D. (2016). Kenneth Clarke 'failed to act' over Lord Janner and Cyril Smith child abuse tip-offs. March 8. *The Telegraph*. Available at www.telegraph.co.uk/news/uknews/crime/child-protection/12188024/Kenneth-Clarke-failed-to-act-over-Lord-Janner-and-Cyril-Smith-child-abuse-tip-offs.html.

41 Greer, C. & McLaughlin, E. (2015). Denial of child sexual abuse. In D. Whyte (ed.), *How Corrupt Is Britain?* (pp. 41–53). London: Pluto Press.

42 I noted in the previous chapter that a variant of cover-up is wilful mismanagement: the claim made by survivor critics of the dysfunctional workings of the government inquiry into historical cases of child sexual abuse.

3

THERE'S NO PLACE LIKE HOME?

Introduction

When I worked in the NHS as a clinical psychologist I listened to many accounts of current and past experience from patients. They taught me that trauma in childhood is highly predictive of a range of mental health problems. The most obvious is when a mixture of symptoms of distress is traceable to a definable extreme event, which can prompt a diagnosis of post-traumatic stress disorder. However, the clinical research literature tells us more than this. It now seems to be the case that a very wide range of symptoms, including hallucinations and delusions, not just the common distress of low mood and variable anxiety symptoms, are linked to childhood trauma. Substance misuse is also a common outcome for survivors of CSA.

One common site for childhood trauma is the family of origin of a patient. Surprisingly, mental health services, despite this knowledge, do not always take detailed histories to enquire about this eventuality. All too often, mental health assessments are directed towards other priorities, such as establishing a psychiatric diagnosis and prescribing a treatment, which is typically medication. However, for those who take the evidence for the traumagenic model seriously, a different line of inquiry is centre stage. This involves a biographical formulation. What has happened to this person in their life? What sense do they make of their experience? How do they cope and what do their symptoms tell us about their sense of self and how it survives?

This formulation-based approach to mental health research has incorporated the viewpoints of service users. Some of them have been prepared to go public about their experiences both as children and within mental health services. One of these is Jacqui Dillon, a psychiatric survivor who has told her story of childhood abuse and traces in detail how the secret world of her family led to her breakdown and memories of it were also needed for her recovery.[1]

Most sexually abused people with mental health problems speak privately to a few trusted friends, relatives and professionals. Many tell no one or their trauma is only manifest many years later. For example, I saw patients who broke down in middle age with depression and suicidal intentions, only when their abuser eventually died. The expectation of a normal bereavement process forced the issue into their consciousness and it became unbearable. Feelings of betrayal, fear and anger flooded in, rather than the socially expected feeling of sadness for their deceased parent.

Emotional and physical abuse are most likely to occur at the hands of parents or those in *loco parentis*, i.e. primary caregivers. The situation is more complex in relation to CSA. Surveys in the USA and Australia concur that most (around 90%) CSA perpetrated by adults is at the hands of people familiar to the victim, in their home or nearby. Thus, less than 10% of CSA involves genuine 'stranger danger'. Of those sexually abusing children and known to them, 13.5% will be fathers or step-fathers. Higher rates are found in a range of adults known to and usually trusted by the victim: other male relatives (30.2%); family friends (16.9%); neighbours (15.6%); or other adults known to the child routinely (15.3%). In this final category, we would find the teachers, youth workers etc. that I discuss in Chapter 5. Adding these sub-groups together, we find that CSA occurs typically in the home of the victim or nearby.[2] As I note later, this means that survivors of CSA are most likely to link it experientially to home life, not strange places for the child.

Another important point about that trend is that victimisation by those already known and trusted creates the added insult of betrayal. If we are assaulted by a stranger, this is traumatic but we are shocked not betrayed. By contrast, if we are assaulted by someone we have come to trust, then the existential implications are different for us and, typically, more distressing. This is why CSA, implicating perpetrators well known to victims, is so important for survivors and can have such long-term implications for their future trust in intimate relationships. It can undermine or distort the latter for the rest of their adult life.

Incest, age gaps and the sexual exploitation of children

Sexual activity involving children in families is generally censured by all human societies. The 'universal incest taboo' was called the 'answer with no question' by the anthropologist Claude Levi-Strauss. The theories about the universal taboo had to be artificially created or contrived for the very reason that, for most of us, it does not need explaining: it is self-evident that sexual relationships between relatives are a bad thing. Moreover, for many of us, that self-evident position applies to all forms of adult–child sexual contact.

When starting to write this book, I occasionally and deliberately asked friends and relatives a faux-naïve question: what is wrong with adults having sex with children? At first, the most interesting part of their reaction was not their words but their faces. Some would screw up in a mixture of fury and utter dumbfounded perplexity for a few seconds. Others would look at me blankly and gravely, as if I was joking about a matter that should not be a joke; implying that even the question itself was part of a taboo. After the funny looks, then the reasons appeared and quite quickly settled upon three matters: harm to the child; the unfair power discrepancy; and the lack of capacity of children to make judgements in their own interests.

Those responses and the offence about sex with children can even extend to consenting adults, when we witness the unspoken scorn revealed in 'dirty looks' poured upon older men with much younger women in tow (and occasionally the reverse of this about 'toy boys'). The veiled contempt in the eyes of those seeing older Western men in public with young Thai brides is an amplified version of this tendency. Maybe this is because the commercial aspect also brings with it resonances of a trade in sex with distressed involuntary younger parties, entrapped by their families in poverty back home.

The 1970s pop star Gary Glitter was eventually brought back from the Far East to face justice in the UK for his sexual attacks on girls because of the Thai authorities refusing him entry. However, this paradoxically signalled the particular role that Thailand has had in the sex trade. It has the highest number of sex workers per capita in the world at present, with that dubious honour being challenged by countries nearby, such as Cambodia and Laos. In that region, widespread poverty boosts the rate of prostitution and some of the latter is an imposed status on children. The term 'child prostitute' is understandably problematic because it indicates the personal agency and knowing responsibility of a child in seeking money for sex. Children do not participate as equal moral agents in sex and when they are used in prostitution that process emerges because of the decisions of adults they are dependent on and who control them. Thus, they are exploited twice over: first by their pimps and their families, and then by individual paedophiles paying to gain sexual pleasure.

A sense of the industrial scale of this trade in the Far East is given by some stark statistics. For example, the World Travel and Tourism Council calculated that, in 2014, sex work generated 12% of the Gross National Product of Laos. By the 1990s, the International Labour Organization estimated that sex tourism was contributing $27 billion to the Thai economy. Thai brides and underage sex work is only one part of this picture, which also includes adult sex workers, pimps and corrupt police officers. But the main point here is that these expressions of sexual exploitation, including that of children, are *normalised* in the poor countries of the Far East, boosting their economic growth by a lax approach to sex tourism.

The Thai bride issue aside, the United Nations has emphasised that child brides still constitute the largest group of sexually abused children worldwide. (I return to this point in Chapter 10.) Although we could explain the concern about child brides as a symbolic extension of the incest taboo, it is not simply a matter of moral revulsion about incest resonating with all evident forms of age gap. For example, children in enforced marriages to men, who might be decades older than them, are exposed to very real physical dangers.

Nigeria has the highest rate of vesico-vaginal fistula (VVF) in the world. Girls and women affected by it are malodorous and so usually become social outcasts. VVF is a fistula extending between the bladder and vagina, which leads to a constant leakage of urine into the vagina. It occurs most in immature girls (with underdeveloped pelvises) who are raped or have hard labour in childbirth. In Northern Nigeria, the practice of forced child brides increases this risk on both counts. In the Democratic Republic of Congo, it arises recurrently from rape as a weapon of war, again leading to raised levels of VVF.

We can see, then, that what starts as a specific transcultural and trans-historical curio about the incest taboo, soon invites our wider interest in the economic and political aspects of the sexual exploitation of young people and children. However, we need still to return to the biological conundrum of incest because it still drives those wider resonances and impacts.

Incest and biology

The examples of the empirical evidence above that the rape of girls is bad for their physical (not just their mental) health are only one biological consideration. The dominant theory of incest, about the biological disadvantage of consanguine relationships, makes sense in relation to evolution. Inbreeding risks disease and it means that genes are not dispersed widely to ensure their survival. We know from animal studies that with pedigree breeds we can create quite horrible defects and vulnerabilities to particular health problems. 'Mongrels' or 'cross-breeds' might be less attractive to the eye but they are more likely to be sturdy. But this evolutionary logic and concern about inherited pathology does not explain the subtleties noted above. For example, why does an extensive age gap between sexual partners elicit consternation, even when and if it is between consenting adults who are not biologically related?

Also, the sexual trauma suffered by pre-pubescent children may raise the risk of VVF but it does not risk pregnancy. We have an offensive scenario, which is not about an introverted and limited gene pool but something more, which is very psychologically unsettling. Indeed, typically it is *more* offensive the younger the child. The rape of a baby is a scene of utter depravity that is difficult to top in real life, even by the barbarity of warfare; and yet procreation is not possible. This is also true of men who sexually abuse their sons. Also, in practice, the commonest scenario today of intra-familial sexual relationships is between men and their step-daughters, where pre-existing genetic ties do not exist. (Some men with a sexual interest in children deliberately form relationships with women who already have children.)

Thus, intra-familial sexual relationships are such a variegated mix that the 'incest taboo' is indeed a blanket mystery. As I noted above, culturally, it seems to become a generalised hostility to *any* sexual partnership where there is an age gap large enough to *signal* discrepant generations. So we are thrown back, speculating about this wider taboo. When we re-focus the generalisation back onto families of origin alone, then concerns about the risk of congenital health problems or weak gene-pool spread are simply not comprehensive enough in their explanatory reach. We have to consider the symbolic generalisation that seems to have arisen in most cultures beyond the family as a social structure.

Nonetheless, the taboo on incestuous contact that transpires to be biologically dysfunctional does apply at times, for example when women have repeated pregnancies in order to produce new sexual victims in waiting for their male partners. This seems to represent the most persistent and perverse attempt at consanguine coupling. Some of the girls re-abused in religious settings in Ireland, I discuss in Chapter 4, were there because they were pregnant by their own fathers and those surviving this scenario can be as confused and hurt about the role of their mother as about their father's actions.

The most dramatic example in recent times of a man fathering children by his own daughter was that of the Austrian Josef Fritzl, convicted in 2008. He imprisoned his daughter Elisabeth in a cellar dungeon of his house, while remaining married to her mother upstairs for a 24-year period. Downstairs, during that time, Elisabeth gave birth to seven of her father's children. The complicity of his wife added to the crime scene. Three of the children were permitted upstairs and were raised by her. The others remained underground with their own mother until the crime was discovered and they were all released. When Fritzl repeatedly impregnated his daughter, she had become post-pubertal and her life as a young woman was in the bizarre imprisoned world of a family that made no distinction between the generations and our normal assumptions about their sexual separation. The persistence of incestuous contact into adulthood for the victim was also evident in the next case.

In Britain, the case of Fred and Rosemary West was comparably unbearable and it involved the murder, not just the rape, of their own and other children. Rosemary murdered Charmaine West, who was from a previous marriage, while Fred was in prison serving a short sentence for theft in 1971. Subsequently, Fred murdered their own daughter, Heather, in 1987. Rosemary had abetted Fred in raping Heather. In 1992, there was a failed prosecution of Fred for raping another one of his daughters on film, who at the time was 13; she would not testify against her father. The removal of the West children by social services then triggered an investigation into the disappearance of Heather and the discovery of her body by the police.

The extent of sexual abuse against children inside and outside the West family has still not been comprehensively calculated but Fred committed at least ten sexually motivated murders and two of those implicated the role of his wife. Rosemary had seven children by West, but one of them may have been sired by her own father. The latter, Bill Letts, was allowed to visit Rosemary after her marriage to Fred, in order to have sexual intercourse with her. This continued a habit from Rosemary's childhood. This highlights a feature of some incest cases in which the father continues to exercise sexual control over an assaulted daughter beyond childhood, indicating this is about general patriarchal control, not merely transient sexual pleasure for the perpetrator.[3]

Another publicised story, though less dramatic or criminal but that still invoked public opprobrium, was that of the film director Woody Allen. He began a relationship with 17-year-old actress, Stecy Nelkin, when he was middle-aged. However, the main controversy centred on his children with Mia Farrow, who were adopted.

In one case of a daughter, Dylan, Farrow accused him of sexual molestation and the court stated that this could not be 'ruled out' and that the girl should be protected from Allen's contact.

A later police investigation failed to confirm the case against him but years later, Dylan repeated her accusation against her father.[4] Later, Allen began a relationship with Soon-Yi Previn. He was 56 and she was 19 and was adopted by Farrow but not Allen. They married in 1997 and had two children. In US law, all of this was legal but the public's reaction to Allen has not always been either trusting or forgiving. Farrow went to great lengths to annul the adoption of those children they had raised together. The age gap between Woody Allen and Soon-Yi Previn and the fact he married his ex-partner's adopted daughter seemed to trigger the generalised emotional resonance to incest I noted above.

Finally, a caveat in this section: incest at times can also involve brother–sister relationships. Then, the taboo is not about the power discrepancy of age but seems to loop back to 'the answer with no question'. However, as a caution against the assumption of a firm and fast universal taboo, we also know that, historically, royal lineages have been maintained by the planned coupling of brothers and sisters. This was practised in Ancient Egypt to ensure royal family political dominance. Marriages to cousins have been common in more recent European royal lineages, in cultural contexts in which such practices were scorned in 'the lower orders' of society and proscribed by religious authority.

All of this suggests that 'inbreeding' can have political advantages at times for some dominant groups. It can also fuel jokes about royalty and the aristocracy (about weak chins and madness). At the start of the twentieth century, this was no joke though for Alexei Nikolaevich, the heir apparent to the Russian Empire. His father was Emperor Nicholas the Second and his mother Empress Alexandra Feodorovna. Her maternal grandmother was Queen Victoria. Alexei inherited haemophilia from that maternal blood line. Royal 'inbreeding' has had its serious disadvantages for some family members.

The political convenience of sexual relationships for royal dynasties was also exemplified by a feudal case which today would be illegal and illustrates changes in norms about child brides. In 1382, Richard II married Anne of Bohemia and she died 12 years later of the plague. After two years as a widower, Richard, as a political gambit to preserve peace across the English Channel, married Isobella of Valois, who was daughter of Charles VI of France. She was six years of age. There was consternation about the betrothal but not because of the matter of her consent but that her young age meant a long wait for the prospect of an heir for Richard. He died three years later with neither wife bearing him a child. Isobella later re-married and died in childbirth in her late teens.

The challenge of estimating incidence and prevalence

Scholarly summaries of estimates of CSA, such as those by David Finkelhor and his colleagues in the USA,[5] suggest that between 1.2 and 4.6 children in 1,000 there are sexually abused each year. As I noted earlier, most of these assaults take place in the home or nearby, at the hands of those known to the child. Most of the victims are girls and most of the perpetrators are adult males.

Finkelhor and his colleagues provide us with three methodological cautions when quoting estimates. First, some estimates only refer to relatives but some include others committing the assaults. Study by study, then, we need to be aware of how CSA is defined. Second, what is recorded by official agencies is only a portion of actual abuse. Much abuse is not reported and some is not proven to the satisfaction of record keepers (see my points below about the 'filtering' of recorded cases). Third, some prevalence studies relate to yearly estimates and others to lifetime cumulative estimates (these are two different versions of what researchers call 'prevalence'). Lifetime estimates suggest that between 3% and 32% of women recollect being sexually assaulted in childhood, with an average estimate being 20% (the average for males is 8%).[6] This wide range probably emerges because of the varied definition of CSA (see next point below).

Moreover, some studies of yearly prevalence are taken from the accounts of children themselves and some from child protection and law enforcement agencies. Also, logically, the estimates about childhood sexual abuse reported by adult survivors provide a picture of the past and not necessarily of the present. Thus, we cannot necessarily use those accounts to clarify current risks to children because norms of protection and risk may have changed.

We can add a fourth methodological challenge as well: that of definition. For example, the British government, for now, is offering the following definition of CSA.

> [CSA] involves forcing or enticing a child or young person to take part in sexual activities, not necessarily involving a high level of violence, whether or not the child is aware of what is happening. The activities may involve physical contact, including assault by penetration (for example, rape or oral sex) or non-penetrative acts such as masturbation, kissing, rubbing and touching outside of clothing. They may also include non-contact activities, such as involving children in looking at, or in the production of, sexual images, watching sexual activities, encouraging children to behave in sexually inappropriate ways, or grooming a child in preparation for abuse (including via the internet). Sexual abuse is not solely perpetrated by adult males. Women can also commit acts of sexual abuse, as can other children.[7]

Studies of CSA vary in their focus and may or may not adhere to this very wide definition. Accordingly, when estimates of incidence or prevalence appear in the research literature, then studies that do not use identical inclusion criteria may be added together.

With these cautions and methodological challenges in mind, the trend seems to be that retrospective reporting has increased but current child abuse (of all kinds) has actually decreased. A caveat to that claim is that *online* sexual offending against children has increased, a point to be picked up in Chapter 10. For our purposes here, we can distinguish policies implied about justice for survivors of abuse from the past, and those which address current and prospective ways of protecting children. The first informs the second, but they are also separate policy considerations. Children are better protected than in the past and poor reporting in the past means that, now, state agencies are dealing with a 'backlog' both in terms of police investigations and in terms of researching the scale of CSA in the past compared to the present.

A repeated methodological problem about estimating the frequency of CSA is that the act is both shameful and illegal. The extremely horrific cases, such as those of the Fritzls and the Wests noted above, might suggest that incest is very rare because it is the stuff of salacious intrigue in the mass media, only 'once in a blue moon' or when its scarcity renders it a 'crime of the century'.

But incest is not that scarce, if we include all intra-familial sexual abuse, with the latter including non-penetrative as well as penetrative acts and with a range of relatives other than biological parents alone (i.e. step-parents, siblings, grandparents, cousins, uncles etc.) Nearly all of this goes unreported in the press and we only know of the cases investigated by statutory authorities that lead to perpetrators being convicted and (in Britain) being placed on the Sex Offenders Register.

The pressures on victims and perpetrators to stay quiet about sexual acts within families come from prospective shame, prosecution and loss of social standing. As most of us know, family loyalties are powerful about most matters, good and bad, and the challenge of incest is the same, when it is known about but then kept as a family secret by all parties. For any party to disclose the secret creates a risk of family disintegration. All of these initial provisos about our methodological challenge might suggest in advance that the estimates below are likely to be underestimates because secrets can, and do, go to the grave generation after generation.

Indeed, before we get to the particularities of estimating rates of incest, criminologists concede a generic problem in their work. When we are presented with descriptions of rates of any type of offence at a moment in time, they are typically based upon police records of arrests and court records of convictions. However, if instead we do community surveys then, typically, we find higher rates based upon lay reports. The latter include events that were not reported to the police for a range of motives. The evidence base for any crime is biased towards the first form of reporting but community surveys will tend to suggest they are underestimates of actual incidence (first cases) and prevalence (cumulative cases).

Prevalence is sometimes expressed as a lifetime estimate and sometimes as the number of cases present in one year: estimating either is challenging because it relies on our confidence in the validity of the data available to us. So, when we read, in academic journals or the mass media, about rates of CSA (or any other crime or disease) it is worth checking whether incidence is being claimed or one of the forms of prevalence (and which type). We also need to look sceptically at our confidence in the validity of the data.

In the case of CSA, the validity of the data is problematic. In popular reporting, the term 'reliability' of evidence is used understandably, as a cue for our general confidence in research data. However, in professional data collection, a useful distinction is made between empirical validity and empirical reliability. The first term refers to whether we are accurately measuring what we are intending to measure. The second refers to whether there is a consistent pattern of findings across time and place and agreement between researchers about their findings. Whether it is about confidence in what is being measured (validity) or confidence in a consistent pattern (reliability), we are mindful that this field of inquiry is shrouded by shame and fear for victims and the need for dishonesty for the perpetrators. As a consequence, *both* validity and reliability are likely to be compromised to a degree which, *ipso facto*, is not easy to estimate.

In the case of CSA, the above methodological challenges have implications for how we get estimates into a realistic perspective. For example, non-reporting of offences and delays in dealing with historical cases create an underestimation of the scale of offending and this is compounded by the attrition of cases as they are processed by the police for court presentations.[8] Thus, we have layers of filtering that produce diminishing numbers as follows, which affect our confidence in the empirical validity of figures about intra-familial sexual abuse. This listing explains the challenge:

1. Most actual incidents of abuse in the family are not disclosed at all as crimes ('family secrets').
2. Some are reported to trusted friends, relatives or authorities, which might be health workers, teachers, social workers or the police (first disclosure).
3. Some of those cases are acted upon by those people to protect the child (referral for police action).
4. There are then those cases that go on to be investigated by the police *and* are credible to the prosecution authorities (cases prepared for court hearings).
5. Some of those cases lead to actual court hearings (cases not withdrawn).
6. Eventually, we end with a fractional sample of point 1 above (those cases which are prosecuted successfully in the court and become recorded convicted cases of CSA).

At each stage, starting from the first, the role of the victim in having the confidence to report what has happened to them is a central consideration in generating data that is valid. If they do not report at all (first stage) then one set of offences is not on the map at all. An exception to this point is the very occasional incident when an adult, by serendipity, witnesses CSA and then reports it to the police. This is a rare scenario because perpetrators normally are very careful to plan privacy for their assaults or are opportunistic about private moments with children.

After this first stage of disclosure, the credibility of the account of the witness, the motivation and available resources of those listening to the account to act upon it and the trust that victims have at all the stages are pertinent to consider. In the latter case, it is not unusual for victims to withdraw their claims because they calculate the risk of continuing for self and others. They may be rejected from the family system or risk intimidation or violence. Also, they may not have confidence that their disclosures will lead to effective action from those in authority. In the light of inefficiencies and the adequate resources required in the criminal justice system, that lack of confidence may be warranted and wise. Thus, confidence in reporting, where the witness is also the victim and vice versa, a particular feature of sex crimes, is a central process, which can alter recorded incest.

The particular risks of step-parenting can be noted. A Finnish study, in the mid-1990s using an anonymous questionnaire with 15-year-old schoolchildren, found that the reported sexual contact with their father or step-father from girls was 0.5%. A division in the data then appeared in relation to a question that separated those two roles: a 0.2% reported rate of contact was reported with biological fathers compared to a 3.7% rate for step-fathers. Thus, according to this study, there is over an 18-fold increase in risk of a step-father abusing a child than their biological father.[9] However, this finding needs to be placed in the context of another noted above: children are over twice as likely to be sexually abused by a male relative who is not a father *or* step-father. This reinforces the interpretation that the more responsibility the routine care role has, the less risk there is to the child. This is why when biological parents, or even step-parents, do sexually abuse their children, the more serious is the violation of a taboo.

I noted in the introduction to the book that a figure of about 1% of adults have a persistent and singular sexual orientation of paedophilia, whereas up to 20% of men express some sexual interest in children, and studies of the use of indecent images of children show that this occurs in family settings not just in the homes of paedophiles living alone. Some 'primary' paedophiles are unwilling or unable to have sex with an adult partner. However, those men who are able and willing to relate to women sexually may do so in order to access child victims. I note this point as well in relation to the grooming of female criminal confederates with children or in childcare roles in Chapter 5. Being a step-father is a role that establishes a bridge to victims for some predatory paedophiles.

The community surveys noted above from North America, Scandinavia and Australia can be compared and contrasted with a summary of data from the Children's Commissioner for England, Ann Longfield, in November 2015. Her report reviewed police and social services information on CSA and concluded that only 1 in 8 victims are actually identified by professionals. (Compare this with an estimated 30% rate of reporting to authorities from both Finkelhor in the USA and from the National Society for the Prevention of Cruelty to Children (NSPCC) in the UK.)

The Children's Commissioner's Report looked at case information across the police and local authorities between 2012 and 2014.[10] Using a methodology called 'multiple systems estimation', it concluded that 450,000 English children were sexually abused during that period, but only around 50,000 cases were officially recorded, with two-thirds of perpetrators being in the home or nearby. The report also suggested that this underestimation (by nine-fold) of the abuse arose because of an over-reliance on self-reporting by victims. As I noted above, the filtering process of underestimation begins with a primary loyalty that children have towards their families of origin.

But there are other factors that might account for this trend of under-reporting, which are not mutually exclusive. For example, some children may be unaware that they are victims, especially if they are very young or have a learning disability.[11] And even some older children may think that sexual contact with adults is relatively normal. Some children are simply disbelieved when they speak out and they might encounter a failure of adults to act even when they do report what has happened to them to more than one party. The cases discussed in Chapter 6 about dismissive police responses to girls exploited in Rotherham and other towns confirms this aspect of the problem of valid recording.

A fundamental problem about relying on the self-reporting of victims is that they would normally turn to their own family as a trusted solution to any problem. Where CSA occurs in the family, then the latter *is the problem* not the solution. The child then has no option but to suffer in silence and tolerate the abuse until it stops or they leave the family system. And that entrapment may be reinforced by threats and intimidation from adult perpetrators or the withdrawal of affection from, or recognition of, the child as a person. These processes of threat and the removal of validation by adult family perpetrators can ensure a silencing of victims, sometimes permanently.

Setting, desire and action

The above discussion highlights the challenge of estimating the frequency of intra-familial sexual abuse. That ambiguity and uncertainty about evidence sets a couple of other hares running, which are relevant to CSA more generally.

First, there is no neat separation between abuse occurring inside families and outside. Sometimes, the arena of the abuse (for example, the family versus the Scout Club) signals the sort of adult perpetrator involved, but not always. Take the example of a child being abused by a regular babysitter or next-door neighbour. The child may experience them as part of their domestic family life but have little or no such association with a gentle and caring grandparent (a blood relative) who they only travel to see twice a year and who lives 100 miles away. Experientially, in this instance, the child may later recall the babysitter as being part of their family, because of the setting of domestic familiarity, but not recall much about their grandparent.

Another ambiguity about the boundary of the family system is that an abuser might enter it very temporarily (say the fleeting boyfriend of a single mother). Again, experientially, the child victim may not describe the man as a family member, even though the abuse took place in their home. And take the example of the father who traffics his daughter or son outwards to a group of stranger paedophiles; again, this disrupts our confidence in making a neat distinction between incestuous and non-incestuous CSA.

Second, since Freud, we have become accustomed to consider the psychological aspects of desire in childhood. Not only might the child be curious about and have feelings about those intimate to them (before the 'latency period' from around five years of age to puberty) but Freud in his early work also encountered evidence that fathers did indeed sometimes sexually assault their children. I return to this point in Chapter 9.

What matters here is the recurring challenge for us as adults that we have, as reflective agents living in a moral order of norms and mores. If the norm is to maintain a benign non-erotic stance in relation to our children, as they grow up under our care and responsibility, and the more is to not act upon any sexual desire we experience about them, then that is what we *ought* to do in good conscience as citizens. On the one hand, in response to this stricture, current in most cultures, what the unrepentant offender might argue is that the norm and more are wrong-headed or unnecessarily repressive. On the other hand, what the defensive ultra-conformist, who may wish to say to banish or execute convicted paedophiles in fury of disgust, maybe fails to grasp (again in the wake of psychoanalytical insights about us all) is that we are *all* prone at times to impulses and fantasies that are at odds with what we ought to do. In between, a mature adult understands that desire and action are both important. It is the way we *act* that matters at all times. An adult who has no sexual preoccupation with children, nor one who has a fleeting sexual interest in them but takes no action about it, nor the genuinely celibate paedophile, will do harm. It is conduct that matters, whether planned or opportunistic.

We should all expect desire but still be obliged not to act upon it, if that would be immoral. We must rescind our wishes and contain our impulses; that is one feature of being civilised. We can be so angry with an enemy at work or the referee on the football pitch that we want to kill them, but we would be wise not to do so. We have our sexual desires, but we should express them carefully, and if we know that they are socially proscribed in our culture then extra care is implied in the interests of both ourselves and others. This is not merely a matter of not being caught (the active paedophile's dilemma) but also a matter of authentically desisting for pro-social, rather than selfish, reasons. I return to this matter in Chapter 10 when noting that genuinely celibate paedophiles desist from action for reasons of conscience.

What happens in CSA, inside and outside families, is that the gap between desire and action disappears for the adult perpetrator, unchecked by conscience. 'Sexual psychopaths' like Jimmy Savile exemplified this, though even he seemed to invest himself in charity work and Catholicism as an insurance policy against his habitual and lifelong amorality, suggesting that at some level he knew what he was doing was wrong. Fred West had even fewer saving graces than Savile, but what they shared in common was a sense of automatic entitlement to sexual self-indulgence, while holding others in complete contempt in the process. These sex offenders understand that their actions are at odds with both the law and with ordinary expectations of sexual probity; their secrecy to avoid detection reveals this point. What they lack is any *emotional* sympathy for laws and social norms.

Many of those being attracted to children and at times acting upon that are not like Savile or West: they are not sadistic and they may have gentle romantic longings. Savile made the point often that he did not actually like children. That was probably true because all of the evidence now is that he found it difficult to be affectionate or caring about *any* other human being, other than his mother. 'Normal' paedophiles, who in all other respects are ordinary conscience-driven citizens, find ways of rationalising their *particular* sexual needs for children and the acceptability of their enactment. Alternatively, they desist from acting on their desires for reasons of conscience. They rarely argue that they *dislike* children (contra the Savile rhetoric) but are often warm and pleasant to those they encounter in the presence of other adults. Indeed, as we will see later in Chapter 9, a collective rhetoric has developed from paedophile advocacy groups that they are true *lovers* of children, concerned with their needs and development. Conveniently, the latter is understood by active paedophiles as being enriched by 'intergenerational sex'. From their perspective, they then turn their sexual desire into a form of unpaid civil duty to improve the quality of life of the children they encounter and groom.

Those who sexually abuse children develop a blind spot of convenience to protect their egos and preserve a sense of general moral worth in their lives, despite that self-deception. (Forensic psychologists and those working with offenders describe the 'cognitive distortions' of perpetrators.) Many perpetrators, inside or outside families, are seemingly upstanding citizens, with this point being at its most evident in relation to those who are clerics or teachers (see Chapters 4 and 5). Analogously, inside families, abusive fathers or step-fathers may emphasise their general responsibility for the development of their victims and believe in their good intentions about parenting. Fritzl saw himself as a proud patriarch in the kingdom of his family and even Fred West reflected sentimentally about his relationship with his children, including (bizarrely) those he or his wife had murdered. These examples demonstrate the degree of self-deceit that human beings are capable of, even in circumstances of their gross immorality and criminality.[12]

This matter of perpetrators justifying to themselves what is unjustifiable in the eyes of others is important and I return to it in Chapter 9. At this point in the book, suffice to say that adults sexually attracted to children, who act upon their desires, are simply trying to excuse their behaviour to themselves and others all of the time, when and if they are detected. Because they are aware that this involves transgression, their first priority is to avoid detection. But we cannot confuse that general evasion of scrutiny about their preferred sexual activity with all paedophiles being evil people or generally 'psychopathic', i.e. being without conscience or remorse for all of their wrongdoings in life.[13] Some are, but many are not. They are people who want to do to children what others condemn and so at best we can expect them to experience shame, even if there is no guarantee that they will experience guilt.

These are closely related emotions. However, the gap between them is important for our topic and its extent will vary from one child sexual offender to another. For example, those attracted to children who desist from acting on their desires seem to have retained guilt (and maybe anxiety) as an internal control on their actions. For those who do not desist, the guilt is either absent or it is minimised by rationalisations (persuasive excuses to the self).

Conclusion

I finish this chapter, then, with gaps and continuities in mind. The gap between desire and action and the gap between shame and guilt are important to consider about CSA. The continuities to reflect on include the fuzzy boundary between family life and non-family life, as well our shared tendency to have a range of anti-social thoughts and feelings. None of us lack those inner experiences completely (where are the true saints in our midst?) but what matters is what we do with them in our lives. And because the content of those experiences is not uniform, we are not all faced with identical existential challenges. For example, I have no sexual interest in children and, consequently, I am not faced with the dilemma of what to do with that desire. By contrast, every step-father attracted to his partner's daughter must choose, on a daily basis, whether to use his power to exploit her or desist from that temptation. The same is true of the paedophile when deciding or not to download indecent images of children and whether or not to extend his voyeurism to contact with children.

The people described in this book inside and outside family settings desist from or succumb to their sexual desires for children. When they succumb, they wreak personal and social havoc, which others see. For this reason, it is not helpful to become focused simply on the truism that sex with children is wrong or on the universal incest taboo and its 'answer without a question'. We need to move beyond these simple but understandable starting points, if the offers of policy progress I put forward in the final chapter of the book are to make sense and be credible prospects.

If home life is not always safe for children, despite our idealised cultural image of that core of our social system, then it is not the only culprit. The next chapter considers the sexual abuse of children in settings which pride themselves on their moral rectitude: religious organisations.

Notes

1 Dillon, J. (2010). Tales of an ordinary little girl. *Psychosis* 2(1), 79–83.
2 Douglas, E. & Finkelhor, D. (2005). Childhood Sexual Abuse Factsheet. May. Crimes Against Children Research Center. Available at www.unh.edu/ccrc/factsheet/pdf/childhoodSexualAbuseFactSheet.pdf; Australian Bureau of Statistics (2005). Personal Safety Survey Australia (Cat No. 4906.0). Canberra: ABS; US Department of Health and Human Services (2005). Male Perpetrators of Child Maltreatment: Findings from NCANDS.
3 Case studies of this type can be found in Middleton, W. (2013). Ongoing incestuous abuse during adulthood. *Journal of Trauma & Dissociation* 14(3), 251–272; and Salter, M. (2017). Organized abuse in adulthood: survivor and professional perspectives. *Journal of Trauma & Dissociation* 18(3), 441–453.

4 In May 2016, Ronan Farrow re-stated the claim in *The Hollywood Reporter* that Woody Allen, their father, had sexually molested his sister when they were children. Farrow went on to argue that past crimes must be highlighted in order that victims of CSA had the confidence to fight their individual cases.

5 Douglas, E. & Finkelhor, D. (2005). Childhood Sexual Abuse Factsheet.

6 Pereda, N., Guilera, G., Forns, M. & Gomez-Benito, J. (2009). The prevalence of child sexual abuse in community and student samples: A meta-analysis. *Clinical Psychology Review* 29(4), 328–338.

7 See HM Government (2015). *Working Together to Safeguard Children* (p. 93). London: Department for Education.

8 Connolly, D. & Don Read, J. (2006). Delayed prosecutions of historic child sexual abuse: analyses of 2064 Canadian criminal complaints. *Law and Human Behavior* 30(4), 409–434; Fitzgerald, J. (2006). The attrition of sexual offences from the New South Wales criminal justice system. *Crime and Justice Bulletin: Contemporary Issues in Crime and Justice Number 92*. Sydney: NSW Bureau of Crime Statistics and Research; Kelly, L., Lovett, J. & Regan, L. (2005). *A Gap or a Chasm? Attrition in Reported Rape Cases*. London: Child and Woman Abuse Studies Unit, London Metropolitan University.

9 Sariola, H. & Uutela, A. (1996). The prevalence and context of incest abuse in Finland. *Child Abuse & Neglect* 20(9), 843–850.

10 Protecting children from harm. November 24, 2015. London: Children's Commissioner.

11 Kendall-Tackett, K., Lyon, T. & Taliaferro, G. (2005). Why child maltreatment researchers should include children's disability status in their maltreatment studies. *Child Abuse & Neglect* 29(2), 147–151.

12 Another infamous example of proud patriarchy from a sexually abusive father is the case of the British artist and typeset designer Eric Gill, whose sexual interest went even beyond his daughters to dogs. He was a moralistic high Catholic but clearly saw no moral problem with having sex with children or animals and his artistic reputation has largely gone unscathed. See MacCarthy, F. (1989). *Eric Gill*. London: Faber and Faber.

13 However, in Chapter 10, I discuss the evidence that incorrigible child sex offenders are more likely to have *general* antisocial tendencies than, say, celibate paedophiles or offenders who then learn to desist subsequent to release from prison.

4

THE RELIGIOUS BETRAYAL OF CHILDREN

Introduction

This chapter considers the sexual abuse of children in religious settings, with a focus on the British Isles. The role of the Catholic Church stands out in its notoriety, which will be addressed in relation to the Irish Republic. In Great Britain (for outsiders, this means the largest of the British Isles, containing England, Scotland and Wales), Catholic priests committing sex crimes against children have certainly been brought to book.

In London in February 2015, Father Anthony McSweeney was jailed for three years for sexually assaulting a boy in care over 30 years earlier.[1] He worked at a local authority residential home as a volunteer and, with its manager, he abused the boy over a two-year period. The home was in Grafton Close in Hounslow and we now know that some of the victims of the Elm Guest House 'VIP' abuse, by those such as Sir Cyril Smith, were supplied from there (see Chapter 1).

The Catholic child abuse crisis is universal, but in this chapter I focus on the case of Ireland because of the enmeshment there of Church and state. Another peculiar feature of Ireland is that it produced one particular order (the Congregation of Christian Brothers) which has had a disproportionate educational influence, and even subsequent global notoriety. For these reasons, the Irish case study reflects both the general features of Catholic child abuse as well as specific national features. Some of the latter were exported with negative consequences to Anglophone Catholic communities in Australia, Canada, the USA and mainland Britain.

The matter of a collective confession has been a particular source of *angst* for the Catholic Church. For an organisation whose core ideology is about the authoritative preaching of moral certainties and the ubiquity of sin, the Church was inevitably hoisted by its own petard.[2] This meant another irony given the metaphor used by organisational theorists about conflicting aims: the 'cruciform effect'.[3] This refers to the inability of those crucified to find peace; whichever way the victim twists a new form of pain arises. The sign of the cross then had a particular significance as a metaphor for the Church's predicament about CSA.

In organisations, the cruciform effect means that every new solution creates a new problem and it seems difficult to find a pain-free compromise or avoid a new form of dysfunction. By switching between the suppression of evidence about abuse, the blaming of isolated perpetrators alone and the eventual admissions of collective guilt and the need for contrition and financial reparation, the cruciform effect was evident in the Catholic Church. Whichever tactical shift occurred, new problems about credibility emerged and financial costs accrued. Some Catholic orders have been nearly bankrupted by the compensation claims of victims, others have survived relatively unscathed. (Although the Catholic Church may seem like a gigantic monolith, in practice it is a highly variegated set of subsystems, despite its devotion to the Vatican and its clerical hierarchy.)

When CSA emerges in *Catholic* settings it is nuanced in a particular way by layers of physical and cultural isolation. The Church has some relevant traditions that, even charitably, we might still call 'sadomasochistic' in character.[4] Pain, suffering, sexual repression, fasting, hair shirts, strict punishments and mortification of the flesh have been strong themes in its cultural traditions. They have become jumbled up in a sort of ball of wax that can be difficult to unpick.

Those intertwining features are not unique (variants can be found in all the Abrahamic religious traditions, for example in the public displays of pious self-flagellating Muslims). However, when they are combined with structured power, these morbid psychological traditions might have some explanatory value in relation to the peculiarities of abuse in Catholic settings.

Global Catholicism and its cultural history

Irish campaigners for justice for victims have challenged the role of the Vatican in failing to accept the full legitimacy of civil investigations into the scale of child abuse reported or even in accepting the belated attempts of the Irish bishops to improve child protection and deal with past criminality. The ambivalence of the Vatican comes from two historical sources. The first is one of the Vatican protecting its bishops and priests, if needs be in favour of the Catholic laity. In this case, in 1997, when the Vatican became aware of the Irish crisis, its officials and with the knowledge of the Pope told the Irish bishops to be 'fathers to your priests and not policemen'.[5]

The second source of historical guidance relates to 'God's Law'. A common ancient rhetoric from all organised religions in the Abrahamic traditions is that God's Law precedes and is more important than secular law. So-called 'canon law' in the Church can then become a law unto itself, unaccountable and in the trust of clerics who are supposedly unerringly wise and just.

The Irish case study presented below suggests that it may be losing the battle to defend forms of traditional authority in the face of secularised civil forms of polity.

An organisation based on older, medieval forms of power structure, such as the Catholic Church, explicitly defends pre-democratic forms of authority, a hierarchy of entitlement and an assumption of automatic lay deference. That traditional pattern of political assumptions now provokes offence in the secular, postmodern or multi-faith present times. We see resonances here of the crisis of traditional authority discussed in Chapters 1 and 2 about our political class.

Irish politics and the role of Catholicism

A particularly enmeshed relationship has existed in Ireland between Church and state.[6] When British colonialism oversaw the six-year potato famine of 1845, with a million dying and a million emigrating, the Catholic Church was there to offer comfort and burials. From then on, its centrality for Irish politics was assured. If the British abandoned ordinary Irish families to their impoverished fate, the Church filled the vacuum.

Not surprisingly, the Irish constitution, created by its first president, Eamon De Valera, emerged in 1937 after extensive consultations with Catholic bishops.[7] Subsequently, the Church established clear lines of influence in political circles and it led to the delivery of public policy, for example in health and education. When that direct authority in relation to Irish public policy was put into practice, it created spaces for religious staff to act with impunity in relation to their authority over children. Many decades passed before the malign version of that authority was exposed. In part, this was because of state/Church enmeshment. The action and inaction of the Irish police exemplified this point.

On October 26, 2005, the Ferns Report[8] was released, triggered by an investigation by the BBC in its documentary Suing the Pope. Victims of clerical abuse had campaigned together in the pressure group One in Four to demand justice and the BBC was giving them a voice. The Irish inquiry looked at over 100 complaints of abuse over a 40-year period, involving 21 priests in the Ferns Diocese (an area in the southeast of Ireland). Most were male victims but there were some sexual assaults on girls. For example, one priest abused a girl in the privacy of the confessional. In the appendix to this chapter I provide victim accounts of one dominant offender, Father Sean Fortune, who abused boys in his parish in County Wexford and before that in Belfast during the 1980s.

In the Ferns Diocese, a pattern of deceit and cover-up was obvious, with successive local bishops not passing on complaints to the police. Those accused were not separated from new potential victims. Until 1990, the police had been unwilling to properly investigate matters brought to their attention. Before then, approaches from victims were not put on record and they were turned away by the local police. Thus, police inaction began by blocking complaints at the outset.

In 2007, the McCoy Report emerged.[9] It documents how 21 children with intellectual disabilities were abused by 18 members of staff between 1965 and 1998. These 21 were a sample: many others were not dealt with in the investigation, which was requested by the Brothers of Charity and commissioned by the Western

Health Board. The perpetrators involved were not named (transparency was thus not a priority at this stage) but there was clear evidence that the order had moved offenders to other locations and not dealt with the abuse.

On November 26, 2009, the then Irish Minister for Justice, Equality and Law Reform, Dermot Ahern, published the Murphy Report.[10] This was the Irish government's commissioned inquiry about clerical abuse in the Dublin Diocese. Ahern pointed out that the report dealt with a past period, in which undue deference had been afforded to the authority of the Church and that Irish culture was changing in that regard.

Judge Yvonne Murphy and her team took accounts from victims and witnesses and scrutinised nearly 70,000 diocesan files. She found that Church authorities knowingly covered up child abuse. The investigation team was prevented from seeing nearly 5,000 files by a named Cardinal in 2008. The report summarises the accumulation of over 30 years of investigation into the matter. It offers a critical analysis of the role of archbishops, bishops, the Irish police force, health authorities and the Director of Public Prosecutions. Four archbishops in Dublin had, one after another, been aware of the abuse but had done nothing to ensure proper investigations.

The report alluded to 320 victims of abuse at the hands of the priests investigated. Of these, 46 priests were studied in detail, 11 of whom had already been convicted for their sexual assaults on children. In another case, 21 people complained of a priest who regularly took boys for car journeys, with complaints of assault. He also encouraged them to bathe naked in his personal swimming pool. When reported to his superiors, he was transferred to a monastery 'for health reasons'. Those at the monastery were not informed of his history, even though he continued to have regular contacts with altar boys there. In another case in the 1980s, a priest used a computer programme which commanded girls to remove clothing, kiss each other and him. When parents complained, their local bishop did not pass the concern on to the police. The latter were eventually informed in 2002.

But the police were not merely kept in the dark; they also connived at times to suppress evidence of wrongdoing. For example, a known clerical sex offender was permitted, with police knowledge, to leave the country. This connivance was only discovered following scrutiny of Church files, not from staff testimonies.

The main police complicity was at a senior level. More junior officers were commended in the report for pursuing successful prosecutions, despite attempts to interfere in their investigations by a named bishop. In the 1960s, a police commissioner failed to investigate a priest who took photographs of children in Crumlin Children's Hospital. In London, Scotland Yard came into the possession of the photographs and passed them to their colleagues in Dublin. On receipt, they were simply relayed on to a named archbishop, without further investigation. After being at large and serially reoffending against children, the paedophile priest was eventually convicted in the 1980s.

The Ryan Report emerged in 2009 and describes abuse in the Irish Church since the 1930s.[11] It documents physical and sexual abuse of children in over 20 schools and residential facilities run by priests or nuns. For example, there was the Artane Industrial School of Dublin, with its regime of intimidation and fear for all children. The report notes that, at Artane:

> sexual abuse of boys in Artane by Brothers was a chronic problem. Complaints were not handled properly and the steps taken by the Congregation to avoid scandal and publicity protected perpetrators of abuse. The safety of children was not a priority at any time during the relevant period.[12]

The second in-depth account is given in the Ryan Report of the Christian Brothers' school, Letterfrack in County Galway, which was an:

> inhospitable, bleak, isolated institution accessible only by car or bicycle and out of reach for family or friends of boys incarcerated there [...] Sexual abuse was a chronic problem.[13]

Letterfrack harboured child sexual abusers for lengthy periods. For example, two offenders were there for 14 years each.

Another important section of the Ryan Report refers to the case study of defrocked paedophile priest John Brander:

> who taught children in the primary and secondary school sector in Ireland for 40 years. He was eventually convicted of sexual abuse in the 1980s. He began his career as a Christian Brother and after three separate incidents of sexual abuse of boys, he was granted dispensation from his vows.[14]

Brander worked at six different schools, where he terrorised the children. Parents frequently reported their concerns about his conduct but to no effect. Complaints to the Church or government authorities simply led to him being moved from one school to another.

The Ryan Report has a special section which illuminates the culture of the Christian Brothers, the main order (called, in this case, a 'Congregation') in Ireland responsible for male education. In the past, many of its recruits were very young themselves. They may have entered the brotherhood as young as 14 years of age and so had no exposure to sexual experiences outside of an all-male culture, in which adult–child power relationships were constantly at the centre of daily activity.

The Congregation, set up by Edmund Rice at the turn of the twentieth century, offered free education to poor boys, encouraged Christian piety and initially eschewed corporal punishment. These expectations shifted over time to being physically punitive but, more importantly, the original day-schooling model gave way to a residential arrangement. This ensured the physical isolation of the schools from daily public scrutiny and that victims were entrapped.[15] The culture of these 'industrial schools' then was of isolated and harsh environments, which became the model for export to 26 other countries by the Christian Brothers. The global mark of Ireland, about CSA in the Church, is now made evident from the surnames of many offenders in the Irish diaspora in these other countries.

By the turn of this century, the cat was out of the bag about abuse at the hands of the Christian Brothers in Ireland, Canada, England and Australia. In the last of these, the Royal Commission investigating historical claims of abuse said in December 2014 that 'Christian Brothers' leaders knew of allegations of sexual abuse of children at four Western Australian orphanages and failed to manage the homes to prevent the systemic ill-treatment for decades'.

The Congregation of Christian Brothers was concerned mainly with the cost of legal proceedings. The commission also noted that 'there was no sentiment of recognising the suffering of the survivors', which suggests that the collective indifference to actual pain and harm was being replayed and the power and reputation of the Church remained a key priority. The pattern remained of seeing the needs of the laity (in this case of child victims) as being secondary to those of Church staff.

Back in Ireland, the tactical ambivalence of the Christian Brothers was evident once the story of abuse became common knowledge. On the one hand, in 1998, it issued an apology placed prominently in Irish newspapers and it offered access to a telephone helpline. On the other hand, when, in 2003, the Ryan inquiry was going to name perpetrators from the order, the latter took legal action (successfully) to prevent this. Thus, the recurring dilemma of balancing transparency and contrition on the one hand with suppression of information and a full confession of guilt on the other was evident.

Clerical abuse discussed in Church circles reflects unwittingly its quasi-incestuous character. Remember that the title of all Catholic religious staff is 'father', 'brother', 'mother' or 'sister' and these terms are often retained retrospectively in official reporting of exposed and proven abuse about the perpetrators. This reflects the ingrained reverence that exists about the clergy, in Catholicism.

The reverence also tended to put religious staff beyond critical scrutiny. For example, the celibacy of religious staff was assumed without question by the average lay Catholic. And yet, research suggests that, at best, only half of the priesthood are truly celibate in relation to avoiding sexual activity altogether; if masturbation is included in that definition of sexual activity, estimates of *true* celibacy drop to about 2%.

This collective charade about celibacy is not important because of its hypocrisy (masturbation remains a sin requiring acts of contrition in the confessional) but because of the watchfulness and subterfuge it demands of priests. Just as the gay life of politicians discussed in Chapter 1 has until very recently required skills of deception (some of which were helpful in politics) so too when priests profess their unending celibacy. When professed convincingly it is a useful cover story when and if sexual activity with children is pursued. Celibacy implies purity rather than danger: surely we can trust our children to the care of Catholic religious staff without question?

Catholicism, like other Abrahamic traditions, prescribes but more importantly it proscribes.[16] Homosexuality is wrong. Pre-marital sex is wrong. Extra-marital sex is wrong. Masturbation is wrong. Contraception is wrong. Abortion is wrong. Divorce is wrong. The arbiters of sexual probity in charge of the Church have put the laity in a constant state of anxiety about their actual or potential wrongdoing. The opportunity and tendency to point the finger in the other direction have thereby often been closed down within the culture of Catholic deference.

In the Catholic regimes of care and control of Irish children, the particular role of the religious 'cloth' also became evident for victims. The children were faced with the expectations of trust and the experience of awe in relation, not only to a daily secular world of adult power, but also of a spiritual power, claimed and believed about those in religious garb. The 'trauma bond' peculiar to abuse in Catholic settings was infused with a mystical or supernatural element for victims; their entrapment was spiritual, not just physical.

The research to date does not confirm clearly that paedophiles enter the Church with the clear purpose of abusing children. But if some abusers are not purposeful in their planned career then the abusive conduct of this group must be shaped by the circumstances of Church life instead. One aspect of that has been strict gender separation. This, of necessity, entailed same-sex contact. The complementary implication of this would be that heterosexual CSA would be a low probability in Catholic settings, which seems to have been the case.

This ambiguity about the sexuality of the perpetrators is extended further when we return to the sadomasochistic culture of Catholicism. This uncertainty is evident in the case of cruel nuns. Clear-cut cases of sexual abuse of girls by nuns are in the minority in the Irish reports (but were present). The intersection of physical abuse and eroticism is not unpicked in the reporting. For example, the Ryan Report cites this as an example it gives of *physical abuse* from the actions of the ironically named 'Little Sisters of Mercy'. Nuns working in pairs would strip girls naked and tie them to a bed with rope so that they could not move:

> She would beat you with the leather strap and count to 100 as she was beating [...] If you cried you got worse, so I learned not to cry.[17]

This is a fairly clear pornographic scenario of sadomasochism but is not labelled as such in the Ryan Report. As the latter noted, 'there were no reports of sexual abuse alone and almost all reports were of sexual abuse, combined with physical abuse, neglect and emotional abuse'. However, this amalgam abuse included forced anal and vaginal penetration with fingers and objects, naked beatings, extensive voyeurism and recurrent private and public humiliation.

All of this suggested that many of the abusive nuns were paedophiles with strong sadistic tendencies. Their existence cautions against explanations of abuse in Catholic settings, which are reduced singularly to patriarchy or to 'paedophile priests'. And, unlike the bulk of female offending against children in other settings (see Chapter 5), where the woman's role is supportive and complicit of male offending, in the case of residential Catholic facilities, such as convents and industrial laundries, the offending had no male involvement.

Thus, the opportunity for heterosexual paedophiles to operate in Catholic settings is highly constrained by their tradition of gender segregation. Heterosexual paedophiles would be likely to look elsewhere to exploit children (for example, in sports' organisations or via planned step-parenting). The Murphy Report noted a couple of parish priests with girl victims. However, these heterosexual perpetrators were in the minority overall. For example, of the 347 reports of abuse against girls recorded in the Ryan Report, only 4 involved assaults from visiting priests.

The implications of the above findings and headline messages for the Irish State have been considerable at the turn of this century.[18] The enmeshment noted between state and Church in Ireland meant that there would be political consequences. One was the emergence of secular pressure groups challenging the traditional power and role of the Irish Church. The other was that cases previously brushed under the carpet could now topple politicians. In late 1994, the child abuse crisis led to the fall of the Irish government. This was a consequence of it mishandling the case of a notorious offender, Brendan Smyth, who was wanted in Northern Ireland for crimes against children.[19]

In 1991, Smyth escaped arrest in Northern Ireland (part of the UK) by moving south across the border and was harboured for much of the time at Kilnacrott Abbey in Cavan. The British police demanded his return but the extradition was blocked and delayed by both the Irish Attorney General and the Church authorities for three years. Past failures by the Church had enabled Smyth to offend for over 40 years, with an estimated number of 143 child victims in Ireland. His favoured *modus operandi* was to befriend families of intended victims and then take the latter on trips where the abuse took place.

This case highlights that the trust and deference of the Catholic laity in some cases can be a determining factor in making children vulnerable. But the institutional and cultural setting of Smyth, *after* his offending took place, also reminds us of the complicit context that is required in order to hide and sustain crimes against children. Earlier chapters have emphasised this point repeatedly in relation to any setting of offending against children.

And as a reminder of the impact of CSA on the viability of the Church itself, Kilnacrott Abbey was closed in April 2015 to be sold off to pay compensation to the victims of Brendan Smyth. Smyth died one month into his 12-year sentence for sample crimes against children. He was buried in a private pre-dawn ceremony in the grounds of Kilnacrott Abbey in 1997; an embarrassed scenario of shame at the end of a shameful period for the Church in Ireland. Smyth was by then oblivious to its meaning, but his remaining Catholic brothers and sisters were not.

Lessons about systemic complexity and multi-factorial reasoning

The Irish case study illuminates again that when we come to understand the sexual abuse of children by adults, there is really little point in seeking single causes (and, by implication, the prospect of single solutions), hence I set out three horizontal frames to consider. At the macro level, the history of the Church and current authority in the Vatican are pertinent to think about. The endemic sadomasochistic culture that has permeated the Church is also a past–present link that is relevant for rendering suffering a virtuous norm.

The middle or meso frame reminds us that we do have to think about contemporary norms and local circumstances. In the Irish case, the enmeshment of Church and state after the formation of the Republic of Ireland shaped the settings of child abuse. Given that the Church took charge of the planning and delivery of educational and health facilities, then, when and if abuse emerged in those settings, this was likely to be at the hands of religious personnel.

The macro and meso levels then provided the particular features when, at the micro level, the interpersonal features of child abuse emerged. For example, the harsh culture of the Christian Brothers was a macro consideration but it had micro implications for perpetrator motivation and the experience of victims. Similarly, the cultural aspects of the tangles the Church has got into about sex and sin has filtered from the distant features in time and space to particular acts of abuse in the here and now.

Within this multi-layered reality, different forms of isolation are important to consider. For example, Church law and authority were separated from the civil rule of law. The police connivance was, in part, about them handing authority to the Church instead of taking responsibility for crimes against children. The separation of canon law from civil law undoubtedly played its part in making children vulnerable to physical, emotional and sexual abuse. When power went unchecked, these three forms of abuse could readily interweave.

But of most importance were the forms of separation that were physical in nature. The facilities were residential and so closed off from the daily scrutiny of outsiders. The aphorism that 'sunlight is the best form of disinfectant' is pertinent here. These institutions were often in isolated rural settings, making it difficult to access for visitors. In those settings, the arbitrary authority of adults was unchecked. Also, they permitted further times of separation in dormitories or the private rooms of staff, where abusive acts could take place. That is why the shift in the model of provision in the Christian Brothers' schools (from day to residential) was such an important historical moment. Isolated residential settings increase the risk of the abuse of power; a point noted repeatedly by investigators of a wide range of institutions, secular and religious.

The corruption of care

The case study of Irish religious abuse reflects a wider public policy challenge for developed societies, which created institutional care for vulnerable people. In his review of the scandals surrounding large 'mental illness and mental handicap' hospitals in the 1960s and 1970s, John Martin wanted to understand what he called 'the corruption of care'.[20] How was it possible that those with the power and responsibility to look after less powerful and vulnerable individuals went on to neglect and abuse them? How was it that places designed to put care at their centre were taken over by oppressive, unsavoury and even illegal forms of practice?

Martin's answers were not about 'bad apples', though he did not deny staff wrongdoing. Of more importance than malevolent individuals were the conditions possibly created by the culture and the sort of system they and their victims shared. Also, the history and purpose (or 'function') of institutions were important to take into account. In the case of the Catholic Church in Ireland, we can consider the following that increased the chances of the sort of corruption of care that culminated in child abuse *and* the damage limitation exercises then stimulated for political reasons:

1. There was a centralised authoritarian organisation that encouraged a top-down rule of obedience about hierarchical clerical authority.
2. The centralised form of power in Rome is long-standing, dating back to the fourth century. Reports of child abuse at the hands of priests and nuns were highly threatening to the global public reputation of the Catholic Church and its very long clerical tradition. The scale of abuse admitted to now put the reputation and viability of the Church at risk. This led to political ambivalence balancing confession with damage limitation.
3. At the national level, in Ireland, the truth was obscured for decades by a lack of candour and sometimes downright deceit on the part of Irish bishops and archbishops. There was also active connivance at times between Church authorities and the Irish police. When the civil authorities eventually demanded transparency, the Church still claimed its right to withhold its records. The enmeshment of the Church and state in Ireland nuanced a more general problem about child abuse on the global stage for the Vatican.
4. At the micro level, where the actual enactment of the abuse was found, the children would suffer the same range of personal troubles as any other survivors of sexual abuse. However, they might also experience the extra burden of the 'trauma bond' linked to religion and their abusers being men and women of 'the cloth'.
5. In those particular Catholic settings, we can also identify the recurrent features of abusive isolated settings that John Martin perceptively argued underpinned the 'corruption of care' in any institution. These forms of isolation were multiple. In those settings, like in the scandal hospitals where those with mental health problems or learning disabilities were abused, the client group was deemed to be inferior and unrewarding. As Harry Ferguson, one of the leading researchers of child abuse in Britain, has noted, institutionalised children were considered to be 'moral dirt'. These were not *any* children, but those already deemed to be problematic in some way: poor, wayward, delinquent, orphaned, disabled or pregnant (or some combination of these). This created a starting point of seemingly warranted harsh authority by adults. And when forms of isolation were the context of that starting point, the benign care of children would be easily shattered. Victim blaming was waiting in the wings as a first line of defence for the abusers. If these children were indeed 'moral dirt' then why should we treat them with respect and why take their complaints

seriously? A feature of the problem in English towns of CSA on the streets (see Chapter 6) was that the testimonies of children were not believed.

6.   The multiple isolation in Irish Catholic settings involved several co-existing strands. They were geographically remote and, as closed settings, they had little or no scrutiny from the outside world. These were desolate and self-defining fiefdoms for the local religious staff. Within the buildings there were areas of privacy ready-made for abusive scenarios. The religious personnel were also culturally and intellectually isolated from the wider world. They remained in a closed world of abstract theological concerns and moralisations and their tasks were solely concerned with the care and control of children. They could remain for years with no wider cultural exposure or altered intellectual horizons. In the case of some of the Christian Brothers, this peculiar world may have begun at puberty. These were people whose norms and moral compass were created in an insulated environment, with little or no understanding of how they were perceived by wider society.

Comparisons with non-Catholic settings

Because of the cultural peculiarities of Catholicism and the unusual political position of the Church in the young republic of Ireland, we must be cautious about assuming that religious settings were safe elsewhere. They were not. For example, the Anglican community in Ireland (called the 'Church of Ireland') has had its own share of abuse scandals but they have received far less mass media coverage and even less state interest. Arguably, non-Catholic children have been proportionally *more* at risk in Ireland because state authorities took less interest in them.

And when we come to look at non-conformist and anti-clerical ('low Church') Christianity, we still find CSA. In May 2015, the Methodist Church in Britain released a report about its own similar challenges. In a three-year investigation, it looked at accusations of CSA going back to 1950. The Church apologised for the 2,000 staff in its midst accused of CSA during that period.[21]

This comparison suggests that religious power can become bound up with abusive power in adults enjoying both in *any* denomination. Maybe religious staff can use the cover of moral purity to have malign contact with children; this suggests that this is not a peculiarity of Catholic culture. For example, in England in 2014, the Archbishop of Canterbury wept publicly when discussing the evidence of CSA admitted to in Anglican settings.[22]

Moreover, the sinister institutional settings exposed by the Irish investigations were not limited to religious organisations. The fact that I adopted a model about layers of isolation and the corruption of care from John Martin's favoured form of systemic analysis in secular state institutions is pertinent. *All* complex forms of institutional care (long-stay hospitals, care homes or orphanages) run the risk of abusing those they allegedly care for.

If all forms of segregation of vulnerable people, be they children or adult, have run the risk of diverse forms of abuse of the weak by the powerful then we need to stop and think about the relative risks of caring for children in open rather than closed settings. Studies comparing foster care with residential care found a level of sexual abuse in both, but there was a significantly greater risk to children in the second form of care financed by the state. However, foster care is not problem-free and neither is ordinary living in our families of origin, where most child abuse takes place. This highlights that child-rearing in most settings involves privacy and an expectation that external scrutiny is minimal.

Home life for us all is *expected* to be private – and, therefore, in its own way isolated – and thus carries its particular risks (see Chapter 3). One of the greatest policy challenges in modern democracies is to protect children from harm inside their *particular* families, without turning *all* families into scrutinised clients of the state. This conundrum remains unresolved in public policy, even in the most developed and resource-rich countries of the world. Basically, complex societies, rich or poor, offer sites of privacy for child abuse to emerge.

Finally, a risk of focusing singularly on child *sexual* abuse in religious settings (drawing us into a 'paedo priest' form of reductionism) is that we can lose sight of the more general distorting impact of power in isolated systems. Much of the abuse of power by adults in the examples given in this chapter was embedded in a general ethos of humiliation and belittlement of children. This emotional abuse alongside, in the past, a commonality of physical abuse, when corporal punishment was considered to be both ethical and legal in childcare settings, can be forgotten easily if our critical attention is limited to sexual abuse alone. Sexual abuse, then, can be a variation on a theme, bound up with more general domination of adults over children in closed settings.

One relevant circumstantial feature of Catholic residential facilities was a cultural assumption that there was legitimate and complete adult authority over children. Children were seen as ill-formed and full of sin. Their assumed moral deficit was dealt with by their 'elders and betters', encouraging a pious sensibility by teaching them godly habits. This was a scenario ripe for arbitrary and unaccountable authority: children deserved what they got, when and if the adult in power and control considered it appropriate. Priests and nuns had the authority of God as a stick to beat children with, metaphorically and often literally.

However, this theocratic authority can be overemphasised: in non-religious care settings, children were still abused and held in contempt as 'moral dirt'. That attribution seems to be a risk factor in *all* childcare settings, secular or religious. It confirms the point made by John Martin that the corruption of care is more likely if the client group involved is unrewarding and deemed to be in some way defective (morally, psychologically or physically). The disturbing scenario of disabled children being sexually abused described in the Murphy Report is, thus, not that surprising, when we think about structured power. Those in the Church protesting that they were being picked on given these wider trends had a point of sorts, because the 'moral dirt' approach to children could be found in secular, not just religious, forms of childcare.

Given this overlap of features across all providers of childcare, the challenge for organised religion may be more about the *particular* credibility problem created by

its history of self-righteous moral authority. Given its tradition of recurrent moralisations, maybe the Catholic Church has deserved the criticism it has suffered for
this reason alone. Moreover, it was an ethical tradition that paid more attention to
sin as rule breaking rather than the human and emotional consequences. This may
be one reason that perpetrators were treated as sinners in need of confession and
repentance, while the child victims and their distress was ignored. Catholic ethics
has to catch up with forms of moral philosophy that deal with emotions and the
recognition of the humanity of vulnerable people, not simply rules. The probity of
the powerful is only one aspect of ethics. Ethics is also about relating with consideration and respect to all fellow human beings.

That culture of moralisation, especially about its obsession with sexual matters
(any of us can easily forget that there is more to morality than sexual probity) set
the Irish Church up to become an idol with feet of clay. The sexual problem for
the Church was created by the grey and hypocritical world of professed celibacy.[23]
As Marie Keenan, an Irish researcher about our topic, noted, sexual misconduct in
the Church was on a continuum in that grey world.[24] Boundary violations of Irish
priests have included sexual relationships with women. Heterosexual priests have
sex with their housekeepers and have, at times, even fathered children.

And many priests are gay and act upon that while retaining their role. Indeed, gay
relationships ensure that the clergy are kept away from the temptations of the flesh
they moralise about and that exist between men and women in relation to favoured
Catholic proscriptions: contraception, abortion and divorce. 'Heteronormativity'
(the cultural assumption that to be heterosexual is to be normal) means that the gay
priest is excluded from facing these lived dilemmas.

The pretence of chastity obscures the actual presence of the range of sexual
conduct of priests and nuns, with true celibacy at one end of a spectrum and CSA
at the other. In between, there are priests and nuns who do what all adults do at
times: have sex with other adults. The false and unattainable standard of genuine
and permanent celibacy for most adults means that Catholic clergy have a long fall
from grace, when they act sexually in any way.

Another part of the context in Ireland is the high prevalence of sexual abuse
reported retrospectively by victims in wider society. This has been recorded as 30%
of women and 20% of men reporting childhood sexual abuse of some kind. This is
a much higher prevalence estimate than that reported in the USA (10%) or the UK
(5%), suggesting that Ireland more than others in the past has abused its children.
However, we can also note that, in those estimates, only 4% of the abuse was by
religious personnel (leading some in the Church understandably to ask why clerical
abuse is singled out for scrutiny).[25]

What we need to think about in relation to clerical abuse is its institutional
features, which are separate from the wider challenge of intra-familial abuse (see
Chapter 3). The Irish Catholic Church, for the complex reasons rehearsed in this
chapter, is a good case study for us to understand CSA beyond simply fathoming
the psychological pathology of perpetrators, despite their hypnotic fascination for
us all.

If, according to research, 4–8% of Catholic priests sexually abuse children, then 92–96% of them do not, but that group is still collectively responsible for child protection. This again reminds us that the scandal about child abuse in Irish Catholic settings occurred within a wider ethos of adult power, which could be benign much of the time. And even when it was malignant, the child victim was not always sexually abused: they may have been only treated harshly or cruelly. This was awful for them, but it reminds us that sexual abuse is only one form of child abuse.

To finish this chapter on a positive note, because the Catholic Church, more than other religions and denominations, has now been evaluated extensively in the past 20 years, it has lessons to share with others about child protection. Some of those lessons are pertinent to all settings in which children exist for varying periods of time outside of their family. In complex modern societies where adults act *in loco parentis*, then children are always at some degree of physical, sexual and emotional risk. This is a cue for the next chapter.

Appendix: A victim's accounts of Irish Catholic abuse

The account below is an excerpt from the full transcript of the BAFTA Award-winning BBC TV documentary Suing the Pope, broadcast in March 2002. It is from Colm O'Gorman, in his thirties, who was abused and raped as a boy by Father Sean Fortune for over two years in the 1980s. Fortune was not brought to justice until 1999, when he was charged with 66 sexual offences against 29 boys. He committed suicide while awaiting trial. The programme notes that four of his child victims also committed suicide. O'Gorman made the programme with the BBC and said:

> He would pick me up and be the priest in front of my mother and my family. Five minutes later in the car he'd have me perform oral sex on him. And then, five minutes after that ended, stop off and again be the priest and walk into somebody's house with me in tow behind […] The one thing that I always wanted was for somebody to take this back, for somebody to take responsibility, for somebody to say, 'Actually, we should have done something here, we didn't […]'.
>
> On Sunday mornings, after Fortune had abused me on Saturday night, he'd leave me in his bed in the bedroom in the house there and come down and say first mass. And I remember that he used to come back after saying first mass and sometimes abuse me again, and then I'd have to go downstairs with him and have breakfast and then come down here for the second mass and sit and watch him say mass. It was so hard to make sense of what was happening […] You know, I blamed myself for what was happening. And he was good at that. I mean, he made me feel like he, he, really manipulated me into a position where I accepted total blame for what was happening. He told me it was my problem and he needed to help me. And he actually threatened to tell my parents […] Not only do I, I suppose, have to deal with the fact that I was abused by Fortune, the fact that, ultimately, I feel I was abused by the

Church and the fact that that whole society, that my own society abandoned me because an awful lot of people knew exactly what was happening but chose not to do anything about it […]

Twenty years ago, that bastard raped me. And, I'm still now forced to be in a position where I have to fight to get somebody to acknowledge what they did or didn't do and the responsibility that they had for that. And I meet up with other men who are in exactly the same position and I find out that, that, that young boys and men have died, have committed suicide, I believe because of what he did to them.

Notes

1 Laville, S. (2015). Priest jailed for abusing boy at children's home. March 27. *The Guardian*. Available at www.theguardian.com/uk-news/2015/mar/27/priest-tony-mcsweeney-jailed-abusing-boy-childrens-home.
2 Faulkner, M. (2003). *Supreme Authority: Understanding Power in the Catholic Church*. New York: Alpha Press.
3 Gowler, D., Legge, K. & Clegg, C. W. (eds). (1993). *Case Studies in Organizational Behaviour and Human Resource Management*. London: Paul Chapman.
4 Hidalgo, M. (2007). *Sexual Abuse and the Culture of Catholicism*. New York: Haworth Press.
5 Cited in Keenan, M. (2012). *Child Sexual Abuse & The Catholic Church* (p. 194). Oxford: Oxford University Press.
6 English, R. (2006). *Irish Freedom: A History of Irish Nationalism*. London: Macmillan.
7 The separation of the Irish Republic from the six counties in the north, which remained in the UK, left Protestants in a tiny minority south of the border (only around 4% of the population). They were 'left as orphans', when the Irish Free State emerged in 1922. Despite Catholic children being exposed to the vagaries of Church-dominated forms of schooling and childcare, Protestant children were at additional risk. This was because sources of overview and regulation from the Irish State were weak or non-existent for that minority. Many non-Catholic children suffered their own abuse in privately run institutions. See Meehan, N. (2015). Tuning out the Troubles in Southern Ireland: Revisionist History, Censorship and Problematic Protestants. Unpublished PhD Thesis. A recent confirmation of the lesser story of non-Catholic abuse evading proper state scrutiny was of the failure of the Church of Ireland (the Anglican Church) to deal with abusers in its own midst. See McGarry, P. (2016). Child abuser volunteered at St Patrick's Cathedral after conviction. November 10. *Irish Times*. Available at www.irishtimes.com/news/social-affairs/religion-and-beliefs/child-abuser-volunteered-at-st-patrick-s-cathedral-after-conviction-1.2863192.
8 Ferns Report (2005). *Report Presented to the Minister for Health and Children*. Dublin: Government Publications.
9 McCoy, K. (2007). *Confidential report presented to the Western Health Board in relation to Brothers of Charity Services in Galway*. Available at www.hse.ie/eng/services/Publications/services/Disability/MCoy_BOC.pdf.
10 Murphy Report (2009). *Report by Commission of Investigation into the Handling by Church and State Authorities of Allegations and Suspicions of Child Abuse against Clerics of the Catholic Archdiocese of Dublin*. Dublin: Department of Justice, Equality and Law Reform.

11 Ryan Report (2009). *The Commission to Inquire into Child Abuse Report.* Dublin: Government Publications.
12 Ibid., p. 3.
13 Ibid., p. 4.
14 Ibid., p. 5.
15 Raftery, M. & O'Sullivan, E. (1999). *Suffer the Little Children: The Inside Story of Ireland's Industrial Schools.* New York: Continuum.
16 Greven, P. (1992). *Spare the Child: The Religious Roots of Punishment and the Psychological Impact of Child Abuse.* New York: Vintage Books.
17 Ryan Report (2009), p. 144.
18 Rigert, J. (2008). *An Irish Tragedy: How Sexual Abuse by Irish Priests Helped Cripple the Catholic Church.* Baltimore: Crossland Press.
19 McKeown, L-A. (2015). Brendan Smyth: Paedophile priest 'told doctor he may have sexually abused hundreds of children'. June 23. *The Mirror.* Available at www.mirror.co.uk/news/world-news/brendan-smyth-paedophile-priest-told-5932125.
20 Martin, J. (1984). *Hospitals in Trouble.* Oxford: Blackwell.
21 Strangwayes-Booth, A. (2015). Methodist Church apologises for abuse spanning decades. May 28. BBC News. Available at www.bbc.co.uk/news/uk-32909444.
22 Graham, G. & Bingham, J. (2014). Justin Welby: I broke down in tears at horror of Church child abuse. October 27. *The Telegraph.* Available at www.telegraph.co.uk/News/Religion. In 2015, ex-bishop Peter Ball was sentenced to 32 months for child molestation and, by 2017, Welby was expressing criticism of a previous Archbishop of Canterbury, George Carey, for not dealing with Ball's extensive abuse.
23 Sipe, A. (2003). *Celibacy in Crisis: A Secret World Revisited.* New York: Brunner-Routledge.
24 Keenan, M. (2012). *Child Sexual Abuse.*
25 Ibid.

5

THE TROJAN HORSE

Working with children

Introduction

In February 2015, Simon Harris was jailed for 17 years and 4 months for sexually abusing boys in Gilgil, Kenya, between 1996 and 2013.[1] The UK court insisted that at least half of the sentence must be served. Harris had headed a youth charity based in Britain which organised placements for volunteers in Kenyan schools. What made this case unusual was that it was one of the first prosecutions of a British citizen who had committed a sexual offence abroad. The abuse came to light as a by-product of a British Channel 4 TV documentary about the lives of street children in Gilgil.

West Mercia police officers visiting Kenya built up a picture of the emergence of the abuse. There was a foreign charity supporting under-resourced childcare in Kenya. The prevalence of street children, who were often viewed with contempt locally, provided a population for a paedophile to target. Harris used money and food to lure the boys he preferred off the street and into his local residence, where the abuse took place. His local presence was assumed to be benign because the charity he headed was respected. The judge in the case noted a 'veneer of respectability' emerged from the latter but also Harris' personality and background; he was intelligent, well-educated and 'charismatic'.

Harris had previously been a classics teacher in England in the 1980s. During that period, he abused pupils (boys aged 13 or 14) at Shebbear College in Devon, but this only came to light in his statement to police on being arrested in 2013. The abuse had been investigated by police in Devon at the time, but the cases were dropped after the parents opted not to pursue their complaints. Harris resigned from his post at the school during the investigation period. As a result, he went under the radar of police surveillance. This was also a time (pre-2003) when the Sex Offenders Register had yet to be established. However, the risk prevention potential of the register is questionable. For example, its powers to prevent international travel were invoked but were circumvented by Harris' appeal in the UK.

Before saying more about the risks posed to children in education, we can look at a different institution, where power over them has been celebrated. This case exemplifies why we should approach an adult preoccupation with youth work with some scepticism. Some wanting to work with children in a paid or voluntary capacity will also have a sexual interest in them. It is not surprising that organised youth work has contained its fair share of CSA. We can start with Scouting, which is the largest non-religious international movement in modern times. Its popularity brings with it an assumption of its safety. But if it is not safe, then such popularity also makes it an extensive site of risk to children.

Scouting

The Scouting movement did not get off to a good start as far as child protection is concerned. Its founder and continuing role model was Lord Baden-Powell who had a voyeuristic interest in young boys, while proscribing sexual activity, including masturbation. In 1911, he proclaimed that 'a Scout is clean in thought, word and deed' and warned boys not to give in to temptation.

On leave from his career in Hussars, Baden-Powell would stay regularly at the elite Charter House public school with one of its masters, Alexander Todd, an old friend who regularly took photographs of naked and semi-naked boys, which fascinated the soldier. He enjoyed pig sticking and saw it as an example of British superiority in Imperial India. It involved killing running pigs with a pointed stick until they bled to death, squealing. Baden-Powell also relished watching executions. We can fairly deduce that maybe he was a sadistic voyeur and that his voyeurism was orientated in part towards young boys. Regimentation and control of young men in his military life then spilled over into his civilian interests, which took organisational form as the Boy Scouting and Girl Guide movements.[2]

Inquiries into large-scale sexual abuse of boys in the USA exemplify how at times the mass media can be a source of useful investigation, not just demonisation and hyperbole. The *Washington Times* had journalists who spent two years examining records of sexual abuse inside the Boy Scouts Association.[3] By 1991, they were in a position to report that paedophiles were indeed attracted to work in the movement. The investigation found that, between 1975 and 1984, 231 Scout leaders had been dismissed from the organisation following revelations of CSA. Between 1971 and 1990, there were 1,151 cases of sexual victimisation (and this was considered to be an underestimate by informants). Given the litigious culture of the USA, it is not surprising that some of these cases triggered large compensation payments: in 50 cases of lawsuits investigated it was estimated that, between 1986 and 1991, the US Boy Scouts Association and its local supporting councils paid out more than $15 million to victims.

In the UK in December 2014, the British Scouting Association (BSA) issued an apology for the expanding number of cases of men who were reporting sexual abuse in their younger lives as Scouts. These cases had been triggered by police inquiries into Jimmy Savile, discussed in Chapter 1. But in the 1990s, a larger and proven example came to light. A splinter movement from the BSA was the UK Baden-Powell Scout Association. The latter focused on returning to the original interest of their founder Baden-Powell on the outdoor, Spartan backwoodsman exploration prescribed in his classic text *Scouting for Boys*. This quasi-military and authoritarian ethos imposed on children is surely a framework for controlling the latter. Such an ethos is not inherently abusive, though some liberals might argue that it is and consequently invented the Woodcraft Folk as a non-authoritarian alternative. However, it creates the conditions of possibility in which control can become deployed for malign purposes.

A police inquiry in 1998 found that, for over 30 years, the Association had harboured an extensive paedophile ring which victimised up to 30 children.[4] The reach of the splinter group was substantial (it had 100 lodges and a membership of 2,000 boys). Both this group and the BSA continue to exist at the time of writing. A newcomer to the current Scouts website would have no sense of the gravity of this recent dark history. Both offer hagiographic accounts of Baden-Powell and there is a silence about wrongdoing, though child protection policies are mentioned.

If we set up a structure, such as Scouting, when men look after boys *and* we unwisely operate a heteronormative assumption *and* we give permission for privacy and physical isolation (such as camping in distant rural areas), then we are creating particular conditions of possibility for sexual offending. Therefore, we should not be surprised when and if gay paedophiles are attracted by the role of Scoutmaster or want to teach in same-sex boarding schools. As I note often in this book, our hypnotic focus on perpetrators has diverted our attention, too readily at times, from the importance of their *contexts* of offending. What matters are the circumstances that adults who wish to have sex with children contrive, or opportunistically seek out, in order to succeed.

Schools: access to ordinary (and extraordinary) children

Given that day schooling is the norm, then we would expect CSA to be limited to the isolated settings of fee-paying boarding schools (confusingly, in Britain, these are called both 'public' and 'private' schools). Indeed, residential schooling is a greater risk factor than day schooling.[5] However, the physical and geographical isolation of residential schooling is only one consideration about risk. Another is to deploy secret methods of voyeurism.

Voyeuristic paedophiles

'Non-contact abuse' is well known in the folklore of schooling, especially in relation to some teachers with a reputation for habitually observing naked children in shower rooms. In a recent case, this was aided by new technology but also detected by the same.[6]

In April 2014, Gareth Williams, a deputy head teacher from Cardiff, was jailed for five years for voyeuristic crimes. He installed secret cameras in the toilets of two private homes and his own school, Ysgol Glantaf, to watch children. He captured the images of 31 boys between the ages of 11 and 16. This discovery was a spin-off from a police investigation of men purchasing indecent images of children from the Internet. Williams was found to be in the possession of 16,419 images of children and 691 videos. He was married, indicating that, outwardly, such a risk was not apparent and more generally his teaching record was exemplary. On detection, he admitted that he had always had an interest in the development of boys but could not explain why. This was a paedophile who stayed in his area of origin. But it is commonplace for child sex offenders to move around so that their local reputation does not haunt them and to seek pastures new for further offending.

Contact offending in teaching

The case of William Vahey, a teacher, starting in the USA indicates how paedophilia can have a global reach from parochial beginnings. His offending began as a Boy Scout in 1963, when he later admitted at his arrest in 1969 that he began seeking opportunities to fondle boys. He was jailed for three months and given five years' probation but was permitted to leave the country. He moved around the world abusing boys in a variety of schools where he worked until he was detected in March 2014 at the American Nicaraguan School. His flash drive discovered there by a housemaid contained images of 90 boys he had filmed after drugging and abusing them. He secreted sleeping pills in soft drinks and biscuits offered to victims.

Prior to that appointment, he had worked at the Southbank International School in London between 2009 and 2013. The FBI alerted police in Britain and an inquiry found that his trademark *modus operandi* had been at the Southbank School too. The Met, arresting him at his flat in London, found similar evidence on his laptop and 11 flash drives. The case did not reach trial because he fled to the USA, where he committed suicide.

Subsequently, parents of his victims sued Southbank International School, noting poor record-keeping and a failure to take action about claims against Vahey in the past. The head of the school had dismissed these complaints as being from disgruntled and vindictive parents. Vahey isolated his victims by volunteering to head field trips abroad. In less than four years he took 17 groups abroad with the full knowledge of his superiors. When on these trips, students and other staff noted that he favoured isolating those becoming sick by placing them in separate rooms, where he would assault them.

The complicity of other staff can be noted. The head failed to pass on four serious complaints to the police or social services locally. Vahey also urged colleagues on trips not to tell parents about their children becoming ill. After the reports and his suicide, colleagues of Vahey recalled his suspicious behaviour. But those suspicions did not lead to corrective action prior to his death. For example, one teacher did report Vahey's habit of isolating sick children to the deputy head, but the latter took no action. Vahey developed a reputation on the trips for slapping the backsides of students and insisting that they slept only in their underpants. He would awaken them by whipping sheets away. This pattern was reported by students subsequent to Vahey's suicide. The theme of contrived isolation is exemplified in this next example, but also note the recurrent theme of the complicity of others in offending behaviour.

The perils of music tuition

Music teaching is a subsystem of schooling that is a particular site of risk. One-to-one tutoring is commonplace. Sometimes, this occurs in soundproofed rooms. The process of music teaching involves a mixture of perfecting playing skills and an encouragement of emotional expression and sensitivity in performance. This process is psychologically demanding both for the teacher and pupil. And the emotional field between them is more likely than in class teaching to evoke intense personalised feelings in both directions. The pupil may start to feel a bond of gratitude and adoration, making them more compliant than the norm. In this setting, then, there is a particular onus on the teacher to remember their power and responsibility. If that duty is abandoned, then there is a risk of both power and erotic desire becoming unbridled and fused. Here are some recent publicised examples of this occurring with criminal consequences.

In February 2015, Philip Pickett was jailed for 11 years for rape and indecent assault.[7] His victims were teenage girls and the cases went back to the 1970s and 1980s. Pickett worked at the prestigious Guild Hall School of Music in London. The assaults occurred during one-to-one teaching in soundproofed practice rooms. After one pupil's parent complained, the head took no action and simply advised that the girls took lessons elsewhere. After the complaint, Pickett was retained and continued to tour abroad. His prestige was unabated, becoming musical director at the Globe Theatre.

Michael Brewer worked as head of music at the prestigious Chetham's School in Manchester between 1975 and 1994. A criminal investigation into his activity followed a complaint from an ex-boarder, Frances Andrade, who was taught by Brewer between 1978 and 1982.[8] What made this case unusual was that Andrade was also assaulted by Brewer's then wife, Kay. The case was unusual in another way. Initially, Andrade did not make a complaint to the police but instead confided in a friend, who herself worked with children's choirs. She took the information to the police without Andrade's advanced permission as a child protection matter. After leaving Chetham's, Brewer had continued to work with young musicians and so this was an understandable concern.

However, this hearsay reporting to the police may have increased the sense of Andrade herself being at the mercy of the actions of others; in court, it transpired that detectives had persuaded her to testify. This signalled a concern from her about the process, not the content, of the complaint: her sexual victimisation by Michael and Kay Brewer. They were put on trial in January 2013 with Michael Brewer being charged with 1 case of rape and 13 counts of indecent assault, and Kay Brewer 1 count of indecent assault and aiding and abetting rape. They were sent down for 6 years and 21 months, respectively.

The case opened up accusations from former pupils that sexual abuse was endemic at Chetham's. The complicity of the headmaster in 1994 became evident during the investigation. Brewer resigned then in the wake of a complaint of sexual assault by another female pupil. The complaint was not relayed to the police at the time. Andrade's past childhood had been troubled and the re-living of the experience during the case took its toll; she committed suicide a week after giving her evidence and before the verdicts were announced.

Elitism and exceptionalism in classical music

The environment of classical music teaching is more middle and upper class than lower class, both in its origins and its current character. This creates an atmosphere of presumed power and exceptionalism. The normal rules of equity do not apply because extraordinary talent *ipso facto* is not normal, but is shaped by the presumed subtle entitlements of cultural elites. This inflects decision-making about those extraordinary talents, who are appointed for their musical expertise under competitive conditions. This was apparent in the Brewer case and the culture of Chetham's School.

During the course of the Brewer trial, Professor Malcolm Layfield, head of strings at the Royal Northern College of Music (RNCM), resigned. He had admitted at the time of his appointment in 2002 that he had had relationships with six former pupils at Chetham's, where he had taught. Two senior teachers at the RNCM resigned immediately in protest, at what seemed to ordinary outsiders to have been a bizarre and unwise appointment. Layfield was subsequently arrested following claims from former pupils at Chetham's, as were two other Chetham teachers, Wen Zhou and Christopher Ling. (In one case of alleged rape, Layfield went to trial but was found not guilty.[9]) Under Operation Kiso, 30 women came forward to police claiming that they were sexually assaulted at Chetham's. In September 2014, Nicholas Smith, former head of choir there, was jailed for eight months for sexually assaulting a female pupil in the 1970s.[10]

At the time of writing, the case against Chetham's past culture of endemic CSA continues. But the investigation has spread to all five main elite music schools. Apart from Chetham's, these are Purcell school in Hertfordshire, Wells Cathedral School in Somerset, St Mary's Music School in Edinburgh and the Yehudi Menuhin School in Surrey. After the Brewer trial, Channel 4 took accounts from women who, as girl pupils of the latter, claimed they were sexually abused by its founder, the world-famous pianist Marcel Gazelle. The violinist Nigel Kennedy confirmed in the report that Gazelle was a serial offender against his girl peers and he was of the view that some of their later mental health problems were linked to his abuse of them.[11]

Before leaving this section, I would emphasise again some themes beyond the sexual motives of the criminal perpetrators described in school settings. In addition, we have particular forms of systemic isolation and the complicity of third parties. In this case, the role of the board of the RNCM in 2002 stands out. We also have the particular emotional field of adult–child teaching which intensifies in one-to-one tuition compared to class teaching. In the case of music teaching, where there is a constant striving for optimal or ideal performances, perfectionism readily blends with an obsession with power and control. And as the 'BDSM community' knows well, power and control can become eroticised. The cases of sexual abuse of these music students had all the elements of sadistic pornography, even though the crimes were not filmed.

Sports coaching

Many of the characteristics that make music teaching a site of risk for talented youngsters also apply to sports coaching. Success in sport is an exciting prospect for many children and so to discover an aptitude and ability for a particular set of skills linked to one of its forms makes the child feel very special from the outset. A drive for achievement then boosts the child's willingness to adhere to adult authority. None of this is problematic in principle, provided that those coaching young sports talent are task focused and do not exploit the scenario for personal reasons.

Some children are particularly vulnerable within a coaching setting. For example, Andrew Faulds was sentenced to 15 years in prison. Faulds had worked as a learning mentor for the Ealing tuition service based in Southall and as a youth worker at Brentford Football Club Community Sports Trust. Apart from possession of indecent images of children, Faulds was discovered in possession of a video of him raping a 13-year-old girl with severe learning difficulties.[12]

Until 2016, this sort of case study of sexual abuse at the hands of soccer coaches was relatively rare, but then a nationwide scandal erupted in England with ex-professional footballers coming forward in large numbers to make allegations against youth coaches at top clubs, such as Chelsea and Southampton. By the end of that year, the police confirmed 155 potential suspects implicating 148 clubs at all tiers of the game (the police used 'impacted' to signal that all were not necessarily under investigation). The police provided a figure then of 429 alleged victims, the great majority (98%) being male. The figure also contained some cases above the age of 16, with the youngest noted at just 4 years of age. Following this news breaking, the NSPCC set up a dedicated football abuse hotline and received 1,700 calls within a month.[13]

Turning from soccer to tennis, the matter of extraordinary youth talent being vulnerable to sexual exploitation is also relevant. For example, in May 2015 Bob Hewitt, the Australian tennis grand slam winner, now living in South Africa, was jailed for six years for sexual offences against three children he was coaching in the 1980s and 1990s.[14] As with many brought to trial, he pleaded not guilty to the charges (two of rape and one of sexual assault).

This theme of talented children being particularly vulnerable was exemplified by the scandal at Penn State University, Pennsylvania in the USA. In 2011, Jerry

Sandusky was indicted on over 50 counts of child molestation of boys in the football teams he had coached, between 1994 and 2009, though it was claimed by prosecutors that his offending had been ongoing since the 1970s. By the time of his trial, 48 specimen charges were considered in court.[15]

Sandusky had set up a sports charity, The Second Mile, which became the main site for his sexual exploitation of children. This case was relatively unusual in going beyond the typically limited focus of the criminal wrongdoing of the perpetrator. Other school officials implicated in covering up Sandusky's activity were also investigated. Some resigned or were fired for their complicity. As with Hewitt noted above, Sandusky protested his innocence throughout but, in October 2012, he was sent down to face a minimum of 30 years and a maximum of 60 years in prison.

These case studies exemplify how sports settings are an important part of our *ecological* understanding of how the sexual exploitation of children emerges. That focus has prompted an increasing interest in dedicated child safeguarding policy in sport.[16]

Health and social care settings

In September 2014, Dr Myles Bradbury, a paediatric haematologist at Addenbrooke's Hospital in Cambridge, was tried for offences against boys aged 8–17.[17] He pleaded guilty to 25 offences including sexual assault against 18 children and the making of more than 16,000 indecent images. He received a 22-year prison sentence, though this was subsequently halved on appeal, much to the anger of his victims.[18] Bradbury's victims were not just children, but children suffering from cancer. Despite this extreme offending (or maybe because of it), the ex-doctor was visited by the police in jail and was consulted about child protection advice. This matter of the police being deferential to those in traditional authority is a recurring dynamic; they do not consult any run-of-the-mill detained paedophile. It mirrored the reluctance of the police to challenge politicians about sex offending noted in Chapter 1.

The deference towards medical practitioners is then a special contingent feature to consider. Addenbrooke's Hospital did have a chaperoning policy in place at the time of Bradbury's offending, but he circumvented it in plain sight of both his nursing colleagues and of parents bringing their children for examination. He insisted on seeing the boys on their own and no one, other than a grandmother who eventually raised the alarm about an assault by him, challenged him. Just as it is absurd to deny that politicians could be paedophiles, the same naïve credulity applies if we think about the complete probity of doctors. That naïvety can also be seen in the next couple of case studies.

In February 2015, Dr Michael Salmon, a retired child specialist from Stoke Mandeville Hospital, a favoured hunting ground of Jimmy Savile, was jailed for 18 years for two rapes and indecent assaults on his ex-patients.[19] A month later, Dr Raza Laskar, a junior registrar in paediatrics in Manchester, was jailed for 7 years.[20] He was caught with over a million indecent images of children and found guilty of a sexual assault in a hotel room with a young boy. While Dr Bradbury and Dr Salmon sexually exploited their patients, Dr Laskar offended outside of his place of work.

What emerged in the trial was that Laskar had an 'affinity' for children. This reminds us that, for one group of paedophiles at least, there seems to be a general personal immaturity or a fixation in their psychological development, preferring to relate to children rather than their ageing peers. This is not about measured intelligence (as we see from some of the highly clever paedophiles on record) but the social and emotional maturity of perpetrators. This is more than just about sexual desire but is an apparent inability to relate well to adult peers; at times, this is described as personal 'inadequacy', though this is a tautology rather than an explanation.[21]

Another example in this section to note involved a medical practitioner who abused children but who also was part of the intellectual leadership of the Paedophile Information Exchange, which I discuss further in Chapter 9. He may also have been part of the tangled web of the politics of Northern Ireland and the security services. Morris Fraser (full name Roderick Morrison Fraser) was a child psychiatrist who practised in the 1970s and 1980s. In 1972, Fraser pleaded guilty to abusing a 13-year-old Belfast boy in London a year earlier. He was not jailed but 'bound over' and the police did not inform the hospital where he was working in Belfast.

In 1973, Fraser was prosecuted in the USA for offences against children in New York. When the General Medical Council (GMC) came to consider another allegation by a boy from Belfast that Fraser assaulted on a Scouting trip, the UK arrest was noted but the GMC ignored the US prosecution, by then on record. He was allowed to carry on practising by the GMC and he moved from Northern Ireland to London to work as a psychiatrist at Springfield Hospital.

During the 1970s, Fraser published work that looked at the activity of children during 'The Troubles' of the period, when a civil war was raging in the six counties of Northern Ireland. His book *Children in Conflict*[22] was serialised by the *Sunday Times* in 1973. In 1977, he published *The Death of Narcissus*[23] about paedophilia and famous writers. It was reviewed favourably. Fraser presented an item on BBC Radio 4's series on Peter Pan and J. M. Barrie in 1978 and was a regular contributor to the *New Statesman* and *New Society* between 1978 and 1985. His first piece in the latter was about 'child pornography'.

This writing, along with other contributions, including to the edited collection by Brian Taylor *Perspectives on Paedophilia*, which appeared in 1981,[24] meant that neither his clinical, nor academic, nor media careers were diminished, despite him being a convicted paedophile. Fraser's criminality then was barely reported on by the mass media but he negotiated the successful use of the latter for his own self-promotional purposes, including the opportunity of serious outlets to dignify and legitimise paedophilia. Here was, like the Savile case, a sex offender hiding in plain sight.

In 1988, Fraser set up the sailing charity – for 'disadvantaged boys' – the Azimuth Trust in Cornwall. Its co-founder, Michael Johnson, was jailed for four years in 1994 for abusing boys in the project amidst accusations that the police did not investigate claims against him.[25] In 1990, Fraser was charged in London with taking and distributing over 1,000 indecent images of children. He was jailed for one year in 1992,[26] but he remained as a registered medical practitioner and only left the profession voluntarily in 1995 and was not barred by the GMC at a hearing after his jailing.[27]

Female offenders in childcare settings

One factor that structures the type of sexual offending against children in childcare organisations has been gender segregation. This was apparent in the cases I discussed in relationship to offending inside the Catholic Church in Chapter 4 and in the Scouting movement noted above. It may reflect our heteronormative cultural history: boys were put in the care of male staff and women took care of girls. This assumed that sexual desire was also thereby pre-emptively kept safe because heterosexuality was the one and only sexuality. But if a gay paedophile wanted a site of opportunity to explore, then working within that traditional gender division of, for example, the Scout Movement, or a male-only boarding school, was an ideal scenario.

The patriarchal skew in CSA in such settings is very evident, though female perpetrators are not unknown. In 2011, the NSPCC in Britain reported that 'hundreds' of calls to their helpline were from victims of women, not men. The British helpline Childline reports that 17% of calls refer to female perpetrators. When the victim was male then the reported perpetrator rate was equivalent, whereas female victims only reported that 6% of perpetrators were female.[28] Despite this reporting, studies examining the rate of female perpetrators of CSA estimate that they constitute between 1% and 5% of cases. These are low rates compared to men but it reminds us that the 'patriarchy' thesis is not the whole story.

In 2011, paedophile Colin Blanchard was jailed for a minimum of nine years when working with four women to offend.[29] One of them (Vanessa George) did so in her role as a nursery worker. She was one of three that he worked with online – only one of them (Tracey Dawber) had a direct physical relationship with him. This case highlights that the plots that paedophiles are involved with now are of a different type to, for example, the PIE-linked rings of the 1970s. Online grooming is not just of child victims but of co-offenders.

Female offending against children is complex because of this frequent matter of submissive collusion with male partners. For example, in the 1960s, the serial child killer Ian Brady was able to access his victims by using his girlfriend Myra Hindley to approach them. They tortured the children before murdering them; Brady had inducted Hindley into enjoying the works of the Marquis de Sade. The case of Ian Watkins I discussed in Chapter 1 had resonances of this case, though murder was not involved.

This leaves the female offending role as ambiguous. On the one hand, usually the women may not *initiate* the crime (suggesting that, generally, their own sexual interest in children is latent and weak) but subsequently they clearly become active participants. This suggests that they are then beneficiaries of a particular criminal variant of BDSM. Myra Hindley, Rosemary West, Kay Brewer, Vanessa George and other female confederates of men who sexually offended against children were not merely dupes. They were active participants, who enjoyed what they were doing. The notion of 'grooming' used throughout any discussion of CSA, in relation to those other than the victim, is a useful starting point. However, it may hide some important nuances about the agency of third parties; it might assume that the primary perpetrator's agency and manipulations represent the end of the matter.

This co-offending in male–female partnerships is still only a partial picture of female offending. For example, there have been cases of women teachers jailed for developing relationships with pupils. In 2009, Helen Goddard, a music teacher in London, was jailed for 15 months for her relationship with a 15-year-old pupil.[30] In 2007, Claire Lyte, a professional tennis coach in Leicestershire, was jailed for three years for a relationship she developed with a 13-year-old girl pupil.[31] Heterosexual female offenders also emerge occasionally. For example, in June 2015, Anne Lakey was jailed for eight years for the sexual exploitation of two underage male pupils during the 1980s.[32]

These examples of hebephilia, where female teachers or coaches are the offenders, offer popular culture the alternative narrative to that of *Lolita* by Vladimir Nabokov. For example, the scenario is explored in Zoe Heller's novel and film *Notes on A Scandal* (with the US prefix, *What Was She Thinking?*). Both of these novels are relatively scarce populist explorations of hebephilia, where sexual titillation and moral dilemmas are woven together; indeed, controversially, both have become famous for their erotic, rather than criminal, narratives. Critics have noted that, in the first, the emphasis is on the pubescent girl victim being seductive, but the female perpetrator is held up for critical scrutiny in the second. When women do offend, maybe they are judged more harshly, at least morally, though sentencing of offenders seems to be inflected more by time and place than by gender considerations.

The very possibility of women sexually abusing children may seem so offensive that it may be flatly denied. For example, feminists are prone to idealise benign female care for others and point to patriarchy as *the* source of oppression in intimate relationships. Empirically, their case holds water most of the time but there are exceptions that prove the rule. For example, the cases of cruel nuns I pointed up in Chapter 4 demonstrate that women can be sadistic towards children and other women. The rare cases of female offenders, such as Vanessa George, Myra Hindley, Rosemary West, Kay Brewer or Woman A and Woman B, noted in the Ian Watkins case in Chapter 1, highlight that their collusion with male perpetrators is part of some offending.

Culturally, the incompatibility between maternalism and child sexual offending is discomforting, and not simply for the ideological bias created by dichotomising forms of feminism about the complexities of being human (women good/men bad). When Michele Elliott, the founder of the child protection charity Kidscape, published her book *Female Sexual Abuse of Children: The Ultimate Taboo* in 1994, she received hate mail.[33]

What this section demonstrates though is that any denial of the prospect of female offending against children evades some tough questions about female agency deployed for malign purposes. A flat denial of female agency and criminal responsibility does not help us either to protect children or understand the complexities of CSA. In a recent case of a paedophile ring involving a woman, Marie Black, and two men, Michael Rogers and Jason Adams, the trial identified Black as the ringleader.[34] They had raped and abused two boys and three girls over a ten-year period, moving the children around between Norwich and London to sex parties, where they were raffled as playthings for the adults present.

At the trial, their individual lawyers traded arguments about whether Black manipulated Adams or vice versa. However, the judge placed Black clearly at the centre of the conspiracy. All three received 24 years in prison. At the sentencing, Black denied all of the charges and maintained that she had been 'stitched up'. During the trial, she did not even enter the witness box to defend herself. She denied that she had ever acted abusively and so there was nothing to defend. She joined the ranks of the self-deceiving male perpetrators who come before the courts or hide undetected in society.

Residential settings

An intractable dilemma for those genuinely intent upon protecting children from abuse at the hands of adults is in relation to residential care. As far as the tabloids are concerned, social workers are damned if they do and damned if they don't, when leaving a child to be abused in a family (see Chapters 3 and 8) or trying to prevent that risk by removing them. And the dilemma does not end there. Foster care and residential care for children are not risk free, even if the latter is riskier for children than the former.

Paedophiles insinuate their way into those settings and a certain level of CSA inevitably ensues. Poorly paid residential social work involving antisocial hours provides a ready cover for paedophiles, where alternative forms of pay-off await them. Financial motives may drive fostering for some, and with that lack of focus upon the need to care may come indifference to the long-term welfare of children passing through. But given that residential care has brought with it several scandals about endemic abuse in residential social-work settings over the years, there remains the focus of the several inquiries deliberating at present about historical abuse in Britain, Australia and elsewhere. A good example to offer here is one which demonstrates that organised child sexual exploitation may start within that setting and that it can involve complicity by the state at all levels.

Learning from Irish victims

In March 2015, a survivor of CSA, who was an important linking witness between a residential care scandal and the VIP paedophile ring topic discussed in Chapters 1 and 2, was interviewed by Channel 4 News.[35] Richard Kerr spoke after nearly

30 years about his abuse in Kincora children's home in Northern Ireland. He revealed that not only did the staff at the home sexually abuse him but also that he was trafficked to London in 1977, along with two other boys. Kerr reported that later they committed suicide.

Kerr was taken to Elm Guest House where he recalls:

> I was tied up here. I do remember that. I don't know why I was tied up but I was tied up. With my hands behind my back. I do remember that. They took photographs. Other men were here. Other men came into the room. It wasn't just this one man. There were other men here.

Channel 4 News took Kerr back to the guest house where he became emotional and said:

> I don't mean to be this way. It happened. I just don't mean to be. It's just holding on this sometimes. I can't believe this happened. God help me.

From Elm House in the 1970s he was moved on to Dolphin Square:

> I remember going in with this guy. He told me to sit down and relax and explained about his glasses. He had Waterford Crystal and he wanted me to have a brandy and we had a small one. And then we had a sexual encounter in here.

At the time of the interview, Kerr was travelling more in hope than expectation that the VIP paedophile scandal would be opened up properly:

> I'm still in some fear [...] I need to know that I can have faith in our government but right now, when they're not willing to bring Kincora into Westminster, the message that sends to me, is that there's some kind of cover-up and there has been.

This plea from a victim in 2015 was the end point of a long saga about Kincora that implicated not just the paedophiles operating there during the 1960s and 1970s (it only opened as a local authority home for troubled and abused boys in 1958) but also the British Army, MI5 and a far-right Loyalist splinter group. At the height of 'The Troubles' in Northern Ireland, the army received reports of the abuse of boys at Kincora. However, orders from high-ranking officers were to close an interest down in the reports; note the resonances here of the response in the Met to the early warnings of the VIP abuse in London. Given that boys from the home were trafficked to the latter arena of exploitation, then the link between the dynamics of power around Westminster, at the centre of the British State, were seemingly being replayed across the Irish Sea in the most politically contested part of the UK. There was the same pattern: official inquiries began with some investigating officers trying to report honestly in good faith but were then soon closed down and the latter cover-up itself was then denied.

In this case, the Royal Ulster Constabulary passed on evidence of the abuse (trailed heavily in the Irish press). However, although a range of important people were implicated (senior civil servants, businessmen and military officers) only three perpetrators in the home itself were tried and jailed. In 1981, the warden of the home, Joseph Mains, was given six years, his deputy Raymond Semple received five years and William McGrath four years.[36] The last of these, a housemaster at Kincora, was the connection with the Loyalists that was not followed through in the initial investigation. He was the leader of a far-right Loyalist splinter group called Tara.[37] He was also a firebrand Protestant lay preacher and sadistic pederast.

It was later claimed by Martin Dillon in his book *The Dirty War* that McGrath's sexual proclivities became a point of leverage for the security services. Dillon argues that McGrath was an informant working for MI5 providing useful information on the Loyalist campaign, and that the security services blackmailed him for more and more security details using knowledge of the abuse at Kincora. In exchange, police inquiries about the place were obstructed and limited to on-site staff.

This scenario of MI5 involvement was explored as well in Paul Foot's book *Who Framed Colin Wallace?* He provides testimonies from ex-residents of Kincora which are reproduced in abridged form in the appendix to this chapter below. The account from Foot also traces a series of collusions surrounding Kincora when victims or their parents attempted to raise the abuse as a criminal matter. Those efforts were ignored or suppressed in the early 1970s, the time of the offending. A former drug squad officer, DC Cullen, prepared a report about McGrath's activity in 1972 which:

> exposed not only his assaults on the boys in his care, but the political chicanery and cant which accompanied them. One moment he would be lecturing the boys on the need for Protestant purity, the next, without a word, he would be stripping and raping them in the toilet.[38]

Cullen wrote up his report on the matter and sent it to Assistant Chief Constable William Meharg. When the story began to break, 20 years later, Meharg denied ever receiving such a report. During that 20-year silence, the public were completely unaware of the wrongdoing at Kincora, thanks to the systematic suppression of the information by the British security services.

However, one of the latter who tried to break ranks was Colin Wallace, Senior Information Officer at Lisburn barracks. On receiving accounts of the Kincora abuse in the early 1970s, Wallace passed on the information to his superiors and was told that the matter was being dealt with. In the wake of internal inaction, Wallace prepared his own briefing paper for the press revealing what was known about Tara, its connections with CSA at Kincora and its members' personal affiliations with senior political figures, including 'Dr' Ian Paisley MP, Sir James Molyneaux MP and Sir Knox Cunningham MP.

During the 1970s, Wallace continued to argue for the exposure of these connections and no response came from the police or politicians. However, in 1980, he was arrested for a murder and was sent down in 1981 for the manslaughter of an antiques dealer, Jonathan Lewis, who was the husband of an ex-colleague of Wallace. Wallace spent six years in prison but in 1996 the sentence was quashed after a review of the forensic evidence. Tellingly, after the miscarriage of justice against Wallace was established, the police did not re-open the case of Jonathan Lewis, who was murdered by somebody yet to be identified. That glib absence of action confirmed the suspicion of those like Paul Foot that the murder was actually carried out by an unnamed agent of the security services in order to frame Wallace. Thus, Foot's book elaborates the case of how the British security forces falsified evidence against Wallace to discredit and punish him using the homicide charge.

A series of official inquiries into these allegations into Kincora and the 'political chicanery and cant' surrounding it have still not established the full truth about the home, such that by 2015, Richard Kerr and others still felt that justice had evaded them. An indicator that the cover-up of the full truth was still in play was that, in 2013, under the 30-year rule of disclosure of government documents, those pertaining to Kincora were *not* released to the public or press. Also, the British government announced that its post-Savile inquiries would *not* extend to Kincora. Kincora is then a special case for political reasons for the British State.

Channel 4 News, reporting on the judicial review (June 1, 2015), also noted that, in the 1970s, attempts by those like Wallace trying to formally report the abuse at Kincora were covered up by MI5 and that this would have required British government knowledge. To date, all requests for a full inquiry into this aspect of British modern history have run into the sand, even though before leaving office Margaret Thatcher acknowledged that her government had not properly investigated the serious claims about Kincora.

The campaigns of the Kincora victims and their supporters for transparency about the role of the British State in their abuse culminated eventually in the concession of a short Northern Ireland-only review. The limitations of the inquiry led some key figures, such as Colin Wallace and Richard Kerr, to refuse to present their testimony. Their grievance was that relevant documentation was being withheld from their own lawyers but not those representing the state.[39]

We can see a pattern here reminiscent of the cases of both Smith and Janner discussed in the early chapters. At the time of writing, justice for the victims of Kincora remains elusive, as does our full understanding of the relationship between the rich and the powerful in British society and the 'ordinary' paedophile offenders who entered residential care work with a lascivious interest in children.

Conclusion

This chapter has explored the wide range of settings in which those entrusted to care for children sexually exploit them. This extends some of the points raised in previous chapters in relation to the Irish Catholic Church and the Australian experience about the 'corruption of care' in a range of residential settings. The same features recur. Our understandable fascination with the morality and motivations of the perpetrators always needs to be placed in the context of particular victim vulnerabilities, various threads of social isolation and degrees of third-party complicity. In the case of Kincora, the latter included the inaction of those in authority who had serious allegations of child sexual exploitation put to them.

This chapter, more than the others, also raises some fundamental ethical and emotive questions for all adults about their relationship to children. In particular, we need to support those who are keen to offer genuine benign care in paid or voluntary roles, while operating a healthy scepticism at all times about adults who *want* to do that work. The power imbalance available to exploit, by those in charge of children *in loco parentis*, is a constant condition of possibility for the emotional, physical or sexual abuse of children outside of their homes. And yet, most of the time, most people looking after children do not exploit that power imbalance but act with good intentions and with personal integrity. The wrongdoing in this chapter highlights the personal damage, and even at times political havoc, that can be wreaked by that minority who exploit their childcare role. The next chapter deals with perpetrators whose actions lacked this ambiguity: their motives were singularly malign and exploitative.

Appendix

The accounts below are abridged from Chapter 3 of Paul Foot's *Who Framed Colin Wallace?* They are reports from victims of William McGrath at Kincora.

The case of 'Clive Ramsay' (not real name)

Clive had a mild learning difficulty and was put in the care of Kincora in 1973, when he told his mother about the following:

> I had been in the hostel about two or three weeks when one night there was only Mr McGrath and my brother and me in the hostel. He came to the kitchen where I was standing and grabbed me by the balls from behind. I was scared and didn't know what to do. I told him to go but he didn't. He was laughing when he done it. Next morning, I went and told Mr Mains what happened and he said forget about it and he would see about it. Later that day I went to my sister's and told my mother and father. My mother said she would take it to court.

When his mother indeed took the account to Belfast social services, it was checked by phoning John Mains, who dismissed it to the satisfaction of the social workers involved. Three similar accounts were put to the Belfast welfare services at the turn of the 1970s and all three were dismissed having taken assurances from the perpetrators.

The case of 'Ronald Johnson' (not real name)

This boy was in Kincora for six months when he was routinely sexually assaulted and raped by McGrath. On the day of his departure, when packing and awaiting his foster parents picking him, up he reports this happened:

> I was in my bedroom packing my clothes when Mr McGrath came into the room [...] Mr McGrath said, 'One more time before you go'. I said, 'No', and he said, 'If you don't do it this time I'm going to tell your foster parents what you're like'. I asked him what he meant and he said, 'I'll tell them about the other times'. I was a bit scared. Mr McGrath told me to take down my trousers and get onto the bed. I pulled my trousers down to my ankles and got onto the bed. I was lying face down. Mr McGrath pulled my trousers right off. He got up onto the bed on his knees and took his cock out. He told me to open my legs and got on top of me.

McGrath anally raped Johnson who went on in his account:

> He pulled his cock out and got up off the bed and fixed himself. He told me not to say anything to anybody and my foster parents about what happened in the hostel. He then left the room. I started to cry and went to the bathroom. There was blood on my backside and legs and my backside was very sore.

Notes

1 UK charity boss Simon Harris jailed for Kenya child sex abuse. (2015). February 26. BBC News England. Available at www.bbc.co.uk/news/uk-england-31599524.
2 Lord Baden Powell. Scouting. Channel 4 Documentary 1995. Part 2 of 6 available at www.youtube.com/watch?v=79jItGdGUOo.
3 'Sordid' history of sexual abuse depicted in Boy Scout files. (2015). January 26. www.washingtontimes.com/news/2015/jan/26/lawsuit-against-boy-scouts-could-reveal-sex-abuse-/ (no longer available).
4 Burrell, I. (1998). Paedophile ring's 30 years of abuse. September 16. *The Independent*. Available at www.independent.co.uk/news/paedophile-rings-30-years-of-abuse-1198569.html.
5 Many examples could be given of this but a famous example was that of the Caldicott Preparatory School, a feeder school for the top public schools like Eton and Winchester. In recent decades, its pupils have included the England cricket captain, Andrew Strauss, and the British Deputy Prime Minister, Nick Clegg. In 2014, its ex-headmaster joined a list of other teachers there who were found guilty of sexual offending against boy pupils. See Wright, S. (2014). PE teacher, 82, at Nick Clegg's old prep school killed after being hit by a train two days before he was due to be sentenced for abusing young boy. February 5. *Mail Online*. Available at www.dailymail.co.uk/news/article-2552175/Top-prep-school-PE-teacher-82-killed-hit-train-two-days-sentenced-abusing-young-boy.html.

6 Voyeur teacher Gareth Williams has jail term cut. (2014). October 28. BBC News South East Wales. Available at www.bbc.com/news/uk-wales-south-east-wales-29801543.

7 Quinn, B., Dodd, V. & Pidd, H. (2015). Guildhall school dismissed girl's claims 30 years before Philip Pickett jailed for rapes. February 20. *The Guardian*. Available at www.theguardian.com/uk-news/2015/feb/20/guildhall-music-teacher-philip-pickett-jailed-raping-young-female-students.

8 Pidd, H. (2013). Chetham's music teacher Michael Brewer jailed for sexually abusing pupil. March 26. *The Guardian*. Available at www.theguardian.com/uk/2013/mar/26/chelthams-teacher-michael-brewer-jailed.

9 Malcolm Layfield rape trial: Chetham's music teacher cleared. (2015). June 8. BBC News, Manchester. Available at www.bbc.co.uk/news/uk-england-33053214.

10 Pidd, H. (2014). Chetham's music teacher jailed for historical sexual assault on pupil. September 1. *The Guardian*. Available at www.theguardian.com/uk-news/2014/sep/01/chethams-music-teacher-nicholas-smith-jailed-sexual-assault.

11 Hawkes, R. (2015). Nigel Kennedy: 'Bad things can happen in music schools'. June 1. *The Telegraph*. Available at www.telegraph.co.uk/culture/hay-festival/11643349/Nigel-Kennedy-Bad-things-can-happen-in-music-schools.html.

12 Pinkham, E. (2014). Youth worker who filmed himself raping severely disabled 13-year-old girl is jailed for 15 years. November 4. *Mirror Online*. Available at www.mirror.co.uk/news/uk-news/youth-worker-who-filmed-himself-4567084.

13 Football child sex abuse claims: What has happened so far? (2016). December 22. BBC Sport. Available at www.bbc.co.uk/sport/football/38211167.

14 Bob Hewitt, former tennis champion, jailed for six years for rape. (2015). May 18. Agence France-Presse. Available at www.theguardian.com/world/2015/may/18/bob-hewitt-former-tennis-champion-jailed-for-six-years-for.

15 Gladswell, M. (2012). In plain view: How child molesters get away with it. September 24. *The New Yorker*. Available at www.newyorker.com/magazine/2012/09/24/in-plain-view.

16 Mountjoy M., Armstrong, N., Bizzini, L., Blimkie, J., Evans, J., Gerrard, D., et al. (2008). IOC Consensus Statement: training the elite child athlete. *British Journal of Sports Medicine* 42, 163–164; Vertommen, T., Kampen, J., van Veldhoven, N., Wouters, K., Uzieblo, K. & Van Den Eede, F. (2016). Profiling perpetrators of interpersonal violence against children in sport based on a victim survey. *Child Abuse & Neglect* 63, 172–182. See also the NSPCC's dedicated system for protecting children in sports settings: https://thecpsu.org.uk/.

17 That age range demonstrates the futility of separating neat psychiatric categories of paedophiles and hebephiles.

18 Abuse doctor Myles Bradbury has sentence reduced. (2015). June 12. BBC News, Cambridgeshire. Available at www.bbc.co.uk/news/uk-england-33106492. Note that the anger of his victims and their families was fuelled further by the report published into his misconduct by the NHS in Cambridge (October 22, 2015). They considered it too superficial and that a full public inquiry was warranted. Note that sentencing norms about paedophile medical practitioners have changed. In 1987, the head of paediatric medicine at St George's Hospital London, Oliver Brookes, was sentenced to one year in prison for the possession of thousands of indecent images of children. However, Lord Lane, then Lord Chancellor, released him after six months on appeal. Lane compared Brookes' actions as being like schoolchildren collecting cigarette cards in days gone by.

19 Morris, S. (2015). Michael Salmon, former children's doctor, jailed for 18 years. February 12. *The Guardian*. Available at www.theguardian.com/uk-news/2015/feb/12/michael-salmon-jailed-18-years-jimmy-savile-stoke-mandeville.

20 Junior doctor Raza Laskar jailed for child sex abuse. (2015). March 11. BBC News, Manchester. Available at www.bbc.co.uk/news/uk-england-manchester-31829268.

21 Baden-Powell was fascinated by the story of Peter Pan, and political paedophiles like Tom O'Carroll I discuss in Chapter 9 seem to be caught in a state of perpetual nostalgia about the idealised world of childhood.

22 Fraser, M. (1974). *Children in Conflict.* London: Pelican (reprinted in Penguin edition 1979).

23 Fraser, M. (1977). *The Death of Narcissus.* London: Secker and Warburg.

24 Fraser, M. (1981). The child. In B. Taylor (ed.), *Perspectives on Paedophilia.* London: Batsford Academic and Educational.

25 Police criticised over handling of abuse case. (1994). May 31. *The Independent.* Available at www.independent.co.uk/news/uk/police-criticised-over-handling-of-abuse-case-1419613.html.

26 Doctor Jailed for Indecent Filming. (1992). April 16. *Daily Telegraph.*

27 GMC Keeps Child Sex Doctor on Medical Register. *Sunday Telegraph.* November 26, 1995. In this front-page story, a former member of the GMC, Jean Robinson, expressed outrage about Fraser's continued registration and believed that the Health Committee of the GMC had suppressed information about his criminal activity.

28 Mariathasan, J. (2009). *Children Talking to ChildLine about Sexual Abuse.* London: NSPCC.

29 Levy, A. & Scott-Clark, C. (2011). Colin Blanchard: the disturbing backstory to a crime of our times. January 10. *The Guardian.* Available at www.theguardian.com/uk/2011/jan/10/colin-blanchard-backstory-crime.

30 Sears, N. (2009). Public school teacher jailed for lesbian trysts can still meet victim, 15, on release from prison. September 22. *Daily Mail.* Available at www.dailymail.co.uk/news/article-1215023/School-teacher-Helen-Goddard-jailed-15-months-lesbian-affair-teenage-pupil.html.

31 Sapsted, D. (2007). Tennis coach 'demanded lesbian sex'. October 3. *The Telegraph.* Available at www.telegraph.co.uk/news/uknews/1564946/Tennis-coach-demanded-lesbian-sex.html.

32 Armstrong, J. (2015). Anne Lakey: Acclaimed headteacher found GUILTY of indecently assaulting two teenage boys. June 24. *The Mirror.* Available at www.mirror.co.uk/news/uk-news/anne-lakey-acclaimed-headteacher-found-5935414.

33 Elliott, M. (1994). *Female Sexual Abuse of Children: The Ultimate Taboo.* London: Guildford Press. Elliott's stance on child sexual abuse is not wholly orthodox. For example, she claims that around 20% of perpetrators are female (5% tends to be the consensus, though the range in studies varies from 1–40%). She also denies that paedophilia is a sexual orientation but describes it instead as a 'learned deviant behaviour'. See also Elliott, M. (2009). Our blind rage at women who abuse. June 11. *The Guardian.* Available at www.theguardian.com/commentisfree/2009/jun/11/child-sexual-abuse-plymouth.

34 Norwich woman who used children as sex 'toys' jailed for life. (2015). September 28. *The Guardian.* Available at www.theguardian.com/uk-news/2015/sep/28/norwich-paedophile-ring-marie-black-jailed-life.

35 Kincora: calls for abuse to be included in UK inquiry. (2015). June 1. Channel 4 News. Available at www.channel4.com/news/kincora-calls-for-abuse-to-be-included-in-uk-inquiry.

36 A parallel set of events occurred about the collusion between those running children's homes and state officials at Bryn Estyn in North Wales, when a senior police officer, Gordon Anglesea, abused boys there in the 1970s and 1980s. Anglesea's conviction in 2016 came in the wake of the housemaster at the home, John Allen, being given

a life sentence in 2014 for child sexual exploitation. (See also Bagnall, S. (2016). How Gordon Anglesea went from respected police chief to disgraced paedophile. October 21. *Daily Post*. Available at www.dailypost.co.uk/news/north-wales-news/how-gordon-anglesea-went-respected-12054885.) These cases remind us that the collusion between politicians, agents of the state and paedophile rings was not limited to London in the UK.

37 Tara is a place where the old Irish kings were crowned. This Protestant paramilitary group had a public face called the 'Orange Order Discussion Group', led by McGrath. He believed that the Irish were one of the lost tribes of the Israelites. For Tara members, Protestants were the sons of God and Catholics the sons of Satan. Tara was committed to a united Ireland under Protestant control and independent of mainland Britain. For a fuller account, see Chapter 3 of Foot, P. (1989). *Who Framed Colin Wallace?* London: Pan.

38 Ibid., p. 131. Local political chicanery repeats and repeats; more on this in Chapter 6.

39 Preston, A. (2016). Kincora survivor Richard Kerr brands inquiry 'unfair' and stops giving evidence. June 15. *Belfast Telegraph*. Available at www.belfasttelegraph.co.uk/news/northern-ireland/kincora-survivor-richard-kerr-brands-inquiry-unfair-and-stops-giving-evidence-34802146.html.

6

STREET LIFE AND THE SEXUAL EXPLOITATION OF CHILDREN

Introduction

In recent years, across a range of provincial English towns, a series of police investigations has led to the prosecution of criminal gangs that exploited teenage girls. The gangs were predominantly of men from a South Asian heritage and most (but not all) of their victims were white. Estimates of victims calculated by official inquiries suggest they were not a handful but were numbered in thousands and that male and ethnic minority victims may have been under-detected.

Few parties have come out of this story with their reputations intact. The perpetrators (both the sexual predators[1] and the gang members feeding them with victims) in many ways are the easiest to understand and evaluate. They manipulated their victims and, if resistance was met, they intimidated them or used actual violence to force compliance. The victims were gang-raped and had petrol doused on them, as they were trafficked for sex with man after man. This is all horrible to detail but it is also predictable. Violent criminal gangs do horrible things: that is their stock-in-trade. Organised crime traditionally has used the sexual exploitation of women and children as one of its many 'rackets'. These child victims were a source of money like contraband cigarettes, heroin or crack cocaine. It was ever thus, at least in modern times. Why are we surprised when gangsters act like gangsters? The impact of the violation of victims by these gangs is summarised here by the Jay Report[2] on Rotherham, discussed below:

> the impact sexual exploitation had on them was absolutely devastating. Time and again we read [...] of children being violently raped, beaten, forced to perform sex acts in taxis and cars when they were being trafficked between towns, and serially abused by large numbers of men.[3]

The report goes on to note the raised incidence of self-harm, drug addiction and mental health problems in the victims. Re-victimisation later in life was also noted. These outcomes were not formally acknowledged or responded to by agents of the local state.

The cases discussed in this chapter open up a range of other matters beyond this post-traumatic outcome for victims, from post-colonialism and religious patriarchy to political careerism and police budgets. These matters are then reflected in the mentalities and decisions of local agents of the British State. A theme throughout this book is thus maintained: this is not just about the psychopathology of criminals, whether the latter are perpetrators of sexual abuse or those who supply them with children. Cultures of complicity and silence are part of this story, just as much as they were in relation to Jimmy Savile at the BBC. Below, I explore that intersection of place and cultural habits, which could explain the emergence of child sexual exploitation on the streets, using Rotherham as an example and two concepts from sociology to aid that illumination: habitus and field, developed by Pierre Bourdieu.[4]

'Habitus' reflects the subjective dispositions of human agents learned over time, i.e. their habits and associated attitudes. These emerge from, and are maintained within, particular families of origin, gender, class, culture, time and place. The latter *particular context for action* Bourdieu called 'field'. 'Habitus' and 'field' are interconnected opposite sides of the same coin, with one side representing subjective experiences and behavioural dispositions, and the other side their particular extrinsic conditions of possibility, past and present. This interplay of inner and outer maintains itself over time, unless and until it is displaced or disrupted by new conditions; in this case, the latter might be criminal investigation or a widespread reversal of cultural norms of patriarchy and misogyny.

The Rotherham Inquiry

In recent years, this unremarkable and largely forgotten South Yorkshire town, once associated with steel and coal, suddenly hit the headlines and with that came collective civic shame. Its only comfort now is that a similar story was unfolding elsewhere and others, still untold, may well emerge in currently unblemished towns.

In August 2014, the report of organised sexual exploitation in Rotherham, from Professor Alexis Jay, was released (Jay, 2014). Immediately, the findings were reflected by *The Independent* newspaper on its front page, 'Britain's worst child abuse scandal' (August 27, 2014). The report described a period of 16 years in which it was estimated that 1,400 children were abused. That figure was described by Jay as a 'conservative estimate'. A third of the cases examined were already known to social services and the police. In response to the damning report, the leader of Rotherham town council resigned immediately but the elected police commissioner and head of children's services in the council resisted calls for a few weeks before eventually acceding to public and political pressure.

The Jay Report described victims treated violently as well as being sexually exploited. Children were gang-raped and forced to watch others similarly victimised. Apart from the graphic details of the offending, the report also considers the resistance, apparent over the years, from council officials and police officers to deal with the widespread abuse known to them.

In 2002, a Home Office researcher put on record a pattern of school teachers and youth workers reporting concerns to social services and the police about victims. The Home Office researcher was summoned and reproached by senior police officers and her project in Rotherham was suspended. She alleges that a council official in her absence removed all of her data from her filing cabinet, she was told never again to refer to 'Asian men' and she was instructed to attend a race and diversity training workshop (interview, BBC2 *Panorama*, September 1, 2014).

The Jay Report noted that police officers regarded 'many child victims with contempt'. When, in two cases, fathers tracked down their daughters to where they were being held by abusers and tried to rescue them, they, not the perpetrators, were arrested by the police. In another case, a police officer considered that a 12-year-old girl was having 'consensual' sex with her abuser. Another victim was aware of police indifference and believed that this gave her abuser confidence to continue to act with impunity.

Despite this evidence of early poor due diligence from the police, in 2010, eight men of Pakistani heritage from the town were put on trial for their sexual activity with, and violence against, minors. Three were acquitted and the others were jailed for periods between 4 and 11 years. Other successful prosecutions were to follow in Rotherham and other towns noted in Box 6.2.[5]

In October 2012, the Home Affairs Select Committee criticised South Yorkshire's chief constable, David Compton, and one of Rotherham Council's senior officials, Philip Etheridge, for their handling of claims of wrongdoing. The committee heard evidence of three members of a South Asian family, who were connected with the abuse of 61 girls but were not convicted, and of an un-convicted 22-year-old man, who was found in a car with a 12-year-old girl with indecent images of her on his phone.[6] The committee also noted that local officials had ignored internal research reports of 2002, 2003 and 2008 highlighting widespread sexual offending against minors, implicating gangs of men of Pakistani heritage.

I summarise the various features of the Rotherham case by using the concepts of habitus and field, introduced above, in Box 6.1. We need to consider the motives of the offenders and their cultural and class background. On the margins of the economy in the 24/7 world of taxi driving, these were not a typical sort of workforce. Their acculturated view of women and girls was not always respectful. We also need to consider the circumstances of their offending and web of complicity from non-offenders. The victims were let down by a string of actors in respectable roles in the local state. The formal upholders of the law, the police, were in denial about evidence before their eyes. Local politicians were either of South Asian origin or, if not, were wary of alienating a local community that offered bloc votes routinely.

The bubble of parochial politics meant that intelligent people could not trace relevant processes in a national and international context. Post-colonial Britain, containing as it did New Commonwealth immigrants and their children and grandchildren born in the host nation, was fraught with contradictions and irrationalities. Pakistani migrants and their subsequent generations could only be in that field because of British colonialism. And their access to Britain was encouraged by economic necessity. The migrants found work, often in low wage settings, and the British economy made use of their labour cost-effectively. But culturally, this scenario also contained risks of incompatibility in a range of ways.

On one side was casual white racism fed and preyed upon by nationalist movements, such as the British National Party and the English Defence League. This prejudice had it both ways – migrants were accused of taking jobs but also free-riding on the welfare state. On the other side was a South Asian culture which was often patriarchal, with men assuming their right to have unbridled power over women and children. Their faith was not relevant, but the ingrained assumption of male entitlement was to become a recurring political matter. Moreover, those from this ethnic minority group were typically in poverty. And with poverty comes the increased chance of criminality.

Fears about giving expression to the first of these irrational forms meant that the second irrational form went unchallenged. Friends of mine, knowing I am writing about this topic, even now consider it eggshell territory to even discuss the possibility of racialised forms of criminality. But in this case, I think this is not primarily about race but religiously justified pre-modern forms of politics, based upon an ancient form of 'brotherhood'.[7] More on this below, but lesser reported aspects of the Jay Report are relevant to note. First, South Asian girls approached by men for sex were less likely to go to the police than white girls for fear of jeopardising their later marriage prospects. Second, South Asian women described to Jay their sense of disenfranchisement because when and if the council consulted their community, it was only to ask men their views. Thus, if culturally ingrained patriarchy is a factor to consider about the pattern of sexual offending in this case, it is also relevant to account for who speaks out and who is silenced in local politics. As Jay noted, this complexity was simply ignored by council officials and the police in Rotherham who 'tiptoed around' the sensitive matter of race and cultural values.

BOX 6.1 FIELD AND HABITUS FEATURES IN THE ROTHERHAM CASE

	Perpetrators	Other actors
Habitus	Learned clan loyalty. Patriarchal values and misogyny. Uncertain expectations of income in a low-income local culture.	Learned clan loyalty. Patriarchal values and misogyny. Politicians fearing loss of bloc votes in Asian community.

	Perpetrators	Other actors
	Distrust of or hostility towards Western culture by black and minority ethnic (BME) communities.	Distrust of or hostility towards Western culture by BME communities. Lack of confidence of whistle-blowers. Attachment needs/ psychological vulnerability of victims.
Field	Hostile white context. Unaccountable or marginal male work practices. Relative poverty of families of origin. Police inaction. Norm of lack of credibility of children's accounts. Wider organised criminality.	Hostile white context. Imam protectiveness.[8] Relative poverty of victims and their families. Lack of responsible caring for children. Police inaction. Norm of lack of credibility of children's accounts. Macho culture of politicians and service managers. Backlash against whistle-blowers.

What was clear in the Rotherham case, as with the example I gave of the Catholic Church in Chapter 4, is that focusing on the evil acts of the perpetrators is of limited value. We should expect and, indeed, we will find complexity. We have to think about time and place, cultural norms, patriarchy, police inaction, the lack of confidence of whistle-blowers, poverty, political careerism and confusion over how to fairly discuss racialised criminal activity.[9]

In the latter regard, British policing in particular had learned to avoid policies that were, or might be perceived to be, based upon racial stereotypes. This understandable and legitimate caution risks denying the brutal facts before those who indeed were aware of a pattern of offending. Moreover, our judgements about criminality can at times be legitimately informed by known social-group patterning. For example, criminality is predicted to some extent by three main factors: male gender, young age and low social class. We do not have to assume that *all* young, poor men are criminals when we concede that pattern in principle.

Similarly, there were a particular set of features operating in the field of offending in Rotherham. And one additional factor to the three I just noted was not about race, but it was about Muslim culture. Jay complained that the attitudes of local imams towards male dominance over women and children gave a background of legitimacy to the offending.[10] Muslim men expect women in their families to be modest, chaste and obedient. When the perpetrators encountered young girls on the street who flouted those expectations, victim blaming came readily. The girls could be seen to deserve what they got because they defied family discipline and were willing to be precociously sexual teenagers.

An uncertain racial dimension (supported numerically by the type of typical victim) was that this was an attack upon *white* girls. Jay conceded that correlation, while introducing caution that male victims and girls from the same communities of perpetrators (including those at home) were also present. What is certain is that to deny the ethnic patterning of the perpetrators is anti-rational. Certainly, we then need to check whether the pattern was a signal, not of race *per se*, but of religion, and in turn whether that religious patterning was a signal of an ancient form of patriarchy.

The latter interpretation is supported by another dynamic in the Rotherham case. In many towns of England, especially in the North and the Midlands, where New Commonwealth families settled after the 1960s, there was a transfer of power structures from South Asia to Northern Europe. This became enmeshed with party politics, particularly the politics of the Labour Party, which typically held sway in post-industrial English towns. This might sound like a vague hypothesis until we examine the focused way in which Labour Party leaders have dealt with the voting blocs of British citizens of South Asian origin. This has had two aspects. First, Labour politicians learned that voting loyalty could be encouraged and even ensured at the level of the patriarchal family and the mosque. Second, the more general micro-politics of South Asia might be transferred to England. The phenomenon of the Biradari (clan politics) soon became a challenge for the Labour leadership.

BOX 6.2 A RACIALISED PATTERN OF CHILD SEXUAL EXPLOITATION IN ENGLAND?

In this chapter, the Rotherham inquiry is offered as the core case study. However, events there were not isolated in two senses. First, the children who were sexually exploited were at times trafficked from one town to another. Second, the towns in which the exploitation took place were peppered across England.[11] They included: Accrington, Aylesbury, Banbury, Barking, Birmingham, Blackburn, Bradford, Bristol, Blackpool, Burton, Chesham, Derby, Dewsbury, Halifax, Keighley, Leeds, Littlehampton, London, Manchester, Middlesbrough, Newcastle, Oldham, Ormskirk, Oxford, Peterborough, Preston, Sheffield, Skipton, Slough, Stockport, Telford, Torbay and Yeovil.

The first legally proven case of sex trafficking of children within the UK was in Rochdale in 2012. At the time of writing, cases dating back to 2003 are still the subject of criminal investigation. The case was dramatised in the BBC TV programme *Three Girls* in May 2017. Some key features were shared in the Rochdale and Rotherham cases. There was early police incompetence and indifference, when evidence of the exploitation was with them; at the time of writing, not a single police officer has been held to account for those early failures of investigation in Rochdale. Social workers were found to 'cover their backs' by arguing that their main interest was in intra-familial abuse. The police treated the cases of exploitation as if they were dealing with culpable adults, not children, or they used the term 'child prostitute' to imply that the girls were personally gaining from their involvement with exploitative older men. Even when the police eventually presented their evidence to the Crown Prosecution Service, the latter would not proceed because they lacked confidence in a successful prosecution.

In both Rotherham and Rochdale, a minority of dutiful workers who were trying their best over several years to report the matter to the police were themselves punished as whistle-blowers or dissenting employees by their local authority. The most striking common feature was the reluctance to countenance a racialised form of offending. In Rochdale, it was only when a new local director of the Crown Prosecution Service, Nazir Afzal, changed the ruling of his predecessor to proceed with prosecution that this point was acknowledged. He announced clearly that, although most CSA in Britain outside of the family is at the hands of white perpetrators, they tended to operate alone in their grooming and sexual predation. By contrast, in the cases of Rotherham, Rochdale and some of the other towns on the list noted above, there was a common pattern of organised group activity amongst the men of Pakistani origin.

However, the producer of *Three Girls*, Susan Hogg, considered from researching the programme that there was no clear-cut evidence that racial sensitivities impeded early police investigations, which were undoubtedly dilatory. She suggested that this lack of efficiency was more a function of lack of resources and the police being generally blasé about child welfare in the town. This raises a case-by-case question about race in two quite separate senses. First, when is there evidence that the perpetrators and victims really do come from particular racial backgrounds, which might be a proxy for religious or cultural background? Second, when is there evidence that those investigating cases (the police and social workers) really are affected by the political implications of identifying perpetrators from BME backgrounds? Not only are these logically different questions, the answers to either of them are also not obvious in advance but need to be carefully and honestly clarified empirically.

The racial or cultural dimension to the offending played out publicly at the trial of the Rochdale men. Outside the court, the British National Party used the scene to chant their angry, racist and anti-Muslim slogans.[12] When sentencing took place, the 59-year-old ringleader, Shabir Ahmed, began to swear about 'white lies' and called the judge a 'racist bastard'. Ahmed was convicted of rape, aiding and abetting a rape, sexual assault, trafficking for sexual exploitation and conspiracy to engage in sexual activity with children. He received a prison sentence of 22 years. Ahmed was found guilty of 30 different counts of rape, including against an Asian girl he had dominated for years. As with the Jay inquiry about Rotherham, the Rochdale offenders were shown to target girls of any race, though their favoured prey was white girls on the streets. The trial judge in the Rochdale case highlighted that bias in victimisation.

We can also note, though, that in some of the organised exploitation cases in the list of towns noted above, the perpetrators were white and non-Muslim (e.g. Yeovil). In the Bristol case, the criminal gang were of Somali, not Pakistani, origin (though they shared the same brutal patriarchal contempt for their female victims). These differences suggest that while Nazir Afzal's generalisation about racially inflected offending was fair comment, each case is different and its details need to be clarified. Gender can also be noted as part of the pattern: men dominated the conspiracies as perpetrators and mediators (confirming the centrality of patriarchy) but occasionally female organisers of the exploitation existed (see Chapter 5).[13] In the wake of prosecutions of men, mainly from Pakistani origins, in Newcastle in 2017, Labour MPs Sarah Champion (Rotherham) and Naz Shah (Bradford West) discussed the relationship between race, culture and wider patriarchy in the press.[14] Reactions to these articles revealed a common cognitive bias of identifying single variables in order to explain child sexual exploitation. Anger emerged when commentators disagreed on which single variable was important. Such a failure to agree reminds us that multi-factorial reasoning about field and habitus remains important for our clarity of analysis (see above).

Labour and the Biradari

Clan politics transferred with migrants and continued culturally in subsequent British-born residents. It is a cultural phenomenon (habitus) situated originally in South Asia but now transferred to the localities of receiving countries (field). The word has a Persian origin ('baradar' which means 'brother'). It refers explicitly then to a *brotherhood* and so is intrinsically patriarchal. Accordingly, in part, it is about the control of women and children. But it is also about establishing and maintaining political control in a locality. Migrant Biradari leaders would select from within their own ranks the most literate and politically competent members to become 'community leaders' in their host countries. In the case of Britain, this entailed joining political parties (particularly, but not only, the Labour Party) and ensuring the delivery of bloc votes in local and central elections. This implicit contract created both leverage and, at times, protection for their ambitions. This process was wholly patriarchal. Men were expected to be responsible for women and children. Women were not expected to have a political voice.[15]

Thus, the pre-existing trends of local political control were important for the Biradari to understand and co-opt or infiltrate. That pattern of co-option and influence is not peculiar to the dynamics of the Biradari in England but can also be found more generally in the local politics of South Asia.[16] This has two important implications in the case of Rotherham and other towns with South Asian origin populations. First, it is likely that the Biradari *would* come to predominate in local party politics. Second, they *would* bring with them assumptions of patriarchy, for example in assuming that politics was only for men and in rendering women and children as less powerful in any given situation. Slowly, the leadership of the Labour Party began to understand what was happening and tried to deal with it. For example, Ed Miliband,[17] the Labour leader in 2013, sought to understand the distortions of clan politics after Labour lost to a maverick socialist candidate, George Galloway. In part, this reflected a breakdown in the traditional reliance on bloc votes delivered by patriarchal Biradari.

Why does this cultural background matter in relation to the case we are interested in of child sexual exploitation in Rotherham and other towns?[18] The answer is two-fold. First, there was the inhibition evident in the police and local council officials to deal properly with the facts before their eyes. Second, if women and children were deemed recurrently to be under the political control of men, then, while this was *inherently* an oppressive tendency, it took a particular malign form as sexual exploitation. If the *norm* in a culture is patriarchal, then it sets up the conditions for oppressive action against women and children in forms of incremental exaggerations of that norm.

Violence and coercion then are logical tactical extensions of patriarchal cultures to ensure compliance with male authority. The latter is on a continuum of soft and hard power. At one end of the spectrum is where women and children themselves simply accept that patriarchy is normal and desirable. At the other end is violence, both sexual and non-sexual (including genital mutilation and so-called 'honour killings'). At all points, male authority is maintained and male power is personally achieved and enjoyed.

The particular form of malign patriarchy being considered here can be put into a wider context of previous problems in Labour-controlled local councils, which cannot be attributed to cultural norms out of sync with British life. What connects them is a misguided commitment to equal opportunities policies in employing authorities (see Box 6.3).

BOX 6.3 ROTTEN LONDON BOROUGHS AND LABOUR PARTY POLITICS

The recent exposure of local government and police failings in provincial English towns has many elements in common with activities in the 1970s and 1980s in London. In December 2016, Lambeth council agreed to pay out compensation, totalling £40 million, to residents of children's homes in the borough, who were now in middle age. The Shirley Oaks Survivors Association had succeeded in its campaign for redress. Its own investigation named 27 active paedophiles operating in the homes in the past and gave details of 60 abusers with multiple allegations against their names.[19]

Between 1998 and 2003, Operation Middleton, a joint investigation by Lambeth council and the Metropolitan Police, examined the history of abuse in local children's homes.[20] It considered over 120 historical allegations of sexual abuse. Three identified perpetrators were consequently imprisoned for periods of between 18 months and 10 years. Sixteen alleged perpetrators died either before, or during, the inquiry. In 11 cases, the Crown Prosecution Service decided no further action was possible on evidential grounds. In 19 cases, the alleged perpetrators could not be identified, and in another the victim died before they could give evidence in court.

A few miles away in Islington, abusive staff also operated; according to the Shirley Oaks Survivors report, this was across the two Labour-controlled boroughs. During the early 1990s, officials of Islington council and its leader, Margaret Hodge, at first denied all allegations and accused journalists of unsubstantiated muckraking. The *London Evening Standard* campaigned to hold councillors to account for the abuse but Hodge accused its editor of 'gutter journalism'.[21] In 1985, an abuse survivor, Demetrios Panton, had written to Islington council documenting events in the home he was resident and where he had been sexually assaulted repeatedly by two male staff members. He received a reply in 1989 which flatly denied the events, offering no explanation or apology.[22] In 1990, two senior council social workers, Liz Davies and David Cofie, also alerted their managers and councillors about many children coming to them with accounts of abuse.[23] Their claims were also dismissed by Hodge and her senior managers and provisional local police inquiries petered out.

An independent inquiry in 1995 by two senior social workers, Ian White and Kate Hart, found that there had indeed been likely abuse and certainly poor care in the homes but fell short of confirming systematic paedophile ring activity, though it did name 32 staff who should never work with children.[24] Its main focus was on a chaotic and mismanaged system of care and child protection in the borough, which fostered bad practice. With resonances of later fears of accusations of racism in other local councils, the report identified a reticence about taking accusations seriously for fear of claims of homophobia. Equal opportunities policies had seemed to cloud ordinary observations and common sense about malpractice. Other poor policies identified related to staff training and supervision, as well as a failure to properly investigate specifically reported untoward or critical incidents involving vulnerable children.

Despite her contentious recent past, in 2003 Margaret Hodge was appointed as Children's Minister in Tony Blair's cabinet, prompting a storm of protest.

The complexities of complicity

What is most striking about the unchecked tendency in Rotherham about child sexual exploitation over many years was the variety of complicit actors. The tendency of local and national Labour politicians to turn a blind eye to the Biradari is one aspect of this but there were other fine-grain tendencies: there were parents who varied in their interest in what was happening to their children (which included benign neglect); there were paid carers who saw girls in residential facilities routinely going off to meet men; there were police officers who normalised underage sexual activity (describing perpetrators as their 'boyfriends'); there were council officials who not only turned a blind eye to what they knew was happening but also at times actively excluded and punished those trying to investigate the matter in good faith. The financial context of all this had a role to play as a field factor. Poverty underpinned the lives of many of both the perpetrators and the victims and funding restrictions to the police and local authorities affected their activity levels about child protection. This should be emphasised while cautioning against the temptation to reduce any social policy failure merely to the matter of financial resources (or indeed any other single factor).

The Jay Report (like the Hart Report on Islington noted in Box 6.3) understandably focused on the *administrative shortcomings* of the police and local authorities in Rotherham, but the above wider context of complicity needs to be understood. In summary, those shortcomings were listed by Jay as follows.

First, managers were criticised. The safeguarding board met regularly but did not do its job of challenging those responsible for corrective action about emerging evidence. Many officials were ignorant of child protection procedures and had been poorly managed. There was a regular failure to learn from cases of sexual exploitation already investigated. At times, there was evidence of denial about the problem from senior council officials. This included them turning away frontline staff coming to them with reports of concern about vulnerable children. Some of those staff were also told in no uncertain terms not to raise the racialised pattern of the offending. According to evidence taken by Jay, this suppression was also encouraged by senior police officers.

Second, resource problems increased the risk to children. Budgets for both the police and local authorities were squeezed and at times recruitment into child protection work proved difficult, as did staff retention. The re-structuring of social service departments in conditions of poor resourcing meant that basic child protection work was eroded.

Third, Jay identified a patriarchal and bullying culture in the Rotherham local authority. This was across the system and could not be attributed narrowly to the South Asian cultural tendency I noted above. It included white politicians and officials as well.

Fourth, Jay found that, with one or two exceptions, local services were not designed in ways which would encourage victims and potential victims to seek out help. In other words, the trust needed for children to rely on benign, empathic authority in the local state was, by and large, missing.

Fifth, Jay found shortcomings in the norms of routine practice in social service and police frontline workers. The latter were not always conducting risk assessments properly or thoroughly. In the latter, a numeric scoring system (to alert or trigger a risk threshold for action) was used crudely and substituted for professional (or even common-sense) judgements. Also, child protection work was not given the priority required within the competing demands for both social workers and police officers.

When case discussions of sexual exploitation occurred, they were not always recorded then in case notes. Also, those individual case reviews came to substitute for a wider strategic approach to child protection in the planning and operation of child services. At times, exploited children were moved around from one care facility to another. On the police side, officers were not able or willing to appraise how an arrest might be effectively implemented or prosecuted. Their understanding of the recurring dynamics of grooming was often inadequate. Good procedures existed on paper but officers did not translate them into practice routinely.

Sixth, the everyday attitude of all concerned to both perpetrators and victims distorted a professional understanding of warranted and needed action to protect children, who were at risk. In relation to perpetrators, the sub-culture of taxi drivers and their key role in the offending were both known, but were not acted upon, by the police. In relation to victims, they were often deemed to be promiscuous or mentally deviant. This reminds us again about the attribution of 'moral dirt' when the corruption of care emerges in relation to vulnerable children. Also, frontline workers did not inform parents of concerns they had about children in state care in relation to their sexual activity.

Seventh, Jay identified poor partnership working. Narrow individual case work was not shared with colleagues. Disputes between the police and social services were common about role responsibilities and shared risk assessment and management. Needed inter-agency case reviews failed to occur. The laudable system developed by social workers to map and cross-reference information about victims and perpetrators was not welcomed by the police. The latter failed to act upon information supplied to them about actual or imminent criminal activity.

Eighth, state agencies responsible for overseeing practice completely failed to alert all concerned to the evident failures of service quality. Jay was particularly scathing about this failure of government scrutiny in the form of Ofsted.[25] Jay noted that its report on Rotherham:

> contained the astonishing statement that 'it appeared that vulnerable children and young people are kept safe from abuse and exploitation'. This was not qualified in any way [...] this was not an accurate reflection of the situation, and may have served to give false reassurance to those running the service.

We can see, then, a widespread denial of problems about child welfare. The denial of the scale of child sexual exploitation even extended at times to government agencies, charged with overseeing the quality of child services. Inspection systems are notoriously weak in their impact, but in this case Jay was highlighting that a watchdog was wildly out of touch with reality in Rotherham.

Consequences for victims

This chapter, like the others, addresses the consequences for victims. I reported Jay's own summary position about this at the start of this chapter. In the cases documented from Rotherham, a pattern common elsewhere in relation to CSA inside and outside the family becomes evident.

First, there is an impact on the roles that victims are prone to when becoming adults. Victims are more likely than non-victims to be sexually re-victimised[26] and to enter prostitution.[27] The latter is often entangled with the learned self-medication habits of substance abuse. In the case of Rotherham and elsewhere, the child victims were inducted into the use of drugs and alcohol. Sex work and drug use become a vicious circle encouraged by organised crime. Second, their adjustment to intimate relationships in adulthood can be affected (poor trust in sexual partners). Third, they are at increased risk of substance misuse, self-harm and suicidal action. Fourth, they are at increased risk of presenting with a range of mental health problems; depression, post-traumatic stress disorder and borderline personality disorder are common diagnostic outcomes for victims.

By denying the occurrence and scale of child sexual exploitation in Rotherham, all relevant responsible adults were complicit in the generation of the above scenario of risk to children. Part of that complicity and denial was the failure of local authorities to ensure serious case reviews, learn lessons from them and ensure prosecutions when evidence was clearly available. Another sign of complicity and denial was that these relevant authorities did not offer a system of support for victims (such as counselling services). This absence then is consistent with a picture of widespread denial – why set up a service when there is no problem to respond to? The bizarre conclusion of Ofsted, that children were being properly protected in 2006, is symptomatic of this state of denial in the system as a whole, relevant to child protection in Rotherham.

The Rotherham abuse case spawned an autobiographical account in the book *Violated* from Sarah Wilson, helped in its writing by the journalist Geraldine McKelvie. At school, she was an outsider and had been subjected to bullying. At the age of 11, she was befriended outside her school gates by young men of Pakistani origin, who used another girl already groomed to hook Sarah in. They fed her drugs and alcohol, which she quickly craved. Within two years, she was being trafficked from town to town and made to have sex with man after man.

It started with young men (for a needy girl this brought with it the prospect of the status and care of a true boyfriend) but soon the men were older and anonymous. By 2005, when she was 13, she was being driven to London and Manchester by her 'boyfriends' to be exploited by a series of older men. Her combined cocaine and alcohol habit locked her in to the gang that controlled her. She remembers that:

> Most of the time when I was being raped, I didn't cry. I was too numb with drink and drugs and it seemed pointless because it wouldn't change anything and the guys would think I was a wimp.[28]

An important sub-plot in Sarah's account was that she had been helped by only one agency, 'Risky Business', an outreach service for children at risk on the streets. To Sarah's fury, she discovered that Rotherham Council had closed down the service.[29] Risky Business reported 1,700 cases of grooming to the police and council over a 15-year period but met constant resistance. The Jay Report noted pointedly that Risky Business was the only part of the local state that really grasped the gravity of the situation about the sexual exploitation of children:

> By its nature, the project's style made a bad fit with the more structured services involved. The failure of management to understand and resolve this problem has been a running flaw in the development of child protection services relating to sexual exploitation in Rotherham.[30]

The extent of abuse was eventually passed on to a journalist from *The Times* in 2012 but when the latter confronted the authorities in Rotherham about the claims they were flatly denied. A full account of the role of Risky Business in the Rotherham case can be found in *Broken and Betrayed*, written by Jayne Senior who headed up the agency.[31] She was harassed and blocked in her efforts to make the council and police accountable for their inaction, given the evidence she had systematically recorded about child sexual exploitation in the town. Eventually, she was vindicated (and named as *Good Housekeeping's* 'Woman of the Year' in 2015).

By October 2014, Senior was appointed as an expert to head up the counselling service for the victims, whose existence and problems had been acknowledged after the Jay Report.[32] But this after-the-horse-has-bolted recognition for Senior could not hide the story she had to tell, which reflected not just the indifference of the police and council officials to what she knew and told them, but also an active cover-up and their punishment of her.

Although the police pretended to receive her information gratefully, they ignored it in practice. It was never accessed for use by either local police or other forces. When it was leaked accidentally, Senior was reprimanded and Rotherham social services buried it. An academic researcher, Adele Gladman, was seconded to work with Senior to gather evidence about gang exploitation of children. When Gladman provided a report of her evidence in good faith to Rotherham Council and the police, this led to Senior's office being raided by council officials and her files confiscated. Gladman was sacked.

It was not until 2010 that the cover-up in Rotherham began to truly unravel in the wake of the murder of 17-year-old Laura Wilson by a young gang member.[33] Laura was Sarah Wilson's sister and one of many that Senior had flagged to Rotherham Council. The council closed Risky Business and took over all files. However, the council still needed to report something about the high-profile murder of Laura Wilson. The report was supplied to journalists who noticed that it had been very heavily redacted. One of them was Andrew Norfolk from *The Times* who, in 2012, began to tell the story.[34] Eventually, Alex Jay was brought in to provide her report.

Conclusion

The Rotherham case, which shared similar features to the offending in other English towns, contained a number of learning points. First, collectively, adults failed children.[35] Second, some of that failure was about turning a blind eye, some of it was about being party to an active cover-up and, of course, some of it was about criminals violating children for pleasure and profit. Third, the denial of the racial (and, I would argue, mainly cultural) aspect of the offending was, to say the least, unhelpful. Fourth, the social administrative lessons pointed up by Alexis Jay in her report are important but they are only one part of the more general challenge evident in my first point above. We seem to be facing a collective denial of the problem of CSA and that in turn encourages *specific* forms of denial. These might be passive (complicity) or active (collusion and cover-up); more on this to come.

Notes

1 Most of the victims were post-pubescent and here we can recall the technical but rarely used notion of 'hebephiles'.
2 Jay Report (2014). *Independent Inquiry into Child Sexual Exploitation in Rotherham*. Rotherham: Rotherham Metropolitan Borough Council.
3 Ibid.
4 Hilgers, M. & Mangez, E. (2014). *Bourdieu's Theory of Social Fields: Concepts and Applications*. London: Routledge.
5 For example, in February 2017 at Sheffield Crown Court, six men of South Asian origin were jailed for a total of 81 years for their part in the sexual exploitation of two girls over ten years previously. Nineteen offences were committed by the men (three of whom were brothers) including rape and false imprisonment. (Reported in the *Rotherham Advertiser*, February 2, 2017).
6 South Yorkshire Police 'must get a grip' on child abuse. (2012). October 16. BBC News, Sheffield and South Yorkshire. Available at www.bbc.co.uk/news/uk-england-south-yorkshire-19966721.
7 The former head of the Commission for Racial Equality, Trevor Phillips, has been criticised (but supported as well by others) for conceding the empirical data on some forms of racialised criminality. See also White, M. (2015). Trevor Phillips says the unsayable about race and multiculturalism. March 16. *The Guardian*. Available at www.theguardian.com/uk-news/2015/mar/16/trevor-phillips-race-multiculturalism-blog.
8 Some progressive Muslim leaders argue that patriarchy and misogyny *are* relevant culture trends that must be tackled by their community, with sexual exploitation being a malign expression of this problem. See Dugan, E. (2013). Imams to preach against grooming of girls for sex. May 17. *The Independent*. Available at www.independent.co.uk/news/uk/home-news/imams-to-preach-against-grooming-of-girls-for-sex-8621655.html.
9 It remains a moot point whether fears of accusation of racism or fear of losing Asian bloc votes was the main issue in Rotherham. Given the wider macho and rather backward local political culture, Jay thought that it was not 'political correctness' that dominated decision-making, but potential vote loss. The programme makers about the Rochdale case came to a similar conclusion but also emphasised the norm of criminalising rather than protecting children in the town.
10 In one of the eventual Rotherham prosecutions, a gang led by a South Asian family involved the active co-offending of two white women, Karen Macgregor and Shelley Davies. The first woman received a sentence of 13 years and the second a suspended sentence of 18 months.
11 The proneness of the Conservative government at the time (2015) to overly focus on Rotherham and its local government culture reflected a failure to admit the national

complexities of CSA. This long list of towns suggests that, while case-by-case local politicians *should* be held to account, one authority alone was not the whole picture. For an omissive critique of this narrow focus, see Crossely, S. & Leigh, J. (2017). The 'troubled' case of Rotherham. *Critical and Radical Social Work* 5(1), 23–40. They also challenge some of the premises of the Jay conclusions about the backward parochialism of Rotherham but they rely on moral panic reasoning as part of their analysis. I take that reasoning to task in Chapter 8.

12 Ultra-right groups in the UK have been inhibited from direct expressions of racism since the emergence of legal constraints. As a result, they have tended to shift to being anti-Muslim in their rhetoric.

13 At the time of writing, a similar case to that of Rotherham and Rochdale has come to light in Newcastle. In August 2017, 18 people were convicted of sexually exploiting 20 female victims, the youngest of whom was 14 years of age. The sole female defendant was white (and charged with trafficking, not sexual assault). The rest, though mainly British-born, were from Bangladeshi, Pakistani, Indian, Iraqi, Iranian and Turkish heritage. See Operation Sanctuary: Newcastle child sex network convicted. (2017). August 9. BBC News. Available at www.bbc.com/news/uk-england-40879427.

14 Shah, N. (2017). We need to dispel the dangerous myth that it's only Asian men who sexually assault young women. August 12. *The Independent*. Available at www.independent.co.uk/voices/newcastle-grooming-scandal-exploitation-victims-sarah-champion-race-a7890106.html.

15 Pervez, S. (2015). How clan politics grew in Bradford. February 27. BBC News, Leeds and West Bradford. Available at www.bbc.co.uk/news/uk-england-leeds-31600344.

16 See Chaudhry, A. & Ahmed, A. (2014). Biradari's function and significance: An anthropological study of gender opinions. *Abid Science International* 26(4), 1863–1865.

17 Has Labour learned lessons from Bradford West byelection defeat? (2013). January 29. *The Guardian*. Available at www.theguardian.com/politics/the-northerner/2013/jan/29/bradford-west-byelection-2012-georgegalloway.

18 Note that Ann Cryer in Labour's ranks did try to alert the police, social services and local community leaders to the risks of criminal gangs in her Keighley constituency in 2002, all to no avail. See Pidd, H. (2014). Rotherham report 'reduced me to tears', says MP who exposed abuse decade ago. August 30. *The Guardian*. Available at www.theguardian.com/uk-news/2014/aug/30/rotherham-girls-could-have-been-spared-ann-cryer.

19 Laville, S. (2016). Lambeth council to pay tens of millions to child abuse survivors. December 15. *The Guardian*. Available at www.theguardian.com/society/2016/dec/15/lambeth-council-pay-tens-of-millions-pounds-child-abuse-survivors-shirley-oaks.

20 Hopkins, N. & Morris, J. (2016). The council that employed an abuser to look after children. March 1. BBC News Magazine. Available at www.bbc.co.uk/news/magazine-35686482.

21 Norman, M. (2015). With a past like hers, Margaret Hodge might show a bit more humility. March 10. *The Independent*. Available at www.independent.co.uk/voices/comment/with-a-past-like-hers-margaret-hodge-might-show-a-bit-more-humility-10098871.html.

22 Stickler, A. (2003). Paedophile Investigation. November 11. BBC Radio 4 *Today* programme. Available at www.bbc.co.uk/radio4/today/reports/politics/bain_20031111.shtml.

23 Harris, P. & Bright, M. (2003). The whistleblower's story. July 6. *The Guardian*. Available at www.theguardian.com/politics/2003/jul/06/children.childprotection.

24 White, I. & Hart, K. (1995). Report of the Inquiry into the Management of Child Care in the London Borough of Islington. The list of 32 staff members was in a confidential addendum and so was not made public by the council.

25 The Office for Standards in Education, Children's Services and Skill (Ofsted) inspected and regulated UK services that care for children and young people, and services providing education and skills for learners of all ages. Though a government agency, it was not linked to one particular government department.

26 Widom, C. (2008). Childhood victimisation and lifetime victimisation. *Child Abuse & Neglect* 32(8), 785–796.

27 Stoltz, J-M., Shannon, K., Kerr, T., Zhang, R., Montaner, J. & Wood, E. (2007). Associations between childhood maltreatment and sex work in a cohort of drug-using youth. *Social Science & Medicine* 65(6), 1214–1221.

28 Wilson, S. (2015). *Violated: A Shocking and Harrowing Survival Story from the Notorious Rotherham Abuse Scandal* (p. 112). London: HarperCollins.

29 However, this grateful response was overshadowed later when Wilson attacked Senior about her version of events in *Broken and Betrayed*. Wilson was threatened with a restraining order by the courts. Senior was subjected to other subsequent criticism, including from some disaffected survivors and those cynical that she had used a ghostwriter for her book. See Forrest, A. (2017). CSE victim handed restraining order against whistleblowing councillor. March 21. *Rotherham Advertiser*. Available at www.rotherhamadvertiser.co.uk/news/view,cse-victim-handed-restraining-order-against-whistleblowing-councillor_21960.htm. The recriminations in Rotherham are one of many aftershocks still being felt today, in terms of public confidence in the competence of local government.

30 Jay Report (2014), para 9.13.

31 Senior, J. (2016). *Broken and Betrayed*. London: Pan.

32 South Yorkshire Police officers to be investigated by IPCC. (2014). October 14. ITV News. Available at www.itv.com/news/calendar/update/2014-10-14/risky-business-manager-appointed-as-rotherham-cse-specialist/.

33 Laura Wilson murder: Rotherham children's board reports. (2012). May 29. BBC News, Sheffield and South Yorkshire. Available at www.bbc.co.uk/news/uk-england-south-yorkshire-18244660.

34 Despite his pioneering journalism, Norfolk did admit to some shame, as he had actually delayed his story by seven years because of his fears of giving legitimacy to far-right propaganda. Both his shame and his earlier fears are both understandable, given the exploitation of the crimes for propaganda purposes by the British National Party and the English Defence League. See The Betrayed Girls. (2017). Last on BBC 2, July 22. BBC documentary at www.bbc.co.uk/programmes/b08xdh9r.

35 Obvious exceptions were those trying to be whistle-blowers like Jayne Senior in Rotherham and Sara Rowbotham in Rochdale. The latter was a sexual health worker whose contract was not renewed though her concerns were eventually acknowledged by her local authority and the criminal justice system. This political resistance to whistle-blowers was not new. An innovative multi-disciplinary child protection team was set up by the social worker Peter McKelvie in 1988 in Hereford and Worcester. In 1993, McKelvie sent a report detailing evidence of paedophiles operating in social work and other parts of the local state to ministers in the Department of Health. No action was taken about the report, but two years later McKelvie's service was closed down abruptly. See Buch, M. (2014). More evidence that the Department of Health were told of Peter Righton paedophile network … and did nothing. January 19. Spotlight, Home/Islington. Available at https://spotlightonabuse.wordpress.com/2014/01/19/more-evidence-that-the-department-of-health-were-told-of-peter-righton-paedophile-network-and-did-nothing/.

7

LESSONS FROM DOWN UNDER

Introduction

On August 30, 2009, on behalf of the Australian government, Prime Minister Kevin Rudd issued an apology for the harm created by the policy of sending children to isolated facilities between the 1920s and 1970s.[1] In 2010, British Prime Minister Gordon Brown also issued a formal apology to the 'lost children'. Brown described it as a 'disgraceful episode in Britain's history' and 'an ugly stain that would never be repeated'.[2] In November 2009, Rudd made the position of the Australian government about the regimes of cruelty to children explicit. He referred to the 'Forgotten Australians' transported as children under duress and conditions of distress. He apologised for:

> the physical suffering, the emotional starvation and the cold absence of love, of tenderness, of care [...] in austere and authoritarian places, where names were replaced by numbers; spontaneous play by regimented routine; the joy of learning by the repetitive drudgery of menial work.[3]

An estimated 10,000 children were sent to the colony to be used as slave labour and to endure physical and sexual abuse. Many were sent to what became the notorious Fairbridge Farm at Molong in New South Wales, to be discussed more below. This was one of a number of farm schools founded by the late Kingsley Fairbridge, a Rhodes Scholar from Rhodesia (now Zimbabwe). He conceived the idea while at Oxford in 1909 and it exemplifies the truism that 'the road to hell is paved with good intentions', rather like the legacy of the founder of the Congregation of Christian Brothers, Edmund Rice, I discussed in Chapter 4.

Kingsley Fairbridge believed genuinely that the skill shortages in the British colonies could be solved by transporting and training children, thereby enabling the latter to be happy Australian citizens and productive labour. The eugenic focus of the scheme was that it was about exporting 'white stock' to the British colonies.

The exportation of British children to the colonies could be traced to the early seventeenth century when destitute minors arrived in Virginia in the United States and yet it received little academic attention until the late twentieth century. Written by Philip Bean and Joy Melville, *Lost Children of the Empire*, summarising the policy, did not appear until 1989.[4] To use their phrase, until then it was an 'untold story'. The story had structural elements of pre-capitalist authority (religious organisations) and contingent triggers involving colonial brutality (such as the Irish potato famine). In Britain, the unemployed and unemployable in workhouses, during the emergence of the capitalist economy, included children who could be exported as a partial solution to the cost of the Poor Laws. In their receiving colony, they could be put to work to sustain the British Empire. This all made functional sense for the rich and the powerful, and even the emergent profession of social work in the twentieth century, but the rights and feelings of the children were an irrelevance to the policy.

By the time Rudd and Brown made their apologies for this colonial experiment, there were still an estimated 7,000 survivors alive in Australia (though note that the scheme was also used to transport some British children to Canada, Rhodesia, New Zealand and the West Indies). A longer personal account of the privations and abuse at the Fairbridge Farm at Molong was provided by David Hill, Director of the Australian Broadcasting Corporation (ABC) from 1987 to 1995, in his book *The Forgotten Children*.[5] Their fate was also summarised in *The Long Journey Home*,[6] an article in the *Sydney Morning Herald* from 2009.

The British Fairbridge émigrés were part of a larger cohort of mistreated children who were to become Australian citizens. Apart from the London Fairbridge Society, which brokered the migration from Britain, a range of Church organisations and charities (such as Barnardo's and the Children's Society) also played their part. This then was a broad government-endorsed scheme, which co-opted the efforts of what we now would call 'third sector' organisations.

The British government fully supported the policy until the mid-1950s. The paternalistic and eugenic experiment to export British children to Australia was part of a two-part story. Another group was the 'stolen children', aboriginal by birth but who were shifted to white families and institutions, which I deal with more below.

In the introduction to the book, I introduced the contested implications of *parens patriae*. The Australian case study highlights why there is such contestation. On the one hand, the positive role of state intervention is to protect children in a valid and effective manner. On the other hand, the state can intervene to transport children for wider policy requirements – in the case here of economics and eugenics. These came into play in relation to both of the case studies I deal with in this chapter.

In the case of the Aboriginal children, they were transported inside their own country by a colonial power, in part to ensure their 'assimilation' into a European culture. That deliberate attempt at assimilation has been called 'cultural genocide' by some critics to add to claims from historians of direct extermination.[7] Whereas the Nazi holocaust in Germany was about the elimination of a racial and cultural group from a power *within* a country, what was different in the case of Australia (and Canada) was that the genocide was from a colonial invader.

In Australia, that genocide had two phases: the assimilation of indigenous children into European-heritage families and institutions after the first wave of direct frontier violence, when the British simply killed aboriginal people. This history can be compared with the Eurocentric narrative that genocide based on race was at odds with *civilised* values. In truth, in both North America and Australasia, Britain presided over genocide during its imperial adventures and it was all done within a claim of civilised concern for native people.

The shared oppression of black and white children in Australian institutions

The forced movement of British and aboriginal children entailed state paternalism and eugenics coming together to enable widespread child maltreatment in a range of receiving organisations in Australia. For example, John Hennessy at the age of ten was already in an orphanage in Bristol when he was put on a ship with others. He was allocated to a Catholic institution at Bundoon north of Perth, where the children were used as slave labour on a building project. The children were fed poorly and, one day, John and others stole some grapes to eat from the vineyard. He was caught and stripped naked before being flogged publicly by one of the Christian Brothers. He was left with a lifelong stutter and recalled: 'I would never, ever, like my childhood days to come back again. It was so cruel, it was so un-Christian, it was brutality at its worst.'[8]

The physical sadism was only part of the cruel baggage for these children. They were told that they were not wanted by their families, but this was not true. Mothers with illegitimate babies were encouraged to let go of them for their own benefit. Sometimes, the children were shipped off without their knowledge.

This leaves us with the difficulty of punctuating responsibility for this child cruelty: it was partly authored by the politicians and social workers agreeing to it in Britain; it was partly about the lack of concern the Australian government had about receiving these children and depositing them in isolated vulnerability; and it was partly the end-point cruelty of those receiving them in isolated institutions.

In 2004, the Australian senate reported on this scandal, unchecked for decades, and detailed 'a litany of emotional, physical and sexual abuse'.[9] Victim blaming was the norm in the receiving institutions. Caroline Carroll spent 14 years in five different institutions and went on to chair the self-advocacy group the Alliance for Forgotten Australians. She recalls:

> We were told every day that we were the scum of the earth, that we came from the gutter, and that's where we'd end up. We were of no importance, there was no individuality, often we were called by a number, not even a name.[10]

The collective story of the 'forgotten children' throws into relief the complexity of child abuse. A core process was that the children (and sometimes their parents) were not being recognised as persons at all. They were simply elements in a social experiment for the sending and receiving agencies. They were slave labour and sometimes sexual objects for those using them at their eventual points of arrival. If their humanity survived it was because of group solidarity; the children cared for one another.

The group solidarity survived in part at least in the organisation the Alliance for Forgotten Australians, which noted in its report of 2008:

> Children experienced: separation, abandonment and loss of family; deception; neglect and exploitation; sustained brutality; sexual assault; poor health including denial of dental care; denial of educational opportunity; removal/loss of identity; drug testing; lack of post care support. Among the lasting effects of institutional care are: a lack of trust and security; a lack of social skills; risk behaviours; inability to form and maintain loving relationships; inability to parent effectively; mental illness. Children in institutions were generally told that they would not be believed if they spoke about their abuse. Many tried and found this to be true. As adults they still feel reluctant to talk about their experiences to anyone who has no knowledge or understanding of the basic facts about their history. Forgotten Australians do not expect to be believed and they have tried to put the past behind them. Forgotten Australians are survivors.[11]

This poignant and defiant summary was in the wake of the report by the Senate Committee of 2004 which listed the reasons for the transportation, including: single parents (usually mother); death of a parent or parents; parents' divorce or separation; parent(s) unable to care for children; economic stress and social disadvantage; children abandoned; sexual abuse by a parent; children escaping domestic violence and parental alcoholism; and the repatriation of children. This was about state power to regulate family life. Some of this was about moral judgements about parental competence which could be unjust (for example, in relation to young single mothers) or a reasonable act of attempted child protection (for example, where the child was being sexually abused in their family of origin).

Grim life at Molong Farm School

The isolation of the British children sent to the Fairbridge farms began at home in the well-intentioned decision-making of the society's initial assessments and negotiations with its referrers. When I gained access to the files of the society at the University of Liverpool to examine this process and the cases of individual children dealt with, a number of pre-migration features were evident to me. The children and their natural parents did not go seeking the transportation: their views as citizens with a stake in the decision were ignored, irrelevant or became, at best, *post hoc* viewpoints (of agreement or dissent).

This prospect of moving children to the other side of the world was a mono-logue of middle-class power, not a dialogue with those of lower socio-economic status. It emerged as an option in the minds of referrers such as the NSPCC, even before the Fairbridge Society played its part. In some cases, parents with large fami-lies were told that one or more of their children going to Australia could lead to them joining them later. This was wilfully misleading. In some of the cases I exam-ined, a father might agree to a child migrating because he wanted rid of them, or a child might prefer the migration to escape from an abusive home life. But these were late-on opinions and were largely irrelevant endorsements of decisions *already made* by others.

More typically, mothers were distraught at the prospect and this would be rein-forced when children subsequently pleaded to return to Britain in distressed let-ters sent back home from Australia. Some went with their children and would try to retrieve them because of their child's distress but were then seen as irrational and meddlesome by the Fairbridge staff. They were only permitted to visit their children three times in total. If, after the late 1950s (until the scheme collapsed in 1966 for lack of a supply of children to the school), parents did want to see their children but had found work in Sydney, this was 200 miles away. They could have their children during the school holidays subject to the Fairbridge staff checking the suitability of the accommodation offered. (This was an irony given the austere and harsh environment of the Molong institution.)

The children were already vulnerable according to their assessors in Britain; indeed, many were typical of the child protection cases seen today by social work-ers. The difference was that state-financed social work was less developed then; this was a period either side of the Second World War. Also, the different moral norms about family life influenced the concerns of the referrers. Children whose mother had died, or who was alive but a single parent deemed to be struggling in her duties, was a particular target of interest. Boys 'running wild' and fathers unable to cope with children without a wife, who had left them or died, also rang particular alarm bells for assessors. These emerged as targeted candidates for enforced migration.

This moral and moralistic separation of 'them and us', or what we now call 'othering', was palpable in the cases I read. The assessors asking Fairbridge to take children drew attention to the failing moral development of children, as well as parental incompetence or fecklessness. What was striking about the files I read was that the moral position of assessors and the Fairbridge staff was taken for granted as being warranted and simply beyond question.

This matter of conceptual separation between middle-class worthy paternalism and the moral failure of poor and dysfunctional families and children is important. Not only did it imply that the latter were 'moral dirt',[12] and so without rights of veto to the transportation, it also meant that those making the decisions were not reflective about the wisdom of their *own* actions.

To them, it was self-evident that their actions were a worthy form of child pro-tection. It transpired that this was woefully mistaken. Not only were the children mistreated – the logic of the move entailed them being used as cheap labour – they were also *de facto* slaves. Whatever were the good intentions, it ended in the hell of the cruel milieu of austere living conditions and staff members who could be abusive to the children without legal redress or outside scrutiny.

The other elephant in the room was about social class as a divider between the professional and the client. Again, little has changed in this regard: poverty still predicts the probability of *parens patriae*. But what that meant in the mid-twentieth-century context of a global aspiration to move 'white stock' to the British colonies was using poor children as slave labour on farms and denying them access to other life pathways. In the same period, rich parents too sent their children away (to boarding schools), which brought with it its own particular deprivations and risks alongside a presumption of eventual supremacy and power. In both cases, a trajectory was set to maintain the British class hierarchy.

And then there were the grim conditions of a loveless world in rural Australia. The British children reacted in a range of ways to the shock of the new. Many were simply and predictably homesick and heartbroken. Some were lucky and found positive attachments to benign house mothers, who might replace the one left back at home or who had died. (Some children were subsequently told that their parents in Britain were dead, when this was not true.) For the lucky ones, they left Molong and adjusted well and would individually report a good experience of the place.[13]

Others were less lucky and faced physical cruelty and sexual abuse. Just as with the Christian Brothers and their scandalous industrial schools, these farm schools had layers of isolation. They were in remote, austere places and the harsh staff culture developing there was unchallenged and untroubled by external scrutiny or changing social norms in wider society. If harm to a child emerged of any sort then it was in the interests of those running these isolated places to keep the trouble in-house. Parochialism and blinkered institutional routines dominated the norms of the staff and their managers.

The 'othering' of 'moral dirt'

The 'othering' process about 'moral dirt' reappeared in some of the less noted cases about the Fairbridge survivors. Most of the latter campaigning for recognition and compensation went on to be the 'new', albeit forgotten, Australians Kevin Rudd above spoke to (as was the intention of the scheme).

However, a few children rebelled and resisted and they did so with the only option available to them: they absconded and became petty offenders. This meant some of them were repatriated after court appearances, with lengthy documentation supplied by Fairbridge staff about the moral failures of the children. Some of the latter were criticised for 'boasting' that their waywardness was simply a way of getting back home, as if wanting to go home was a preposterous expectation.

Thus, when we think about adult power over children (and one scenario that can arise at times from this is sexual abuse) we also see a power struggle. Some of the children exercised their limited powers of resistance in delinquency, as a means to return home. Some of the survivors later came together in solidarity to demand justice and reparation.

All of this shows that the power exercised over children by those able to do so, and often self-righteously, can always invite or incite a political reaction from its victims. It may not always lead to the full truth coming out, but it reminds us that child abuse in general (not just sexual abuse) is about struggles about power: the privileged power of some of us to define the lives and welfare of others, and the protest and resistance that arises in its wake. In this case, that power struggle was largely about the intersection of age and class but colonial power and a binding eugenic philosophy also created the particular arena of possibility for that interaction.

Fact-finding in 1956 and the end of the Empire

In 1956, the British government sent a fact-finding mission to Australia to examine the receiving schools of migrant children. There were two political prompts for this visit. The first was that, since 1951 in Britain, a policy had developed of the intention to run down institutional care, with its displacement by foster care and adoption (though in Britain this took a while to put into practice).

The second stimulus was legal. The Empire Settlement Act of 1922 was due to expire in 1957 and the visiting party fed into a wider decision-making process about what would happen in the future in relation to Britain's traditional role in the colonies and ex-colonies. Australia's separation from British rule during the twentieth century was episodic and gradual. Even now, it is not a republic: it remains a constitutional monarchy and member of the British Commonwealth.

The British visiting party was less than impressed. Its three-man group categorised the quality of the care in 26 institutions in Australia receiving British children, with the worst institutions placed by name at the top in rank order. Overall, the report was highly critical, but at the top of its ten-site 'blacklist' of worst-functioning institutions there appeared the names of the Fairbridge schools at Molong New South Wales and Pinjarra in Western Australia. These were criticised as well in pointed private addenda in the report, such was the dire state of the farm schools. The situation was so severe that the visiting party felt that they could not justify that the British government should fund any more migrant schemes. (Subsequently, some funding did continue for the better-run schools and with the caveat of transporting parents with children, rather than the tradition of splitting families.)

The upshot for Molong was that no British children were sent there after 1966 and, inherently, the place would run down for lack of supply. Attempts at adaptation under the 'Families Scheme' were failing and the fate of Molong was really sealed. Initially, it was decided to shut the place in 1966, but it staggered on and eventually collapsed in the early 1970s, not because of the proven inhumanity of the place but because of depleted sources of funding.

The Fairbridge Society was at the time re-thinking its role; moving from residential care provision to other schemes, such as supporting children in local schooling and academic scholarships. In 1982, that revised role, and altered functioning, were formally announced and the aims of the society were accordingly altered within its charitable status in Britain.

Parochial forms of denial

One might expect then that by the mid-1960s the gravity of the situation about the reputation and viability of Molong Farm School would have been a focus of intense and anxious internal deliberations there, alongside evidence of planned decommissioning in practice. But this was not the case. There were resonances here of the BBC being in denial about Jimmy Savile (see Chapter 1). This time, though, the denial was about the critical messages issued after the 1956 visit. Molong was found lacking in its duty of care and was out of sync with emerging norms about good practice. But, as will become evident, the parochial isolation of those running Molong meant that these reality checks were evaded. In more ways than one, the managers of the farm school were 'in denial'.

I looked at the minutes of the management committee meetings of the school between 1962 and 1976 as well as summary reports of children from the Welfare Officers. There was little in these documents to suggest that either the Molong Farm School was in crisis or that there was any concern about the quality of care it was providing for children. What was striking was not what was said but what was *not* said; financial accounts were recorded and technical information about the functioning of farm equipment noted.

According to these records, all was well: the staff were contented, the farm produce healthy in quality and supply and the children happy with their lot. One minute from 1968 described the Molong children as 'looking the picture of health' (a phrase used repeatedly in minutes). A reader of the documents, with no knowledge of the 1956 blacklist, would have no sense at all of the organisational challenge for Molong. The subtext of the silence was 'Crisis, what crisis?'.

The 1960s, then, was not witnessing any recorded acknowledgement of the critical report of 1956 or the impending closure of Molong. The sense of this denial was of the staff at Molong whistling in the dark; as if recording the happiness of the children and the rude health of the farm made the place of the school, when judged in the history of childcare, as being exemplary. The recent judgements of Kevin Rudd in Australia or Gordon Brown in Britain in this century now make this literal denial of the organisational problems of Molong seem bizarre or even unreal. Indeed, as often happens with isolated organisations, the people working in them become out of touch with reality.

At last the dinosaur dies

The school was closed finally, after 38 years of functioning, in 1974, but no sign of this eventuality was visible in the minutes recorded until very late on. For example, in July 1970, the principal reported the good news that the school would *start* to be used as a placement for trainee teachers. However, in the same report, and with some resentment, it was noted that the State Child Welfare Department was intending to 'examine our licence renewal'.

By November 1970, the biggest problem for the principal still seemed to be one of technical inefficiency – at that time because of the absence of a working 'spirit duplicator' in the office. Eventually, reality impinged and, after 1971, the actual mechanics of closure of the farm school were discussed. This was like a dinosaur taking a long while to recognise the obvious truth that it was fatally wounded.

In March 1971, the retiring chairman of the school council was still talking of the financial backing for the place for another ten years. However, by April 1971, only 70 children remained at Molong and the principal was declining applications for new entrants from within the country (from 1963, new entrants were taken from Australia). The chairman of the council, H. L. Kingsmill, resigned in protest at the imminent closure, again signalling that this predictable eventuality was like a shocking bolt from the blue, warranting his indignation. The principal also resigned, giving ill health as the reason.

By May 1971, active steps were proposed to shrink the school to just two functioning cottages (which by now had no British children in them). However, those working there put up a strong resistance to quick and eventual closure. Bizarrely, by August 1971, the council resolved to *rescind* the decision to close the school. By August 1972, the Molong group was looking for other supply sources of children to 'restore Molong to what it was in its heyday'. This meant the group was in denial that the 'heyday' had involved a blacklisted status from the British government and what was soon to become a successful legal class action by its ex-residents.

However, by June 1973, the council eventually accepted defeat and moved to sell the property. All dinosaurs eventually die. By Christmas, most of the children had been dispersed elsewhere. In January 1974, the wording of a memorial plaque was agreed:

> On this 1500 acre Fairbridge Farm from 1938 to 1973, over 1500 British and Australian Boys and Girls were brought up to love the country, and to learn country skills and ways, in keeping with the ideals of Kingsley Fairbridge, Founder of the Fairbridge Farm Schools of Australia and Canada.

By the turn of this century, that wording could be contrasted with a legal outcome for Fairbridge survivors who would receive the formal apologies from the British and Australian governments noted earlier. By June 2015, the victims were eventually in receipt of $24 million from the State and Federal Governments. The Fairbridge Society made no contribution to this compensation fund.

Moreover, despite Rudd's fine words, government lawyers challenged the class action from victims no fewer than 21 times since proceedings began in 2009 on behalf of 60 Fairbridge victims. Again, there are resonances here with the Catholic Church: apologies are issued but compensation is not offered readily, without a determined legal fight from those accused. This gives moral claims from such organisations about the welfare of victims a resounding hollow ring.

Survivors tell a different story

The minutes of the business of Molong Farm School tell a story of literal denial about an oppressive regime which routinely betrayed children and at times abused them. The story told by its survivors later in adulthood, and summarised eloquently by David Hill in *The Forgotten Children*, was quite different from the official account recorded in the internal documents I examined.

The survivors report that one dominant principal was Frederick Woods, who presided over the school from 1942 to 1966. Claims of his sexual abuse of a girl in 1945 were brushed under the carpet but his bullying ways and claims of him being a 'sexual pervert' led to his eventual sacking. A naked Woods had enjoyed inviting girls to bring him his early morning tea, to their distress and confusion.

But Woods' eventual undoing was that he had acted immorally with other female staff members, not because allegations about his physical or sexual abuse of children were accepted by the Fairbridge organisation. In the immediate wake of his sacking in Australia, the London office supported him and still wanted to retain his services, but to no avail. A previous principal, Richard Beauchamp, had been quickly released from Molong after a two-year reign because of reports of inappropriate sexual contact with some of the older girl residents, but the long and loyal reputation of Woods protected him in the eyes of his allies in Fairbridge.

Ironically, the man in charge of sacking Frederick Woods was Field Marshall Sir William Slim, who was made Governor General of Australia in 1953 and took over the chairing of the London Fairbridge Society ten years later. In 2007, three Molong survivors alleged that Slim sexually assaulted them at the farm school, when visiting in his duty as chairman.[14]

Two successive aftercare officers (Messrs Phillips and Newberry) in the 1950s left the school after complaints about them sexually abusing girls. By the time Newberry left, he, like Woods and Beauchamp, had become the principal at Molong. None of these disciplinary matters were referred to the police but were dealt with in-house by Fairbridge. So too with other cases: early in the 1960s, the garden supervisor at Molong, Ted Roach, had a penchant for grabbing the genitals of boys in his work groups.

Abuse in a loveless world

What dominates the picture, and there was a strong consensus about this, is that the regime was loveless. The individual assaults were important but so too was the heartless harshness of the place that affected all of them, assaulted or not, unless they were rescued by the odd benign attachment to a member of staff. This is captured well here by Janet Ellis who arrived at the age of seven in 1954:

> There wasn't anyone to pick you up and give you a cuddle and say it was alright. They called me scum; they said I was dirty. They said I was the lowest

form of life. I don't remember anyone ever saying to me 'you did a good job, Jan. Well done'. I remember a lot of people hitting me around the head and belting me with whatever they could lay their hands on.[15]

This outcome of a seven-year-old girl being physically assaulted and treated contemptuously was par for the course at Molong. But the scenario arose because the school was being fed by child protection referrals from Britain (typically, the NSPCC or the Scottish Society for the Prevention of Cruelty to Children). Janet's simple and short recollection reminds us that sexual abuse was entwined with both emotional and physical abuse and that victim blaming came readily to adults who enjoyed power over children in a rural parochial institution. It is also a direct and honest recollection of what it is like as a child to be treated like 'moral dirt'.

Finally, in the case of Fairbridge, we can compare the path from literal to institutional denial reminiscent of the BBC discussed in Chapter 1. Whereas, by the turn of this century, the British and Australian governments were issuing apologies and organisations implicated in the transportation, such as Barnardo's and the Children's Society, accepted that the past was a barbaric and shameful period, no equivalent acknowledgement came from the London Fairbridge Society.

Its director, Nigel Haynes, told the British House of Commons Select Committee for Health in 1998 that it had no record of any physical or sexual abuse in its homes after 1938.[16] Haynes also noted that its old form of functioning had ceased and that the new Fairbridge organisational incarnation was no longer concerned with either the direct provision of childcare or the welfare of ex-residents.

It adopted a stance of drawing a line under its moral and political responsibility for the survivors of the Fairbridge regime in Australia, and that was the end of the story from its new perspective. As with the BBC's point of arrival at institutional denial, it was a case of 'that was then but this is now' or 'we are now a different organisation and so we hold no current responsibility for any past misdeeds or mismanagement'; once any organisation prefers to 'draw a line under the past', then the prospect of justice for its victims is undermined, maybe fatally.

And yet, today, the London Fairbridge Society still remains vigilant and cautious about access to its archives at the University of Liverpool. In those archives, there is an account in the society's minutes (July 2, 1965) of a sadistic housemother at Molong, Katherine Johnstone, regularly whipping children with a riding crop and, in one instance, shoving the head of a six-year-old girl down the toilet for bedwetting. This is at odds with the testimony of Haynes in 1998 that there was no abuse in the Fairbridge Farm schools recorded after 1938.

Denial takes many forms, including, it seems, blind spots about records possessed by an organisation. The exact value of political apologies for past misdeeds is understandably debated. But different 'states of denial' require a debate of a different kind, as the case studies of Fairbridge, the BBC and the Catholic Church all demonstrate in their own ways. A denied past catching up with the present is a cue for the next section.

Child abuse in a context of cultural genocide

The Fairbridge scandal was one important aspect of child abuse in Australia in the twentieth century. Another was about the treatment of indigenous children. In particular, those of mixed race invited a policy of integration as part of British colonial rule. By the end of the nineteenth century, the eugenic hope of European-heritage Australian colonists was that 'full-blooded' aborigines were a dying race and that 'half-castes' would eventually become white. A parallel rationale was also witnessed at the hands of the British in Canada from the mid-nineteenth century.

One deliberate effort to absorb the latter group was by taking children and placing them in white-run institutions and families to be raised as white and to be 'assimilated' into a Eurocentric Christian culture. So, although this process was racist, behind that racism was eugenics, at the time the policy orthodoxy across the political spectrum in all advancing capitalist societies. The policy towards the native Australians and the British migrant child slaves noted above were driven by the same political ideology.

The emergence of a mixed-race generation at the end of the nineteenth century was itself a direct product of the sexual abuse of aboriginal girls and women by white settlers, who typically were immune from its legal consequences, when the victims were below the legal age of consent. (This mirrored the emergence of the 'Mulatto' group in the Caribbean, as a result of white slave owners imposing themselves sexually on black girls.) We see here a confluence of patriarchy, slavery and colonialism as sources of oppressive power to enable CSA. But that primary abuse at the hands of white male colonials in Australia triggered the secondary risk of the internal transportation policy.

In 1998, the Human Rights and Equal Opportunities Commission for Australia issued its 'National Inquiry into the Separation of Aboriginal and Torres Strait Islander Children from their Families, *Bringing Them Home*'.[17] The focus of *Bringing Them Home* was past practices involved in taking these children from their biological families and 'under compulsion, duress or undue influence' and placing them in other places. It was also concerned with making recommendations in the light of this investigation, in terms of reparation and compensation.

The reckoning that white Australia was facing here was not about its twentieth-century policy of restricting immigration, but an even earlier one of dealing with indigenous people in the nineteenth century. Ironically, the challenge *was* about immigration but that of unrequested and aggressive white colonials. How were they to deal with native Australians? Apart from shooting Aboriginal people when they encountered any resistance, the other option was to 'assimilate' them into white society so that the pre-existing social order of nomadic Aboriginal life was eroded until eventually eliminated.

The legitimacy of this policy was ensured by passing laws to support it. This began with the Victorian Aborigines Act of 1869, followed quickly by similar legislation in other Australian states. From the outset, this was a policy of social improvement to uplift the morals and health of indigenous people, who were seen, by and large, by the colonial power as being savage and animalistic.

Bodies like the New South Wales Aborigines Protection Board were provided with powers to take custody and control of any indigenous child judged to be in need of protection in their own best interest, in order to improve their moral or physical welfare. Employees of the board used their discretion in this regard and no court proceedings were required nor was the consent of the child's parents. The policy became routine from 1910 and was only fully ended in the 1970s.

Seeking to control the indigenous young not only weakened their bond and identification with their traditional communities but it was also a means of force-fully regulating a nomadic culture that was at odds with the settled socio-economic routines preferred by the European invaders. As with Fairbridge supplying a work-force, these indigenous children were to be absorbed into the urban landscape, mainly as domestic labour, as well as being used for farm work. They were removed to what were called 'training' placements. More girls than boys were removed to decrease the probability of them falling pregnant to Aboriginal partners. By the 1930s, over 80% of the children removed were female. If these became pregnant later, when put into domestic service, their own children would also be removed elsewhere.[18]

The habit of kidnapping children of both sexes for cheap labour had begun by frontier British invaders during the mid-nineteenth century and it was during that phase that the first wave of mixed-race offspring emerged from the sexual abuse of the girl captives. In this context, sexual abuse became a weapon of colonisation. The parallel religious rationale coming with colonisation was the green light given to missionary organisations to take children in order to inculcate Christian values into what were seen as savage heathens.

The terror and distress caused by the policy of forced removals intimidated local indigenous groups and so the harm done was not just to the stolen children but also those left behind. The conditions in the 'training' institutions holding the children were very poor and many died there quickly from disease exacerbated by malnutri-tion. In a parallel process to that endured by the Fairbridge migrants, children were told that their parents were dead and so it was futile to seek a return home.

One difference between the groups was that the British children were tar-geted mainly on grounds of social class (from 'failing' poor families) whereas the Australian children were chosen because of their racial status. Another dif-ference (again reflecting white racism) was that the indigenous children were given new names, whereas the British children were permitted to retain their birth names.

The colonial assumption was that in the face of the supremacy of European forms of social and economic organisation the 'full-blooded' Aboriginal would sim-ply die out. The problem of the 'half-caste' children and their borderline status could now be resolved: they were being 'rescued', not stolen, in order to enjoy a supe-rior white Christian world. The predominant eugenic ethos of Social Darwinism ensured that the Europeans could predict that the survival of the fittest would be those that were as approximate as possible to those who were white in both genes and personal outlook.

Although the policy only petered out in the 1970s, as early as 1948 the UN Convention and Punishment of the Crime of Genocide included in the latter the forcible removal of children from one group to another, in order to destroy their original ethnic or religious community. However, by 1998, the Australian Prime Minister John Howard still refused to apologise for the policy on the grounds that current governors of the country should not be responsible for the actions of those in the past (a variant of 'institutional denial').

The 'stolen children' (sometimes also called the 'stolen generations') reflected a seeming paradox: an invading European power that was self-styled as being 'civilised' compared to the indigenous people they encountered, treated the latter in the most brutal and uncivilised manner. That contradiction was resolved, to the satisfaction of the powerful invaders, by their coercion being justified by a mixture of legalism, the warm glow of Christian piety and arbitrary acts of cruel brute force becoming ones of generosity and welfare against 'the other'.

In this case, 'the other' was defined on eugenic grounds primarily (designating Aboriginal people as sub-human and animalistic) but within that tendency also on grounds of age: children were un-socialised and so still primitive and *ipso facto* not civilised.[19] Indigenous children were de-humanised twice over, for being both black and young.

In summary, this policy background about the 'stolen children' accounts for why indigenous children were put at risk of harm in a variety of ways in the twentieth century in Australia. One specific form of harm risked was from the white people in charge of them during their 'assimilation' into the ways of European Christianity. As with other contexts of CSA, most of that harm was imposed by adult males but in some cases (see the appendix to this chapter) women also were perpetrators.

Conclusion

At the time of writing, the Royal Commission in Australia is still overviewing historic cases of child abuse across a wider range of religious and secular organisations. This chapter has picked out two large and important case studies but it does not exhaust the topic for that country. For example, I alluded to abuse there in Catholic institutions in Chapter 4 and the Church in Australia is still dealing with its own particular legacy, as in other countries.[20] Similarly, Jewish children raised in Australia from a post-holocaust context have found themselves entrapped at times by religious demands not to disclose experiences of abuse in their community.[21]

What the two case studies above offer is a particular formulation about power. Not only do they remind us that beyond the motives and desires of predatory perpetrators lay a range of considerations about the variegated isolation of children; in this case, colonialism and eugenics have to be considered as well. This is not to argue that these complex conditions in a simple sense *caused* CSA. Instead, as is obvious above, what they did was create the conditions of possibility for it to emerge in the way it did in Australia.

These conditions also emerged in part from the Nazi holocaust that propelled part of the Jewish diaspora to the suburbs of Sydney and Melbourne or, say, the politics of Vietnam and its 'boat people'. But the main roots lay in the politics of British colonialism and its impact on both black and white children in Australia, from the mid-nineteenth century to the mid-twentieth century. Structures of power based on colonialism, eugenics and religious conformance all played their part in shaping particular risks to children.

The Australian experience will continue to provide us with evidence of the rich complexity of the conditions of emergence of CSA in contemporary developed societies. Those conditions are not rooted simply in the base motives of perpetrators themselves (though they are always important to fathom) but in a set of self-righteous ideologies based on colonial self-confidence, racial politics and Judeo-Christian assumptions about 'doing good work'. The road to hell is indeed paved with good intentions.

Appendix: Survivors' experiences

The forgotten migrant children

> Bob Stevens, a claimant in a lawsuit against Fairbridge Farm, a school in Australia for mostly British child migrants, said Viscount Slim would arrive in his Rolls Royce and the 'next minute we were sitting on his knee and he's got his hands up our trousers'.
>
> Mr Stevens, who was sent from England when he was eight-years-old, has given private testimony to Australia's Royal Commission into child abuse and is preparing a submission to the commissioner seeking to have Viscount Slim, who died in 1970, stripped of his peerage [...] 'He used to visit Fairbridge and we were all in some cases given rides in his Rolls Royce car, round the farm,' he told ABC News. 'I don't care how brilliant a man he might have been militarily, if he abused children the way I was abused and others, I don't think people like that have the right to continue [...] in terms of peerage that goes on from family to family to family. I think it's outrageous.'[22]

> He [Mr Phillips] treated me like shit, sexually abused me. He would wait till his wife was asleep in the bedroom I shared with his daughter when she was asleep and regularly abuse me. I was then expected to serve him breakfast and clean up after him next morning. I didn't mention it to anybody because I thought it was just happening to me. I had no idea whether other children were having problems.[23]

> I managed to get down to the veggie patch and they had a shed down there and I managed to find the shed and I also managed to find Mr Newberry

too. He didn't – well he didn't actually penetrate, you know he didn't actually – he touched me, you know. It's hard to talk about it – it has to be talked about but it's very hard to talk about that part. And I couldn't go and tell anyone. I was a scared little rat and plus, you know, he said, 'You tell and you get it worse'. Well you're a child. You're just scared. So I just shut up and got on with life.[24]

Jack Newberry touched me up. I had three other people sexually abuse me at Fairbridge other than Jack Newberry. I must have been just one of those people that had 'victim' written on their forehead [...] We were in Molong Cottage and we were allowed in to her cottage [the cottage mother's] quarters to watch a movie on television with her and her husband. It must have been winter and there were blankets over everybody and he was sitting next to me and I mean he even shoved his hands up inside me then [...] She must have known what he was like and she must have known he had me. Who do you tell? Because no one wants to know anyway. And then they don't believe you and then you're accused of being a liar.[25]

He used to grab you and run his hands all over you. It was disgusting. He was a creep. He just thought he had a God-given right to do what he wanted. And what could you do? He used to say no one would believe you. I was angry and then you tell your cottage mother and she accuses you of telling lies. The adults didn't want to believe you. So I went to Woods and he said the same as the cottage mother: 'You're telling lies.'[26]

The stolen indigenous children

I was thirteen at the time Mr E wanted to rape me. I rushed around to his car, pulled out the shotgun and instead of shooting him I pushed him in the bore tank. He never tried anything else since. I told Mrs E and she told me that it was a lie, that he wouldn't touch a black person. I told the Superintendent at Cherbourg. He wouldn't believe me.[27]

I led a very lost, confused, sad, empty childhood, as my foster father molested me. He would masturbate in front of me, touch my private parts, and get me to touch his. I remember once having a bath with my clothes on 'cause I was too scared to take them off. I was scared of the dark 'cause my foster father would often come at night. I was scared to go to the outside toilet as he would often stop me on the way back from the toilet. So I would often wet the bed 'cause I didn't want to get out of bed.[28]

I was being molested in the home by one of the staff there [...] She was telling me all about the time she was with my mother when she died and how my mother had told her how much she loved me. She also had a large bag of puffed wheat near the bed, because she knew how much I loved it. All this time she was inserting this cane into my vagina. I guess I was about 9 or 10. I know she did this to me many times over the years until she left the home when I was about 14 years old.[29]

I ran away because my foster father used to tamper with me and I'd just had enough. I went to the police but they didn't believe me. So she [foster mother] just thought I was a wild child and she put me in one of those hostels and none of them believed me – I was the liar. So I've never talked about it to anyone. I don't go about telling lies, especially big lies like that.[30]

Notes

1 Kevin Rudd's national apology to Stolen Generations. (2009). October 23. News.com. au. Available at www.news.com.au/national/pm-moves-to-heal-the-nation/news-story/ bc17b0684b1df369a87a4d3b3dd1e41c.
2 Gordon Brown apologises to child migrants sent abroad. (2010). February 24. BBC News. Available at news.bbc.co.uk/2/hi/uk_news/8531664.stm.
3 Kevin Rudd's national apology (2009).
4 Bean, P. & Melville, J. (1989). *The Lost Children of the Empire: The Untold Story of Britain's Child Migrants.* London: Unwin Hyman.
5 Hill, D. (2008). *The Forgotten Children: Fairbridge Farm School and Its Betrayal of Britain's Child Migrants.* Sydney: William Heinemann.
6 The Long Journey Home. (2009). November 16. ABC, Programs. Available at www.abc. net.au/tv/programs/long-journey-home/.
7 Moses, A. (2004). *Genocide and Settler Society: Frontier Violence and Stolen Indigenous Children in Australian History.* New York, NY: Berghahn; also, Rowley, C. (1970). *The Destruction of Aboriginal Society.* Canberra: Australian National University Press.
8 Cited in Hill, D. (2008). *The Forgotten Children.*
9 Inquiry into Children in Institutional Care. Parliament of Australia. Available at www.aph. gov.au/Parliamentary_Business/Committees/Senate/Community_Affairs/Completed_ inquiries/2004-07/inst_care/index.
10 Marks, K. (2009). Australia's apology to transported children. August 30. *The Independent.* Available at www.independent.co.uk/news/world/australasia/australias-apology-to- transported-children-1779652.html.
11 Forgotten Australians: Supporting survivors of childhood institutional care in Australia. Alliance for Forgotten Australians. Available at www.forgottenaustralians.org.au/assets/ docs/Booklet/MiniAfaBooklet.pdf.
12 Ferguson, H. (2007). Abused and looked after children as 'moral dirt': Child and insti- tutional care in historical perspective. *Journal of Social Policy* 36(1), 123–139. https://doi. org/10.1017/S0047279406000407.
13 For this reason, some Fairbridge ex-residents have been hostile to David Hill's picture drawn in *The Forgotten Children,* which he notes in the preface of the second edition of the book.
14 Pearlman, J. (2014). Britain's 'finest WWII general' accused of child sex abuse. March 13. *The Telegraph.* Available at www.telegraph.co.uk/news/worldnews/australiaandthepa- cific/australia/10696544/Britains-finest-WWII-general-accused-of-child-sex-abuse- in-Australia.html.

15 Cited in Hill, D. (2008), *The Forgotten Children*, pp. 293–294.

16 Ibid.

17 *Bringing Them Home Report*. (1997). Report of the National Inquiry into the Separation of Aboriginal and Torres Strait Islander Children from Their Families. Australian Human Rights Commission. Available at www.humanrights.gov.au/publications/bringing-them-home-report-1997.

18 Ibid., p. 37.

19 Van Kreiken, R. (1999). The barbarism of civilisation: cultural genocide and the "stolen generations". *British Journal of Sociology* 50, 297–315.

20 By February 2017, The Royal Commission into Institutional Responses to Child Sexual Abuse reported that 1,265 Catholic priests, religious brothers and nuns had been accused of sexually abusing children between 1950 and 2010. Few of these cases had been investigated, documents had been lost by parishes and cover-ups were routine. See Roberts, R. (2017). Australian Catholic Church has abused thousands of children, inquiry finds. February 6. *The Independent*. Available at www.independent.co.uk/news/world/australia-catholic-church-child-sex-abuse-inquiry-a7565326.html. This resonates with the Irish case study I described in Chapter 4. By July 2017, the high-profile case of Cardinal George Pell captured the headlines. He returned to Australia from the Vatican in order to face charges from 'multiple complainants' about past cases of CSA. He denied all the charges and said that he was 'looking forward to his day in court'. See Cardinal Pell will plead not guilty, his lawyer confirms. (2017). July 26. BBC News, Australia. Available at www.bbc.co.uk/news/world-australia-40712528.

21 Marr, D. (2015). Rabbis' absolute power: How sex abuse tore apart Australia's Orthodox Jewish community. February 19. *The Guardian*. Available at www.theguardian.com/australia-news/2015/feb/19/rabbis-absolute-power-how-sex-abuse-tore-apart-australias-orthodox-jewish-community.

22 Pearlman, J. (2014). Britain's 'finest WWII general' accused of child sex abuse.

23 Hill, D. (2008), *The Forgotten Children*. Mary O'Brien's (at Molong from 14 years of age) account of Mr W. Phillips.

24 Ibid. Vivian Bingham's (at Molong from 5 years of age) account of Jack Newberry.

25 Ibid. Liz Sharp's (at Molong from 9 years of age) account of Jack Newberry.

26 Ibid. Janet Ellis' (at Molong from 12 years of age) account of Jack Newberry.

27 *Bringing Them Home Report* (1997). Queensland: woman removed in the 1940s.

28 Ibid. NSW woman removed at 3 years of age in 1946; she experienced two foster placements and a number of institutional placements.

29 Ibid. NSW woman removed to Cootamundra Girls' Home in the 1940s.

30 Ibid. Victoria woman removed at 7 years of age in the 1960s.

8

IS CHILD SEXUAL ABUSE A MORAL PANIC?

The chapters so far have provided an extensive picture of CSA. The remaining chapters examine the intellectual implications of the evidence we have about it and the approaches taken within academia about social problems. Academics address the latter in a variety of ways but, broadly, two approaches stand out. The first is to describe, measure and account for a problem in focus. The second is to query whether the problem is a problem at all or if it has been exaggerated. The first attends in various ways to the real causes and consequences of CSA. The second attends more to the meanings attached to it in society in general, within particular social groups or by individuals. In academic parlance, the first is mainly concerned with ontology, whereas the second emphasises epistemology. The divergence between these approaches is seemingly very marked when we come to address CSA.

On the one hand, many (including this author) are concerned with a focus on the scale, harmfulness and wrongfulness of adult–child sexual contact, inside and outside of families. But this has not been the whole story. There has been a second stance offered by some social scientists that CSA is a moral panic. This chapter unpicks the latter position. The next chapter provides a detailed case study of its implications, when academics become involved in political lobbying to liberalise our view of enacted paedophilia and to argue for the decriminalisation of adult–child sexual contact.

Below, I focus first on the dubious claim made by some academics that CSA is a moral panic. They have argued that the concern about 'intergenerational sex' is a storm in a teacup for modern societies. Essentially, their argument goes that once we introduce historical relativism and we discount the general public's irrational and sexually repressive response to the very idea of sexual adult–child contact, then we are left largely with a 'socially constructed' melodrama created by the illegality of adult–child sexual contact.

Testing the moral panic thesis about CSA

Here is a broad description of a moral panic given by Stanley Cohen, a leading social theorist in the field:

> Moral panics are expressions of disapproval, condemnation, or criticism, that arise every now and then to phenomenon, which could be defined as deviant. The example I took was the perceived misbehavior, which we would now call 'anti-social behavior', of teenagers which was really exaggerated, and out of proportion to the original events.
>
> The moral part is the condemnation and social disapproval, and the panic is the element of hysteria and over reaction. Which subsequently can be applied to all sorts of waves of phenomenon. It is largely created by the media: no media – no moral panic. The media are carriers of moral panics, which they either initiate themselves, or they carry the message of other groups. We see things about unmarried mothers, failing schools, the current crisis about children in care. These are all distinguishable moral panics, and the argument is that the reaction to deviance inflates and increases these groups.[1]

Cohen is an important leader in the field of moral panics and so I will dwell on his definition and its implications. He also is one of the few moral panic theorists who has also expressed some doubts about the implications of applying that theory to CSA (more on this later and in the next chapter). In Box 8.1, I provide an outline of what we should expect from a moral panic in practice.

BOX 8.1 EXPECTED FEATURES OF A PURE MORAL PANIC

A pure moral panic has the following key elements. First, some target group (usually young people, but not always) is reported to act in a way that is transgressive of social norms and *morally offensive*, such as drug taking, sexual deviance or violence. Second, the public majority express an *emotional reaction* to that transgression, of fear, anger or disgust. Third, that condemnatory reaction is viewed as *disproportionate*, when gauged against the actual personal or social harm generated. The reaction is both reflected in and promoted by mass media reporting. Fourth, moral panics tend to be *precarious and ephemeral*, disappearing as quickly as they dramatically arrived, though occasionally the same panic may reappear from time to time. Illicit drug use exemplifies the latter. Fifth, moral panics *serve the interests* of more powerful social groups and so they always constitute a conservative force to preserve the social and political *status quo* when under threat from an alternative and emergent force in society. Additionally, ordinary people (as passive observers) may derive benefits of the emotional security of defending their daily expectations of social norms. Thus, a moral panic performs the function of preserving routine role/

---

rule expectations. This last aspect then has both a top-down and bottom-up dynamic of preserving the status quo.

The term 'moral panic' has been around for a long time. It was emphasised by post-Second World War 'deviancy theorists' such as Jock Young studying illegal drug use[2] and Stanley Cohen, cited above, studying the sub-cultural antagonism and sporadic violence between 'mods and rockers' in the 1960s.[3] Their case studies exemplified the anxiety-provoking nature of rule transgression, which might threaten an established social order. That period was a time when young people were re-shaping cultural norms, especially in relation to defining new forms of freedom and self-defined identities (the seeds of what we now call 'identity politics'). Subsequent moral panics listed in the literature include AIDS, mugging, illicit drug use, girl gangs, CSA and Islamic terrorism.

In the light of the above definition from Cohen and the features outlined in Box 8.1, we can now apply those expected criteria, one by one, to CSA and examine if they work in that case.[4]

A moral offence to the great majority

CSA 'ticks the box' of causing moral offence with most people in society condemning, on moral grounds, sexual adult–child contact. This entails disgust and anger about perpetrators and anxieties about children near and dear. The degree of public offence is so strong and pervasive that in most societies today that contact is criminalised. For some, the hostile reaction even includes the belief that child sexual offenders should be subjected to capital punishment. This is an unusual demand, given that homicide is not involved. This is against the trend of other forms of sexual identity being normalised and proudly declared in most democratic societies (for example, LGBT political progress). Paedophiles who have tried to hitch their wagon to the LGBT cause are now clearly rejected by the latter. (The main attempt to do so emerged in the 1970s and is considered at greater length in the next chapter.[5])

As well as stable forms of social response, such as the criminal law, most societies also develop a range of other policy measures to protect children from sexual predation from adults. These child protection or safeguarding policies include police checks in advance of employment to work with children, powers to remove children from family settings in which they are suspected of being abused and the immediate suspension of employees working with children that are suspected of offending, following complaints from colleagues or others.

The offence expressed is disproportionate

Alexis Jay, the chair of the Rotherham inquiry (discussed in Chapter 6) argued that the *scale* of offending has not been reflected in an overreaction but an *under-reaction* from those responsible for preventing and identifying sexual attacks on children.[6] For Jay, the social problem is not one of a moral panic but of moral indifference. Given that victims of CSA are overrepresented in psychiatric services (see below), it is routinely ignored during professional assessments. This reflects another example of how cultural norms can downplay its occurrence.[7]

Ascertaining the prevalence of CSA is difficult because of dealing with actions that are generally condemned and usually criminal in character. This raises the probability of underestimation (a gap between actual occurrence and the empirical recording of CSA); we cannot measure CSA readily because the activity tends to be clandestine. It not only implicates a form of human action that is typically private in character but also the people involved are motivated to keep silent. Perpetrators want to avoid detection, social censure or prosecution, and the victims may be intimidated from speaking out, or not even aware they are being victimised. If they are abused inside the family, they may want to protect adults they are dependent upon. Moreover, as has been evident in accounts in this book, we have a culture in which children are often not believed when they do speak out.

Another problem of estimating prevalence relates to surface accounts and measured behaviour. For example, one writer in this area, Sarah Goode, makes a distinction between paedophiles (those who are sexually interested in children) and a sub-group of people that act upon that interest and actually abuse children.[8] However, empirically, it is difficult to identify accurately the sub-group within the whole group. Some may not have had any live sexual contact with children but still masturbate regularly using indecent images of children, with the latter, of necessity, implicating the past abuse in practice of those in the images. Paedophiles may deny ever touching children and have no criminal record, but they may be lying. Many paedophiles arrested for the first time have not offended for the first time. All of this picture points to an iceberg of offences against children with the difficult challenge of measuring what is above and what is below the waterline.

In the case of paedophilia, we also have to consider whether our reaction to it is a proportionate response in the light of evidence about its frequency. Methodologically, this is not easy because it is a covert not overt form of deviance. This point tends to support Alexis Jay's argument that the measured prevalence of sexual adult–child contact is quite probably an underestimate.

Similarly, the last thing that paedophiles are likely to do at present is publicly boast about their sexual interests, even if privately those are guilt-free, celebrated and furtively and regularly acted out. Only the most determined political activist or arrogant and narcissistic paedophile will 'go public' on the matter. CSA inside families follows this same tendency – which relative of a child would publicly confess to their activity? Overall, then, this is a scenario in which adult–child sexual contact is likely to be under-reported not overreported, by both victims and perpetrators.

This challenge of accurately estimating prevalence is separate from another matter: does adult sexual contact harm children? Most (but not all) of those arguing that the scale of child sexual abuse is overestimated, because of the moral panic assumption, will concede that *individual* child victims might well be harmed. When we come to consider, then, whether the typical public revulsion about enacted paedophilia is warranted, then that consideration matters, not just the one about contested prevalence.

The evidence is compelling that sexual adult–child contact is harmful, whether it occurs inside or outside of families. The empirical evidence suggests a range of adverse biological, psychological and social impacts on victims. For example, children are exposed to the physical suffering of sexually transmitted diseases and girls to pregnancy. In the short term, sexually abused children are more likely than non-abused peers to show a range of symptoms of distress including anxiety, bedwetting, school refusal, social withdrawal and decline in scholastic achievement. In addition, they are more likely to be sexually aggressive. They may sexually assault their peers, as well as approach adults in a sexual manner.

In the longer term, sexual traumatisation in childhood predicts overrepresentation in psychiatric samples. Adult mental health problems are not limited to post-traumatic symptoms of dissociation and 'flashbacks' to the trauma scene, but also include panic attacks, self-harm, substance abuse, chronic low mood and suicide attempts. Also, psychotic symptoms (hallucinations and very wide mood swings) increase in probability in the wake of childhood sexual victimisation. The chronicity of such a mixed picture may lead to a diagnosis of 'personality disorder'.[9] For example, 80% of female prisoners with a diagnosis of 'borderline personality disorder' were sexually abused in childhood. Survivors of CSA are at higher risk of suicide and are more likely than the general population to receive psychotropic medication. Surveys indicate that over 50% of male and 60% of female psychiatric inpatients have been physically or sexually abused.[10]

Adult survivors might also struggle with personal trust generally, and specifically in relation to sexual intimacy. They also have high rates of re-victimisation in their intimate relationships.[11] We can add to this the treatment costs of responding to the distress of victims and the inquiry costs to the state of police investigations of individual offenders, the detention of offenders in jails and psychiatric facilities and the expensive episodic public inquiries about historical sexual abuse, nationally and locally.[12]

As far as harm and suffering are concerned, some of this is experienced by perpetrators as well. They risk the harm of imprisonment, career damage, family rejection and general social censure. Their need for furtiveness to avoid detection can cut them off from others or make them insincere in their daily routines. Some, like their victims, abuse substances and commit suicide. One solution to this perpetrator distress is to argue that their actions should be tolerated and that norms should change in their favour. This line of reasoning is discussed further in the next chapter.

For now, social norms do not tolerate adult–child sexual contact. Thus, when we frame CSA as a public health question, then it is clearly a recurring source of harm to perpetrators, not just their victims. This means costs to society as a whole.

The transgression is linked to those lacking status and power in society

Adult perpetrators are unlike other social groups who are 'candidates' for moral panic reactions. The groups typically listed in moral panics have an *a priori* label of moral dubiousness. In the case of those offending against children, the public make *post hoc* attributions. Prior to that, the undetected abusers were *not* part of a stigmatised group; they were invisible and unremarkable because of their wide dispersal in society. A recurring public policy challenge about researching or detecting child sexual abusers is that they are 'everywhere' and so 'nowhere' – they are 'hiding in plain sight'. Given that those with a sexual interest in children are (a) adults, and (b) from all strata of society, including the rich and the powerful, then it is not self-evident at all that they generally lack status and power. They are not comparable to the brawling teenagers in the 1960s who featured in the foundational studies using moral panic theory. Adult roles, especially those entailing contact with children, often reflect a socially recognised special and honoured *authority* (intellectual, artistic, pedagogic, political or spiritual). If we then add intra-familial offending to that list, then, traditionally, parents have warranted and routine power over children. With parenting comes a cultural tradition ('sacralisation') of private possession and discretion of action in relation to their offspring.[13] In other words, adults looking after children in any setting are ordinary and legitimate and may even have above-average social status; this is out of sync with the stigmatisation of groups *typically* at the centre of moral panics.

Thus, until they are detected and brought to book, those adults with a sexual interest in children typically are *not* lacking in power or status. They have the ordinary respect of being adults inside families or with access to the labour market, and they may well be in roles which are accorded average or above-average status in society. Academics, teachers, politicians and religious staff have no *a priori* disadvantage in society, quite the reverse. Light entertainers are often awe-inspiring celebrities. Of all the groups, outside of family settings, which have been found to have suffered *pre-detection* prejudice, are only those men of South Asian origin, who were apprehended in the police inquiries of Rotherham and other English towns, discussed in Chapter 6.

A further consideration about status and power relates to that of the child victims (or, in those who defend intergenerational sex, 'participants'). The reason as to *why* the social norm of state paternalism (*parens patriae*) has developed is because of the child's very *lack* of power, normally presumed because of a combination of physical and psychological incomplete development. They also lack direct economic power. They cannot vote, so they lack political power in parliamentary democracies. Given this amalgam of reasons to account for their relative powerlessness, children are not starting from a position of equality with their prospective adult partners.

CSA is a unique form of transgression that entails a relationship with a particular social group (children) who unambiguously *are*, in a variety of ways, lacking in power. Where there is such a structured power imbalance, then personal exploitation is ever present, as both a prospect and an actual outcome. For this reason, we cannot simply discuss paedophilia in the same ethical and political breath as other forms of adult 'sexual preference'. Being a paedophile has no fair claim to an oppressed identity, within a broad culture of sexual intolerance, though this does not dissuade some from making such an argument (see next chapter).

Thus, those who seek and achieve sexual contact with children may well be 'demonised' and their humanity denied post-detection. However, those children who are logically necessary for their sexual gratification are also objectified and exploited by those very 'folk devils' (Cohen's term for the focus of moral panics). If a case can be made that paedophiles are unduly victimised by a hostile public post-detection, then one can certainly be made that they are clearly *victimisers*. Moreover, in adult–child sexual relationships, the asymmetry is not only about power, it is also about desire. The two parties are not starting from an equivalent position of either power *or* sexual interest. This point is conveniently challenged by pro-paedophile groups (see next chapter).

Adult–child sexual contact is an ephemeral concern

There is little evidence that CSA will be seen as a temporary matter of public concern that will dissipate. Ever since the Enlightenment, there has been a progressive trend of protecting the rights of all human beings from harm from others, but especially those deemed to be particularly vulnerable. Today, that entails a stable and persistent public policy consensus about child protection.

Deviancy theorists supporting the moral panic thesis more generally note that a few come and go in fashion and so are not always singular pieces of social ephemera. However, CSA is not like, say, illicit drug use. Even before the Enlightenment there was the universal incest taboo that remains today. It is only by returning to a very specific cultural context historically that adult–child sexual contact can be 'normalised' as being unremarkable. A favoured argument from paedophile advocacy groups is that, in Ancient Greece, man–boy sexual activity was seen as a positive 'rite of passage' for the younger party. The other example I have noted is the historical acceptance of child brides, which has persevered in some developing countries today.

Ironically, some academic arguments which have made a case for tolerance towards paedophilia, which I discuss more below, note that the Greek scenario was inherently anti-Gay (or 'heteronormative') implying that 'normal' adult sexuality was heterosexual in kind and that same-sex contact was a passing and immature phase to give way to 'proper' mature heterosexuality. Part of the logic underlying this stance is to point up historical relativism to legitimise a form of deviance under discussion today. The logic is this: if it can be shown to have happened in other times and places and was tolerated, then we should not presume that our current negative attitudes and policies about it are correct. If it happened before, then it is probably OK (or at least defensible), goes the argument. A related argument from historical relativists is that childhood itself is a modern social construction and, therefore, it is an arbitrary matter to categorise those in one age span as being a different form of human kind to those in another. This can be a springboard argument about equal rights for sexual contact between participants, who are at different points in the life span.

Both counts (allusions to Ancient Greece and a noted modern definition of childhood) miss the point that, for the past 200 years, and for the foreseeable future, adult–child sexual contact has not been, and is unlikely to be, tolerated, nor will childhood be abruptly 'declassified' in our social norms. The pointers are in the other direction, if we consider the national and international policy aspirations about child protection. This is like slavery: the Ancient Greeks had slaves but where today can we find a progressive logic that slavery should now be acceptable or re-introduced with impunity?

Interest work

The final criterion to consider when deciding on the moral panic status of our topic is about whose interests are being served. If we consider active paedophilia, this cuts against the trend of interest work associated typically with moral panics. Rather than its exposure deflecting attention from the rich and the powerful, at times it does the very opposite: the interest work involved has often been about *suppressing* a moral panic not 'whipping it up'. It has been in the interests of the rich and the powerful *not* to investigate the extent of CSA in their midst, as earlier chapters highlighted.

There is a case to be made that the mass media have fed off the child abuse scandals and have sold their products on the back of them. But these stories have not been invented by the press. They were there already and at most a twist of journalistic hyperbole meant that the tabloids gained some increased circulation and populist support. The best example of this was in 2000 when the *News of the World* campaigned successfully in the UK for mandatory reporting by the police of child sex offenders in neighbourhoods. So-called 'Sarah's Law' now exists and may indeed have made parents extra vigilant. At the same time, it has encouraged vigilantism.

But alongside tabloid populism in the midst of a circulation war, there has also been serious investigatory journalism, which has provided a public duty when exposing paedophile rings not detected by the police. Thus, the ambiguous role of the press is evident. They are not only interested in attacking 'paedo' 'beasts' and 'monsters', the language common in the tabloid newspapers, they also investigate matters seriously and thoroughly at times.

The press has shown another form of ambivalence on this matter. On the one hand, they certainly often demonise 'stranger danger', but on the other, there have been major scandals about intra-familial abuse in which the mass media have taken against the professionals investigating them. The most notable example of this was the Cleveland case in the 1980s in which doctors and social workers were pilloried by the press. What was not reported was that the children who the professionals acted to protect by removing them from the particular families suspected of abusing them were largely already known to services; past cases of neglect and abuse were on record. These were not children being taken to A&E services for the first time with a stomach ache.

A further example of journalistic ambivalence is that some reporters and commentators explicitly decry CSA as a moral panic. In Britain, David Aaronovitch has written extensively about his view that there is no evidence base for the scandals associated with VIP paedophile rings and ritual abuse.[14] At the same time, there are others, such as Nick Davies and David Hencke, who have countered the Aaronovitch line of reasoning; journalists on this matter are not of one voice. Accordingly, taken in the round, we cannot discern what the mainstream mass media are 'up to' in relation to our topic of interest.

Social workers in particular are tabloid fodder – 'damned if they do and damned if they don't' – when they act to protect children. This is the final reason why I consider that the moral panic model fits poorly when we are considering the topic of this book. Basically, it is not clear precisely what interest work is at play then in the mass media reporting of CSA because the 'folk devils' are not of one type.[15] Even those supporting the utility of a moral panic position admit this. Moreover, those writers are perplexed when the mass media ignore a warranted concern, such as the increased availability of indecent images of children with the impact of the Internet.[16]

This lack of clarity is relevant because, in many accounts of moral panic, it is the mass media which are considered to be the *main players* in irrationally exaggerating a social problem and manipulating public anxiety and hostility. If the main culprit, the mass media, is not even acting according to what is expected in this regard, then those supporting a moral panic position are now on shifting sands of their own making.

Cohen's ambivalence

Given the above, we can see that CSA is not a good example of a moral panic at all; only the first expected defining feature is fulfilled. For this reason, it is instructive to look at how that poor fit was dealt with by the leader of moral panic theory introduced at the start of the chapter. As will be clear below, he has to make arguments and counter-arguments when forcing CSA onto the Procrustean bed of a moral panic. Essentially, he stretched the latter into something more plausible but no longer the original concept. CSA now becomes *an emotive public controversy* rather than the moral panic expected. At best, a 'moral panic' is now only a loose metaphor to explore CSA.

Stanley Cohen died in 2013 but, before that, gave an interview in which he conceded that maybe there were 'good' and warranted moral panics, with CSA being one of them.[17] In his final written commentary from the Third Edition of *Folk Devils and Moral Panics*, he carefully recaps their ambiguous character. They are new *and* old ('camouflaged versions of traditional and well-known evils'). They are damaging but imply deeper and more pervasive harm to society. They are transparent (any of us can see them) but also opaque as they require expert description, explanation and even intervention.

Cohen goes on in this final preface to his classic book to list seven 'clusters' of moral panics, starting with his original case study and moving to others since: young working-class violent males; school violence (bullying and shoot-outs); wrong drugs used in the wrong place by the wrong people; child abuse, Satanic rituals and paedophile registers; sex, violence and blaming the media; welfare cheats and single mothers; and migrants and asylum seekers flooding our country and services. To my mind, five out of these seven require no critical response as they are fair comment. But for obvious reasons, after giving a little more space to Cohen's views, I will comment on the child abuse cluster but also on that relating to the mass media, as it has relevance for this book.

When Cohen discusses these clusters, his own uncertainty about a consistent set of features of an ideal type of moral panic recurs. For example, in relation to child abuse, he makes a number of key points. First, the term refers to physical, emotional and sexual abuse, with the public becoming more concerned about the last of these, especially in relation to 'atypical cases outside the family'.

Second, he acknowledges that in the past 20 years it has come to light that in residential settings and often in the wake of poor family care, children have indeed *been* abused. This was linked not to panic but what he calls 'chilling denial' (his phrase).

Third, child deaths have led to panic and been typified by a 'familiar criminal triangle of an innocent victim, an evil perpetrator and "shocked but passive" bystanders'. Child protection professionals, as much as the perpetrators, have been vilified for not intervening or at other times intervening in the wrong cases: 'either gullible wimps or else storm troopers of the nanny state; either uncaring cold hearted bureaucrats for not intervening in time to protect the victim or else over-zealous, do-gooding meddlers for intervening groundlessly and invading privacy'. Cohen cites the Cleveland case as typifying this confusion: 'the resulting moral panic became a pitched battle of claims and counter-claims [...] there was not even a minimal consensus about what the whole episode was about'. For Cohen, that ambiguity was superseded by a case that was 'more fictitious and one of the purest cases of moral panic'. Here he refers to the Orkney case; I return to both cases in the next chapter.

Thus, Cohen seems to be stretching the notion of moral panic here effectively to mean 'emotive public controversy' involving competing viewpoints, which goes beyond the original notion of an expression of moral revulsion from the general public about specific 'candidates'. CSA, then, really is like climate change: it is a legitimate public policy concern, not a panic. Indeed, Cohen now seems to be saying we need to panic more, not less. At this point, the concept of a moral panic, used in its original form, seems to be melting like ice in the hot cross-winds of academic and journalistic disagreement and confusion. Cohen is struggling to defend his own theory, when it is applied to CSA.

Fourth, he moves to stranger danger, where the perpetrators are 'pure candidates for monster status'. Here, Cohen emphasises the role of mass media hyperbole and its dehumanising discourse, as well as the tendency illogically to lump together all cases in equivalent moral terms. Online indecent images, the seduction of a 14-year-old boy by his mid-thirties female teacher and the sexual murder of a child are conflated. Also, hares are set running about, driving offenders underground and out of sight of surveillance and beyond the reach of corrective sex offender treatment programmes.

Fifth, politicians were pushed by the overplayed narrative of 'stranger danger' into an ambivalent position of earnest sympathy for anxious parents with their understandable moral revulsion, alongside a rejection of mob rule. 'The rational polity is contrasted to the crowd: volatile and ready to explode', as Cohen puts it, succinctly.

Then, Cohen focuses more attention on these features about child abuse in his next cluster discussed: sex, violence and blaming the mass media. As he puts it, 'for conservatives, the media glamorise crime, trivialise public insecurities and undermine moral authority; for liberals, the media exaggerate the risks of crime and whip up moral panics to vindicate an unjust and authoritarian crime control policy'. CSA is part of these strained and competing positions. Again, the concept of moral panic is stretched to mean 'controversy' by Cohen.

Ever ready to sympathise with ordinary people, he concedes that their concerns are not unalloyed irrationality. He concedes that abused children *are* met with disbelief at times and that *moral stupor not moral panic* can be the true problem. This echoes the view of those like Alexis Jay in response to child exploitation on the streets and many others about the abuse of children in residential settings. Even though mob rule is unwarranted and vigilantism not a good alternative to the rule of law, Cohen understands *why* people might be anxious or angry about the risk to their children.

After describing his seven clusters of moral panics, Cohen moves to a more explicit account of his own ambivalence. He starts with the divisions in social science about social constructivism. The strong version of the latter simply deems everything to be socially constructed, but the weak version endorsed by Cohen himself (and of relevance here for this book) requires that we need a reality check to detect whether or not a response to a problem is either exaggerated or even warranted.

This choice about social constructivism is important for the lay reader, who is often perplexed by its strong version. Typically, he or she is anchored in some form of common-sense realism about their life. For them (and me and, I suspect, Cohen), everything is *not* merely a social construct: there is a measurable or palpable reality to social problems.[18] Some of them, like the risk of exploitation of vulnerable people, are a real and abiding concern for any civilised society. For example, a strong consensus at the time of writing is that the intolerant, violent, misogynistic and homophobic norms of ISIS reflect a lack of civilised values. These are a sort of benchmark for how we *ought* to proceed hereafter as a moral order in our species.

This point about the legitimacy of 'the moral' as part of society thus evokes Cohen's sympathy in his discussion. He is also keen to emphasise that the reality checking noted above should be applied properly from case to case. For example, if a feature of a prototypical moral panic is that harm is exaggerated or even non-existent, then we need to *check* whether this is or is not true in any particular case. Similarly, if we assume in a moral panic that there is always public volatility, then we need to *check* whether that is actually the case. We need to check if child abuse is an ephemeral concern or a persistent and reasonable public policy concern. I have argued at various points in this book that the latter is the case in relation to protecting children from abuse (in all its varieties).

In relation to CSA, Cohen has sympathy for the case made in this book that much of the time we have witnessed moral stupor *not* moral panic, and that vulnerable children have indeed been disbelieved when they were true victims of crimes against them by adults. In the case of our topic, there has indeed been irrational volatility at times (such as vigilantism). However, at other times, volatility has been displaced by denial and suppression. Hence, we also found the moral stupor associated with child sexual exploitation on the streets and the active suppression of evidence of crimes by the state, the BBC and Church authorities in collusion with the police.

For Cohen, then, there is a risk sometimes of using the moral panic tradition to defend social injustice rather than expose it. An ultra-liberal critique about the overuse of risk management by the modern state may become a form of libertarianism, whereby the state is chided or scoffed at for trying to protect vulnerable people. In this book's introduction, I pointed up the work of Frank Furedi and his colleagues in the Institute of Ideas and *Spiked!* which, as I note above, continues to reflect that libertarian stance. In the light of a more nuanced position about cases of moral panic from Cohen, it is not surprising that his later work indeed focused on the *denial* of problems in society, not their fevered amplification. For this reason, we find Cohen's work on 'states of denial' informing the analysis by Chris Greer and Eugene McLaughlin of the Savile case at the BBC.[19] The latter authors have been joined by critical criminologists such as Michael Salter, who notes that moral panic theorists remain wedded to the notion that labelled offenders are an oppressed social group in the face of state power. In the case of CSA, as he notes, the oppressed group are victimised children and so moral panic claims can divert us from recognising that basic fact.[20]

My reading of the third and final preface to *Folk Devils and Moral Panics* is that Cohen's ambivalence reflects an admission that his original work on 'mods and rockers' can be stretched to CSA *but* many inconsistencies and contradictions then emerge in that exercise. In my view, at this point, moral panic theory begins to unravel. Cohen is important because of his totemic status in moral panic theory. At the end of the next chapter, for emphasis, I return to his ambivalence and even his regret that social constructivism has been misused at times to deny human suffering in the wake of torture and CSA.

With Cohen's ambivalence in mind, and his endorsement of the need for careful reality checking and the risk of 'states of denial', I now turn to the intellectual case put forward, not just to argue that CSA is a moral panic but also to make a positive defence of adult–child sexual contact. Political lobbying then becomes a matter of civil liberties not just social theory. Sociological factional disputes enter the world of *realpolitik*.

Notes

1 Cited in LeVrai, B. (2010). Mods, rockers, folk devils, deviants: An interview with Stanley Cohen. *Vice*, September.

2 Young, J. (1973). *The Drugtakers: The Social Meaning of Drug Use*. London: Judson, McGibbon and Kee.

3 Cohen, S. (2002). *Folk Devils and Moral Panics* (Third edition). London: Routledge.

4 This method is called an 'immanent critique'. I elaborate it in Pilgrim, D. (2017). The perils of strong social constructionism: The case of child sexual abuse. *Journal of Critical Realism* 16(3), 268–283.

5 I noted in Chapter 5 that Michele Elliott, who has focused on female perpetrators, refuses to countenance that paedophilia is a sexual orientation and opts instead for a notion of 'learned deviant behaviour'. This insistence on psychologising a sexual interest in children reflects an understandable need to prevent paedophilia from being associated with legitimate forms of identity politics. But paedophilia simply *is* the sexual orientation of some adults. It is its practical expression that is at the centre of political and ethical contention, not its existence in principle. I am grateful to Sarah Goode for pointing out this nuanced distinction in a personal communication.

6 Jay Report (2014). Independent Inquiry into Child Sexual Exploitation in Rotherham (1997–2013). www.rotherham.gov.uk/downloads/file/1407/independent_inquiry_case_in_rotherham.

7 In Britain, mental health services are advised by the National Institute for Health and Care Excellence (NICE) to ask about childhood adversity but we have little up-to-date information on its actual implementation. See, for example, Hepworth, I. & McGowan, L. (2013). Do mental health professionals enquire about childhood sexual abuse during routine mental health assessment in mental health settings? *Journal of Psychiatric and Mental Health Nursing* 20(6), 473–483. Earlier studies of the practice of asking such questions suggest a wide range from 0–30%. See, for example, Wurr, C. & Partridge, I. (1996). The prevalence of a history of childhood sexual abuse in an acute adult inpatient population. *Child Abuse & Neglect* 20(9), 867–872. New Zealand studies found that the questions may be regularly omitted from assessment forms which actually contain them: only 70% of outpatients and 32% of inpatients were asked about childhood adversity. See, for example, Read, J. & Fraser, A. (1998). Abuse histories of psychiatric inpatients: To ask or not to ask? *Psychiatric Services* 49(3), 355–359.

8 Henley, J. (2013). Paedophilia: bringing dark desires to light. January 3. *The Guardian*. Available at www.theguardian.com/society/2013/jan/03/paedophilia-bringing-dark-desires-light.

9 See, for example, Read, J., Agar, K., Argyle, N. & Aderhold, V. (2003). Sexual and physical abuse during childhood and adulthood as predictors of hallucinations, delusions and thought disorder. *Psychology and Psychotherapy: Theory, Research and Practice* 76, 1–22; Ogata, S., Silk, K., Goodrich, S., Lohr, N., Westen, D. & Hill, E. (1990). Childhood sexual and physical abuse in adult patients with borderline personality disorder. *American Journal of Psychiatry* 147(8), 1008–1013; Cutajar, M., Mullen, P., Ogloff, J., Thomas, S., Wells, D. & Spataro, J. (2010). Psychopathology in a large cohort of sexually abused children followed up to 43 years. *Child Abuse & Neglect* 34(11), 813–822; Read, J. & Bentall,

R. (2012). Negative childhood experiences and mental health: theoretical, clinical and primary prevention implications. *British Journal of Psychiatry* 200(2), 89–91; Wilsnack, S., Wilsnack, R., Kristjanson, A., Vogeltanz-Holm, N. & Harris, T. (2004). Child sexual abuse and alcohol use among women: setting the stage for risky sexual behaviour. In L. Koenig, L. Doll, A. O'Leary & W. Pequegnat (eds), *From Child Sexual Abuse to Adult Sexual Risk: Trauma, Revictimization and Intervention* (pp. 181–200). Washington, DC: American Psychological Association; Filipas, H., & Ullman, S. (2006). Child sexual abuse, coping responses, self-blame, posttraumatic stress disorder, and adult sexual victimization. *Journal of Interpersonal Violence* 21, 652–672; Hillberg, T., Hamilton-Giachritsis, C. & Dixon, L. (2011). Review of meta-analyses on the association between child sexual abuse and adult mental health difficulties: A systematic approach. *Trauma Violence & Abuse* 12(1), 38–49; Jonas, S., Bebbington, S., McManus, S., Meltzer, H., Jenkins, R., Kuipers, E., et al. (2011). Sexual abuse and psychiatric disorder in England: Results from the 2007 Adult Psychiatric Morbidity Survey. *Psychological Medicine* 41(4), 709–719.

10 Anda, R., Felitti, V., Bremner, J., Walker, J., Whitfield, C., Perry, B., et al. (2006). The enduring effects of abuse and related adverse experiences in childhood: A convergence of evidence from neurobiology and epidemiology. *European Archives of Psychiatry and Clinical Neuroscience* 256(3), 174–186.

11 Del Gaizo, A., Elhai, J. & Weaver, T. (2011). Post-traumatic stress disorder, poor physical health and substance use behaviors in a national trauma-exposed sample. *Psychiatry Research* 188(3), 390–393.

12 Saied-Tessier, A. (2014). *Estimating the Costs of Child Sexual Abuse in the UK*. London: NSPCC.

13 In June 2016, a case in Japan made national news in relation to parental freedom to treat children at will. A seven-year-old boy who had a habit of throwing stones was punished by his parents by them leaving him alone in a forest. He was discovered seven days later dehydrated and near to death. The BBC reported that 'some have criticised the parents for child abuse'. What is astonishing is that anyone had a view that this was *not* a case of child abuse. See Japanese missing boy Yamato Tanooka found alive in Hokkaido. (2016). June 3. BBC News, Asia. Available at www.bbc.co.uk/news/world-asia-36441612.

14 Aaronovitch, D. Don't look now. (2003). January 19. *The Guardian*. Available at www.theguardian.com/society/2003/jan/19/childrensservices.comment; cf. Hencke, D. (2014). Why Theresa May was right to ignore David Aaronovitch over child sex abuse in North Wales. December 2. Available at https://davidhencke.com/2014/12/02/why-theresa-may-was-right-to-ignore-david-aaronvitch-over-child-sex-abuse-in-north-wales/.

15 The preface of Stanley Cohen's *Folk Devils and Moral Panics* (Third Edition) emphasises this inconsistency. Also, in the case of the Rotherham scandal, moral panic claim makers have noted that the usual suspects (social workers) were more evident as honourable whistle-blowers and it was *the police and council officials* who this time were the folk devils: see Meyer, A. (2015). The Rotherham abuse scandal. In V. Cree, G. Clapton & M. Smith (eds), *Revisiting Moral Panics*. Bristol: Policy Press.

16 Jenkins, P. (2001). *Beyond Tolerance: Child Pornography on the Internet*. New York: New York University Press.

17 Le Vrai, B. (2010). Mods, rockers, folk devils, deviants.

18 Note that even ardent moral panic theorists do not argue that a social problem is simply created from thin air. Instead, an emerging real problem is *amplified* by an emotive public reaction.

19 Greer, C. & McLaughlin, E. (2015). Denial of child sexual abuse. In D. Whyte (ed.), *How Corrupt Is Britain?* London: Pluto Press.

20 Salter, M. (2017). Child sexual abuse. In W. Dekeseredy & M. Dragiewicz (eds), *Routledge Handbook of Critical Criminology*. London: Routledge.

9

POLITICAL DEFENDERS OF 'INTERGENERATIONAL SEX'

Introduction

Those working in the field of child protection are familiar with the personal rationalisations used by perpetrators of CSA. Their cognitive distortions turn their sexual crimes into legitimate and benign forms of intimacy. The child was not a victim but a willing participant. They wanted it. They enjoyed it. We were friends. We loved one another. I cared for them and helped them to mature. It did them no harm. This self-deception may seem absurd or even pathetic but it is common in offenders. Such specious justifications have sometimes been bolstered by an authoritative case set out by intellectuals. The heyday of that reasoning was in the 1970s, but a weakened trace of it can still be found today, as will be made clear below.

In 1977, there was an unsuccessful lobby from intellectuals in France, including Jean-Paul Sartre, Simone de Beauvoir, Jacques Derrida, Roland Barthes and Michel Foucault, to decriminalise 'non-violent' adult–child sexual activity.[1] In the USA, the North American Man–Boy Love Association (NAMBLA) emerged and made similar arguments, as did the René Guyon Society, which proclaimed 'Sex before eight, or else it's too late'. In Britain, the Paedophile Information Exchange (PIE) emerged as a refuge for men and women with a sexual interest in boys and girls, though it was dominated by pederasts.[2]

What all these had in common was the use of academic authority to lobby governments to liberalise policies in relation to adult–child sexual contact. We see, then, a parallel process between the child sex offender, with their self-serving rationalisations, and more abstract and seemingly respectable arguments from their intellectual allies. As will become clear, in some cases these were not separate groups, because we find evidence of intellectuals who themselves were offenders.

The Paedophile Information Exchange (PIE)

Although the moral panic thesis discussed in the previous chapter was at the centre of the intellectual case to defend enacted paedophilia, the *political opportunity* for it emerged in the counter-cultural period between 1960 and 1980. The political case for identity politics provided a unique opportunity during the 1970s. Paedophile advocates positioned themselves as an offshoot of Gay Liberation, even though the leadership of the latter resented the tactic and would not endorse the position of paedophile activists. Women's Liberation, or second wave feminism, was to react with even more hostility, given that most of the intellectual lobbying was being done by men. Numerically, men dominated groups like PIE and NAMBLA. Organisationally, numbers were also relevant: PIE gave one to each new member, so that they could communicate anonymously in print (see below).

An important academic product, which was to be a coded lobbying device for PIE, was the controversial book *Perspectives on Paedophilia*, which had the explicit aim of enlightening social workers and youth workers.[3] The editor, Brian Taylor, was also the research director of PIE, where he had used the pseudonym 'Humphrey Barton'. PIE itself was not mentioned by Taylor but he does allude to 'paedophile awareness groups' in his introduction. Much of the text of the latter can be traced to an earlier piece on the politics of paedophilia written by Barton.[4] Taylor (PIE member 54) had also offered his arguments about 'guilt-free pederasty' in the *Sociological Review*[5] in 1976. The editorial introduction for the book set out its stall:

> Paedophilia is not an easy subject to talk, or to write about. Difficulties immediately arise through the combined influence of prejudice against dispassionate investigation of it and ignorance of its nature and manifestations. These two factors, prejudice and ignorance, are not unrelated. Prejudice bedevils any reasoned discussion of paedophiles, their sexual preferences and practices, because of the negative and often hostile social definitions which such behaviour conventionally attracts. As a result, ignorance of the complexities of the phenomenon – both in the sense of a lack of knowledge about and indifference to information which challenges accepted views of it – is widespread. The common intention of the chapters which comprise this volume is to assist in mitigating ignorance about one aspect of human sexuality, and hence, possibly, to inhibit or at least to inform, antipathy toward its discussion, its indulgence, or even its existence.[6]

Not only did Taylor fail to mention his membership of PIE, as the editor, he also failed to note three other members, who contributed chapters.[7] One of these, Ken Plummer (member number 236), referred to self-help groups and he noted PIE by name but not his own reason for membership of it; years later this was to be clarified (see below). Plummer suggested in a piece published at the same time as the Taylor collection that 'By applying sociology to the field of paedophilia we may partially relativise it, humanise it, normalise it, and politicise it'.[8] The same omission was evident in the case of the next two chapter authors. Morris Fraser was a child psychiatrist who had already been prosecuted in both the USA and the UK for sexual offences against children (see Chapter 5).[9]

Another contributor and undeclared PIE member (number 51) was Peter Righton. He was a key intellectual figure in PIE and an acknowledged national expert on child protection. He worked at points in his career for the National Children's Bureau, the Institute of Social Work and several British universities. Righton was subsequently prosecuted for his possession of an extensive archive of indecent images of children, though he did not receive a custodial sentence. He was the focus of a BBC exposé about his work as part of an elite paedophile ring ('Children at Risk: the Secret Life of a Paedophile', *Inside Story*, BBC1, June 1994). That pivotal role was noted in Tom Watson's parliamentary question in 2012 that triggered the ongoing inquiry into historical cases of child abuse (see Chapters 1 and 2).

When alluded to, fleetingly, by Taylor and Plummer, PIE was the subject of only an arm's-length sociological commentary without reference to their insider status. Fraser and Righton were more detailed. Righton offered a typology of 'dispositional paedophiles' (caring and harmless) and 'sexual molesters'. This binary was of course without empirical foundation, given what we know about grooming – now a sexual offence, but not then.[10] Righton asserted his position with cool academic certainty but without reference to his own offending, which had yet to come to light publicly. Similarly, Fraser, in his chapter, which includes a set of clinical case studies of children (based on his own patients) who had had sex with adults, provides a sense of *faux* objectivity reflecting a deceitful but seemingly quasi-scientific agenda and strategy of PIE members.[11]

Just another self-help group for an oppressed sexual minority?

As a network, PIE shared views in print about guilt-free rationales for paedophilia and, as transpired, it also created sub-groups, which could exchange indecent images of children and physically meet to plan and enact sex with minors. It had a regular publication, *Magpie*, which provided articles on the benign thrill of the sexual need for children and the harmlessness of that desire, despite it being for now criminalised, when put into practice. To signal its normality, *Magpie* contained news items, book reviews, a letters column and even a regular crossword.

Here is a flavour of the content in a review of an art exhibition:

> I hope I was not the only one among us to visit the exhibition of drawings and paintings by David Remfry at the Mercury Gallery, Cork Street, London. Entitled Images of Childhood these paintings and drawings, mostly of little girls, have a calm beauty and subtle eroticism of great appeal. More often than not posed against a blank wall, barefoot on carpet, barekneed on chairs, simply dressed or not at all, playing hide and seek in a birthday suit behind the jardiniere, these children are caught, frozen in mid-dance, reclining on day

beds, leaning listlessly, lost in sadness, pouring tea or simply playing, exempt from time yet dimly aware each day is one day nearer the gates of the Garden of Eden. Full of foreboding for the end of childhood, *knowing they must grow up and what growing up means*, these still nymphets are filled with unease and recall those many portraits of the Virgin looking wistfully at the Christ Child, as a mother protective, yet as the Mother conscious of, and resigned to, the Cross. For all their charm and apparent innocence, these paintings never lapse into sentimentality, and never do so because *the subjects are clearly as aware as the painter of their potential appeal.* Yet the eroticism is muted, not blatant as in Balthus' paintings of pubescent girls, curiously English, reserved, belonging indoors, *unrequited.* It is precisely the eroticism of paedophilia, the attraction of the unattainable, the charm of cool remote children, the yearning to touch the untouched, tenderly. The distance between us and childhood is the hallmark of paedophilic yearning, the rosegrey dream which dooms us, for when it is eclipsed in intercourse, there is the worm in the bud. Despair inevitably follows, not at once in the flush of passion, but later in twilight when we dimly perceive that our dream can never be incorporated in the smooth precise flesh of any child, not because children grow up, but because they must never cease to be distant. This is our dilemma: the child possessed is no longer child. Possessed, and a sword shall pierce the heart. So Remfry's children, solitary especially in company, remain aloof, retain their distance, which is precisely their presence, *and beckon us, only to ask us to go.* [My emphasis is added to highlight the paedophile's wish or assumption about children being knowing sexual agents gaming their desiring voyeurs.][12]

In the same issue, a letter from another member made the normalising point that:

By producing an 'educational' rather than 'sensational' magazine, paedophiles will, I believe, gradually begin to come across as a caring rather than corrupting breed. Only by striving to achieve a cloak of respectability will we be able to gain a place in society, we will never reach our goal by adopting a 'don't give a damn what you think of us' attitude. This, I think is where the Gay Liberation Front failed to gain support because the media and most of the public have a built in defence against these kind of tactics. You go out there saying 'Bang! Crash! – Here we are, and we don't care' and what happens – cries of 'My God, how dare you do this?' from the Press and T.V. etc. The result being that, far from furthering the cause – you frighten would-be members off! No, I think to continue the magazine in its present format is far the wisest thing – after all we can all get hold of these other publications if we really want them. If anything, there could be a little more variety, perhaps more girls – and I am sure many members would not object to seeing boys in the 12–18 age group too. I think the inclusion of short stories or a serial would be a good idea, perhaps members could submit their own contributions, and I don't see why members couldn't contribute their own favourite photographs too – provided of course that they fit in with the objectives of the magazine [...] It must also bring about new tolerances from the public, which at the end of the day will mean the gradual re-shaping of society's attitude towards us.[13]

The public and private life of PIE

Because of the illegality of paedophile activity, scheming and secrecy were unavoidably the group norm.[14] PIE developed a twin narrative: one public and the other private. The former offered the world an intelligent public relations exercise. Academic publications explained the harmlessness of adult–child sexual contact. Earnest representatives appeared on the BBC news explaining that erotic contact between adults and children was about the *rights* of the latter, not their abuse.[15]

We now know that some PIE members were part of the elite group discussed in Chapter 1, such as Sir Cyril Smith. Others were spies such as Geoffrey Prime who confessed to his wife that he was a KGB agent and was sexually attracted to young girls; she contacted the police. In 1982, he was sentenced to 38 years in prison for his espionage and sex offending. He was found guilty of three attacks on girls he stalked in his neighbourhood.

Prime demonstrated the grim and nasty reality of the private life of some PIE members. However, a number of key figures emerged from respectable and respected professional backgrounds, who were PIE members. These men were emollient and skilled in their public plausibility. The most important of these were Peter Righton and Tom O'Carroll, both of whom were employees of British universities.

The most public activist was Tom O'Carroll (PIE member number 50), who was initially imprisoned for corrupting public morals and repeatedly later for possessing indecent images and molesting boys. He remained unapologetic about both his sexual orientation and the right to express it in practice, despite imprisonment[16] and a barrage of arguments condemning him and his ex-colleagues in PIE. A celebratory autobiography about his life appeared in a film produced by David Kennerly (*A Decent Life: The Dissenting Narrative of Tom O'Carroll*) in which O'Carroll lays out a series of arguments that paedophiles have used to defend their cause:

1. Paedophilia is a sexual orientation[17] like any other and it is not a form of pathology and does not arise necessarily in the wake of abuse in early life. (O'Carroll emphasises his benign family and loving parents and that he simply finds boys attractive and that is not a problem.)
2. Sex play in children is normal. (O'Carroll went to an all-boys school, enjoyed it, and this led to a persistent interest in 10- or 11-year-old boys.)
3. Benign rather than coercive paedophilia is about nurturance and paternalism towards children and involves a love of physical contact and does not necessitate an obsession with penetrative sex. (O'Carroll emphasises this is his particular orientation.)

4. Many paedophiles can retain a friendship with children when the latter grows past the age of sexual interest to the adult. (O'Carroll does not indicate whether he has personally achieved this.)

5. Sexologists like Kinsey demonstrated that paedophilia was part of the rich tapestry of human sexuality, as was children acting sexually, sometimes with adults and without harm. (O'Carroll is reassured by those like Kinsey that sexual adult–child contact is natural and appeals to his lasting scientific authority.)

6. The repression of a sexual orientation leads to violence. (O'Carroll invokes the work of the psychoanalyst Wilhelm Reich to confirm this point.)

7. The Gay movement were right to turn their identity into a positive identity and paedophiles should do the same. (O'Carroll invokes Michel Foucault's notion of 'reverse discourse', to turn a psychiatric label into a legitimate and proud identity. This recalls the progressive role of new social movements.)

8. PIE wanted to separate civil disputes about harm from criminal law because they are always contested case by case. When a paedophile is arrested and taken to court this traumatises their child 'partner'. (O'Carroll argues that this more discerning legal convention and the abolition of age of consent would lessen the prospect of harming the child. He invokes the example of Anti-Social Behaviour Orders, introduced by Tony Blair, as a legal analogy to this proposal.)

9. If a child is assaulted then this is a criminal act (as with adults). However, if the child gave consent then this should be permitted lawfully in society. (O'Carroll asserts this argument and claims that harm to children is simply an artefact of current heavy-handed legal arrangements. He suggested that becoming verbal, at around the age of four, then warranted the capacity for consent.)

10. Feminists have noted that breastfeeding is an erotic experience. *Ipso facto* mothers have natural erotic feelings about their children. Men too can have such natural feelings. (O'Carroll notes that he is one of those men. He bemoans those feminists though who are 'repressive' towards paedophilia.)

11. It is normal for parents to feel that their children are physically attractive. Because this makes them feel guilty, they project their impulses onto paedophiles. (O'Carroll argues that paedophiles are honest about finding children physically attractive but parents are usually dishonest.)

By the mid-1970s, discussion of the rights of sexual minorities had become a mainstream rallying point on the political left. As a young left-wing student at the time, I recall a norm of protecting the emerging views of sexual minorities from right-wing prejudice and hostility. Organisations like the National Council for Civil Liberties defended PIE's right to hold public meetings to discuss their policies. 'Radicalism' then, in this context of sexual freedom during the norms of the 1970s, referred to the guilt-free expression of sexual desire. This was seen as both healthy and a fundamental individual right. To deny the demands of *any* sexual minority was thus an offence against civil liberties and it was psychologically morbid. This prompts the aphorism that 'the past is a foreign country; they do things differently there'.[18]

Later regrets and current implications

In retrospect, it is clear that the rhetorical cleverness of academics became a resource to defend enacted paedophilia, in the context of the liberal norms of the 1970s.[19] The emphasis in these texts was of *normalising* not only enacted paedophilia but also its calm and tolerant social scientific investigation. This aimed to allay purported unwarranted fears in a general population, which was allegedly ignorant and confused by what Taylor called 'myths' and 'stereotypes'.

The Taylor collection dominated the pro-paedophile cause but it was not unique. Other academics mainstreamed notions about cultural relativism, the harmlessness of adult–child sexual contact and the role of children as participants, not victims. These views aimed to counter moral censure and promote degrees of decriminalisation. Examples could be found in the published work of an academic social worker at Brunel University, Len Davis, as well as that offered by the prestigious Cambridge criminologist Donald West.[20] In Australia, Paul Wilson evinced the same arguments about the socially created harm of criminal investigation intruding upon benign and mutually loving boys and men. As with other intellectual pederasts, such as Righton and Morris noted above, for Wilson, boys were a singular preoccupation; their personal sexual orientation drove their obsessive intellectual focus.[21]

However, more recently, this academic liberalism has shifted. Some of the contributors to *Perspectives on Paedophilia*, who are still alive, have expressed regret publicly about their older views. For example, the clinical psychologist Graham Powell, who co-authored a chapter querying the harmfulness of adult–child sexual contact, told a journalist in 2014 that:

> what I wrote was completely wrong and it is a matter of deep regret that it could in any way have made things more difficult [for victims] […] The literature [scientific evidence] was so poor in 1981, people just didn't realise what was going on. There was a lack of understanding at the academic level.

In the same newspaper report, Ken Plummer told journalists that:

> I would never want any of my work to be used as a rationale for doing 'bad things' – and I regard all coercive, abusive, exploitative sexuality as a 'bad thing'. I am sorry if it has impacted anyone negatively this way, or if it has encouraged this.[22]

Plummer, by now an eminent qualitative researcher of sexual lives, went further and published an open letter on his personal website. This made clear that he did not support any position that might do harm to children but, by implication, did not explicitly reject in principle the *possibility* of benign consensual adult–child sexual contact in society.[23] To my mind, moral arguments about paedophilia should revolve around wrongfulness, not just harmfulness.[24] Harm might be unintentional and emerge from morally acceptable and well-intentioned conduct. Analogously, immorality does not always, and necessarily, cause harm.

The changes in the academic output of Plummer mirror a normative shift over time about paedophilia and its legitimacy as a sexual minority, akin to being gay. In 1991, he argued that 'As homosexuality has become slightly less open to sustained moral panic, the new pariah of "child molester" has become the latest folk devil to orchestrate anxieties over the moral and political life of Western societies'.[25] In the 1981 Taylor collection, Plummer had made three claims to support those seeking to legitimise paedophilia in modern societies.

First, professional researchers pay no sympathetic heed to experiences of those who sexually desired children. Plummer, like other authors in the Taylor collection, alludes to those adults, not their sexual objects of interest. By the time of his 1991 chapter, noted above, he still suggested that the nuances of childhood sexuality were a mystery because we do not understand the subjective lives of children from their first-hand accounts. Plummer noted that a weakness of the paedophile case is that it assumes the power of paternalism by speaking for children and their putative right to 'sexual citizenship'.

He joined PIE in order to investigate the views of its members as an ethnographer. The PIE members' view he relayed in 1981 was that children were the beneficiaries of older sexual partners. By implication, the absence of 'intergenerational sex' meant children were missing out on a developmental opportunity.

Second, he argued that paedophiles were oppressed by social stigma and ageism. The latter was relevant because it suggested that 'intergenerational sex' was not tolerated for unjust ageist reasons. Again, this intimated the ideological point that paedophilia should not be a crime but, instead, given consideration as a reasonable human right that is being denied by a repressive society.

Third, paedophiles found themselves isolated and without sympathetic human companionship. For Plummer, the answer to all three challenges was provided by the Paedophile Information Exchange, a social network, lobbying and 'support' group which he was studying at the time as an ethnographic insider.

Plummer also raised a matter that even many of those opposed to paedophilia being 'liberated' would agree with. After nearly a hundred years of psychoanalysis, it is unrealistic to depict children as lacking in sexuality or desire. For Freud, the struggle with our inherited sexual energy starts at birth. Freud actually encountered recurrent evidence of childhood sexual abuse in his early clinical work but he could not deal with the implications of its scale, modifying his theory to assume that it was the result of the patient's fantasy life.

The research psychoanalyst Jeffrey Masson[26] criticised Freud for this change of mind because he thereby missed an early opportunity to identify the psychologically corrosive impact of incest. Other early analysts though, such as Karl Abraham and Sandor Ferenzci, continued to adhere to the original sexual trauma model of psychopathology. Another analyst, Wilhelm Reich, argued that children should enjoy sexual play (and the common outcome in both masturbation and peer-group exploration) but he did not condone paedophilia and was particularly critical of the pornography industry. Reich's emphasis was on sexual de-repression but also on the child's right to discovery in benign relationships with others. That Reichian ambiguity meant that some of his followers moved towards the paedophile cause. One of them was Valida Devila, a social worker who began the Childhood Sensuality Circle in San Diego California and argued for a 'Child's Sexual Bill of Rights'. She was happy to be an adviser to Tom O'Carroll when he came to write his *Paedophilia: The Radical Cause*.

PIE: the aftermath

Although PIE petered out organisationally in 1984, a well-respected academic review of sexualities appeared the following year which broadly represented the position adopted by the authors in the Taylor collection. Jeffrey Weeks' book *Sexuality and Its Discontents: Meanings, Myths and Modern Sexualities*, in a long section on 'intergenerational sex[27] and consent', replayed the arguments of the Taylor group of authors. However, Weeks also introduced some important balancing cautions from feminism.

The paedophile activists of the 1970s did not dwell on women's rights. Most of them were men wanting to justify their sexual appetite for children, especially boys, and arguments about the patriarchal oppression of girls were at odds with the personal needs of heterosexual PIE members. *Ipso facto* gay paedophiles were no threat to girls and so could not stand accused by feminism, at least in relation to their individual personal conduct. (Men tend to take CSA less seriously than women.[28]) Weeks, quite correctly, rehearsed feminist objections in order to temper the earlier enthusiasm for paedophile rights he relayed from the coded PIE position from those in the Taylor collection.[29] It is obvious to anyone researching this field that men have driven the paedophile advocacy movement. Some women have been present in those organisations but are a tiny minority. Weeks also conceded a central and obvious point: on average, children have a limited cognitive capacity compared to adults.

At that point, Weeks did not deal with the empirical question of the demonstrable harm to children or adult sexual predation, nor with fundamental moral questions about respect and recognition, at least if feminist objections are tested to their limits. By the end of the twentieth century, Weeks' work represents, with others, a current of thought derived from the radical days of sexual liberation. The avalanche of evidence since then about the impact of CSA on its survivors means that there is now more at stake morally than the right to be part of a free sexual minority.

In a later work in 2007 (*The World We Have Won*), Weeks moved much more strongly to a value-based position about sexual activity: that it should not do harm and that it should demonstrate genuine reciprocity, thereby now creating a moral consideration of *wrongfulness*. Weeks also conceded the vulnerability of arguments used by his colleagues, who were strong cultural and historical relativists. Instead, Weeks argues (and I think he is right on this point) there must be an ongoing dialogue about sexual ethics, but one which starts with core values about care and mutuality. In the case of some sexual practices, such as paedophilia, bestiality and necrophilia, these two core ethical features are inevitably absent or highly compromised. (In personal correspondence with me about this topic, Weeks agreed that such practices were indeed unethical.[30])

It is noteworthy that Tom O'Carroll's *Paedophilia: The Radical Cause* and the Taylor collection defending paedophilia, which Weeks had drawn upon in *Sexuality and Its Discontents* (from 1985–1995) were no longer prominent in *The World We Have Won* (in 2007). In the first part of this century, the social progress achieved in this 'world we have won', via worthy liberation struggles, does not now seem to include any remaining serious intellectual defence of adult–child sexual contact from libertarian sexologists.

Thus, Weeks toughened his existing doubts and Plummer by and large recanted his earlier position. However, O'Carroll carried on regardless. Nonetheless, the argument that the harm from adult–child sexual contact is an exaggerated panic has still not disappeared completely, nor has the assertion that such contact is neither wrong nor pathological, as the next section demonstrates. In current times, there is a new wave of moral panic claim makers about both CSA and enacted paedophilia.

Since the leading academic work of Weeks was developed (his *Sexuality and Its Discontents* was reprinted in 1995, which is now over 20 years ago) much has happened, which he starts to acknowledge in *The World We Have Won*: the Catholic Church has been embroiled in an unresolved scandal about enacted paedophilia; both the BBC and the NHS have admitted being unwitting hosts to the abuse of children on their premises; and a scandal has erupted about groups of paedophile politicians.

More recent moral panic claim makers

A new wave of intellectual interest has arisen in relation to active paedophiles and has exposed a particular division in the academic community, especially in Scotland, which at present is conducting its review of institutional CSA separately from the one in England and Wales. This new wave may reflect the turbulence created by the social-work profession in Scotland being embroiled in criticisms about abuse in its own midst.

Some researchers studying CSA have tested the limits of a moral panic position. For example, in the late 1990s, Jenny Kitzinger, a feminist sociologist, examined paedophilia using the moral panic lens and found that it worked poorly.[31] She noted the expected demonisation in the tabloid press about those detected, convicted and then released after their sentence. However, she also noted that resource-poor local communities were starved of information and they had personally witnessed investigatory police incompetence. They had understandable fears about the capacity of the state to act efficiently about child protection. This point was well founded – see examples of police inaction and corruption in my earlier chapters. Although within critical sociology the moral panic thesis predominates, some resist it strongly. In addition to Kitzinger's feminist response about CSA we also find the critiques of

Ross Cheit and Michael Salter.[32] The presence of the feminist icon, Simone de Beauvoir, in the French lobby noted at the outset, might now be a source of embarrassment for the movement she supported.

This then is a complex matter and has left moral panic theory standing but also attacked strongly in the academy. This mirrors Stanley Cohen's personal ambivalence about CSA. He conceded that the public have *grounds* for worrying about transparency and competence from the police and other state agencies, even though public anxiety and cynicism can sometimes culminate in dysfunctional vigilantism and rough justice in localities. Also, treating released child sex offenders as subhuman (calling them 'animals', 'monsters' and 'beasts' etc.) has had consequences for our understanding of paedophilia as a sexual orientation. This process of dehumanisation diminishes the accuser as well as the accused, not just morally but also intellectually; it limits their critical appraisal of what is happening and why. Paedophiles are often unremarkable, when they are hiding from us in plain sight. They are not the un-smiling, bulging-eyed monsters appearing on police arrest mug-shots, and gratefully blown up for effect on tabloid front pages. In reality, they could be anyone. In the thrall of an orgy of mass contempt, we can close down our calm and critical understanding of sexual offenders as ordinary human beings in their range of ordinary complexity.

Also, a central insight from Kitzinger's work is that the skewed interest in 'stranger danger' has tended to deflect our needed curiosity in the bigger picture about child protection priorities. Most sexual abuse of children actually takes place in their home (see Chapter 3). We can miss that obvious point when focusing on 'stranger danger'. The patriarchal family unit is culturally assumed to be part of the sacred not the profane; it is idealised and sentimentalised. This might explain why the Orkney and Cleveland cases produced the media responses they did. The journalists favoured the parents over the professionals, assuming the former were obviously innocent victims and the latter crassly insensitive agents of the state. This is not helpful when we are appraising the real and immediate presence of sexual risk to children, which is often not just close to home, but actually is *in* the home.

Recently, some academic social workers have reanimated the British legacy of the work of Jock Young and Stanley Cohen by issuing a set of published briefing papers on moral panics in relation to the family, children and the state.[33] These were underpinned in large part by the outcome of a series of seminars organised by a group from the University of Edinburgh (Viviene Cree, Guy Clapton and Mark Smith). The seminars were funded by the Economic and Social Research Council in 2012.[34]

In one of these short collections a contribution was made by Frank Furedi, entitled 'The moral crusade against paedophilia',[35] in which he argues that the latter represents a 'permanent focus of moral outrage'. But if it is that, then it follows that 'a permanent focus' undermines one criterion of a prototypical moral panic (that it should be ephemeral). We are also told scornfully that 'according to the cultural script of virtually every western society child abusers are ubiquitous'. But he offers no empirical evidence to support paedophilia being the mere social construction of a common story ('cultural script'), rather than an actual phenomenon. Surely, those who sexually abuse children *are* ubiquitous: a predictable rate of offending (both reported and unreported) is indeed present across society (see my empirical points in the previous chapter). Furedi provides no hard counter-evidence to that from those studying the incidence and prevalence of CSA. Instead, he simply offers us hyperbolic rhetoric.

Furedi tells us that the moral panic about paedophilia is 'symptomatic of a world view that risks losing the capacity to understand the distinction between fantasy and reality'. But, again, he offers no evidence to demonstrate that concerns about CSA are a fantasy. He does not rehearse Stanley Cohen's profound ambivalence in relation to child abuse being perhaps a *warranted* moral panic, nor Cohen's later emphasis on 'moral stupor' and 'states of denial', in particular relation to CSA. Furedi does not follow Cohen's stricture that we should do a reality check, case by case, to see if a panic is warranted or not. Indeed, the whole position adopted by Furedi is an evidence-free zone. He does not cite a single empirical study to support his arguments. They hang together as a rationale but, ultimately, they are no more than a set of assertions.

Furedi goes on to argue that some interest groups (politicians and child protection experts) seek to promote anxieties about threats to children in a moral crusade. Again, he offers no evidence to support this assertion. What we know instead is that it is an under-reported phenomenon, children are disbelieved and evidence to police and social workers has at times been ignored and suppressed. Cohen, discussed in the previous chapter, conceded this point when expressing his ambivalence about his core concept of a moral panic to child abuse: 'panic' morphed instead for him into the less contestable notion that child abuse is a recurring and understandably legitimate *controversy or concern*.

By contrast, Furedi argues that such a concern is unwarranted and is actually damaging to the proper responsibility adults have towards children (again, an assertion with no evidence attached). And, in my view, this leads to the most perverse aspect of Furedi's logic: he claims that the putative moral panic and moral crusade about CSA now *weaken* the confidence and effectiveness of adults to protect children. He argues that adults are now disengaged from children, who are viewed as an 'inconvenience' (again, no evidence offered for this claim). The consensus on the evidence we do have, reported in the past decades, is that before the rise of internet offending, the incidence of child abuse was decreasing for the very reason that collectively we became *more* concerned to involve ourselves in strategies to protect children. Surely, overall, we are now more, not less, engaged with the matter of child protection, though internet offending may now be creating a losing battle.

Finally, Furedi draws a comparison between paedophiles and witches (with child protection experts thereby becoming new sorts of witch-finders, backed up by politically motivated moral crusaders). But isn't there a clear empirical distinction to be made between the unwarranted trial of harmless reclusive women and that of adults who stand accused of sexual contact with children? Some adults do actually sexually molest children, but what did witches *actually do* that was comparable? To my mind, this comparison by Furedi is simply silly.[36] Also, the disjuncture about patriarchy is not spotted by Furedi. In the case of women, their emerging power was a *threat* to patriarchy, and the attribution of witchcraft reflected that threat. By contrast, paedophilia is (in large part) an *expression* of patriarchy, not a threat to it.

Furedi's concern about child protection priorities having a paradoxical and negative impact on confident and mutually supportive forms of social relationships echoes a wider claim by the editors of the series 'Moral Panics in Theory and Practice':

> the lens of a moral panic highlights the ways in which social issues that begin with real concerns may lead to the labelling and stigmatising of certain behaviours and individuals; they may precipitate harsh and disproportionate legislation; they may make people more fearful and society a less safe place.[37]

These editors go on to make it explicit that moral panics can mean that concerns about internet pornography can undermine individual freedom and child protection policies can 'inhibit our capacity to support families'.

These are strong claims, but where is the evidence that they are true? Indecent images of children always imply that the latter have *already* been sexually victimised in practice. Whose individual freedom is important here, the adult user of the Internet or the child abused to create indecent images? Moreover, there is the implication from these libertarian academics that parents *only* require 'support' and never constraint. However, in practice, families sometimes need support and sometimes they are sites of crimes against children. At that point, crimes need investigation. In some cases, the non-abusive members of families need support to nurture children who have been sexually victimised and so social-work interventions might, quite legitimately, mix both an investigatory and a supportive role.

We need evidence, case by case, to understand this varied picture, which cannot be discerned in advance by rhetorical claims about the damage allegedly inflicted by the routine activity of child protection workers. The latter do not *create* CSA, they *identify* it. Typically, they then struggle with what they have found when considering the child involved and their particular situation, with the risks of false positives and false negatives being ever present in any form of human decision-making (see Chapter 2).

Reading these moral panic claim makers reminds us that they, like the objects of their interest, can be irrational in their reasoning. If a classic moral panic involves a disproportionate reaction to a social problem, then those adopting moral panic reasoning have to deliver the evidence that the reaction studied is truly irrational and unwarranted. If they cannot deliver this evidence, then their *own* moral posturing is itself irrational. Any theory worth its salt needs to be confirmed by empirical evidence. In this case, moral panic claim makers certainly state their rationale clearly; Furedi's *logic* readily makes sense. But this is not enough to persuade. This is about crimes being committed against children (or not). It is not an exercise in pure logic alone. Instead, it requires supportive evidence. What we are offered by Furedi and other moral panic claim makers is not proof but self-assured rhetoric.[38]

The keenness of some social-work academics to invoke moral panic logic reflects professional special pleading, and then a problem emerges about their rhetoric. Self-organising groups of survivors of sexual abuse have a clear view of what social justice means; and it does not mean social-work practice guided by moral panic theory.[39] If the latter is 'emancipatory' in this context, then who exactly is being emancipated?[40] How precisely does it help vulnerable children or bring justice to those who were abused in childhood? To be clear here, not all those proposing a moral panic theory approach to our topic are also those acting as pro-paedophile advocates. Political libertarians like Furedi and the Edinburgh social-work group focus on defending the moral panic position discussed in my previous chapter. We can see that their work and the pro-paedophile case are *aligned* in their logic because they both problematise whether or not CSA is a social problem and its harm is being exaggerated. The link between them is moral panic theory. However, the pure pro-paedophile arguments linked to PIE above did have a more recent resonance which we can now note.

The more recent pro-paedophile case

A controversial pro-paedophile research study emerged in 2004 that reanimated a libertarian position from academia.[41] In 2004, Richard Yuill was awarded a PhD by the University of Glasgow, entitled 'Male age-discrepant intergenerational sexualities and relationships'.[42] For short, Yuill calls the latter 'MADIS' in order to contrast it with the dominant or 'hegemonic' discourse of CSA.

Yuill reports that he posed as a 'boylover' and made contact with the International Paedophile and Child Emancipation (IPCE) group. This was a continuing example in The Netherlands of PIE in London, showing that in this century still there are pro-paedophile organisations in Europe. Yuill reviewed their literature and interviewed both paedophiles and boys who had sex with them. IPCE was coordinated by a Dutch academic researcher (Frans Gieles). One of its political strategies was for members to attend academic conferences in order to promote a permissive view of paedophilia.[43] Yuill joined that academic movement not only as a researcher of it, but also by willingly transmitting its dominant ideology.[44] Three familiar themes were reported by Yuill:

1. The pro-paedophile social movement is opposed to the common assumptions of most people today that adult–child sexual contact is wrong and harmful. (Yuill's thesis explores 'the way in which such relationships have been constituted within hegemonic child sexual abuse discourses'.[45])
2. These assumptions have been constructed in recent times by particular repressive and illiberal social forces. (Echoing the moral panic logic, Yuill argues that our dominant anti-paedophile view has been created by 'the growing professionalisation of education and welfare institutions; the increasing problematisation of child and youth sexuality; and finally the popularisation of taboos on such relationships through a series of media and political campaigns'.)

3. As a counter to this 'hegemonic' and orthodox view, the sexual rights of paedo-
    philes could be extended by responding to the positive messages advanced by
    pro-paedophile organisations. (For Yuill, these include 'young people's sexual
    rights, to boylover identity groups stressing the positive and beneficial aspects
    of such relationships'.)

Drawing upon the academic authority of Foucault, Bourdieu and Queer Theory,
Yuill quite correctly places side-by-side for our consideration a choice. We either
go with the orthodox view that condemns enacted paedophilia (the 'hegemonic
CSA discourse') or we listen sympathetically to the proponents of the 'MADIS
discourse', who were given an extensive voice in Yuill's thesis.[46]

A reminder of Cohen's cautious ambivalence

This chapter has argued that the moral panic claim *alone* could not be the basis
for pro-paedophile lobbying; other civil libertarian arguments also needed to be
invoked by advocacy groups like PIE, NAMBLA or IPCE. Indeed, logically, it is possible to defend moral panic reasoning but oppose enacted paedophilia. Nonetheless,
the ready alignment of moral panic theory with a libertarian policy stance about
adult–child sexual contact was noted above.

   With the exception of Yuill, the more recent contrarian libertarians in the
academy (such as Clapton, Cree and others like Furedi) have returned primarily
to the moral panic orthodoxy discussed in the previous chapter. For this reason,
the centrality of moral panic theory for this chapter as well as the previous one
remains important and so we need to return to the mixed views that Stanley Cohen
expressed about adult–child sexual contact.

   To confirm Cohen's anxiety that the moral panic thesis might be misused, I cite
here his cautions at some length because they are so important; he remains a totemic
figure in moral panic theory. He moved from his initial interest in the amplification
of social problems by media hyperbole and the irrationality of the masses to a different one: the processes of denial in society about atrocities and suffering. This led
to him expressing a serious doubt about a full-blown social constructionist position
about moral panics, when interviewed by fellow sociologist Laurie Taylor:

> You and I wrote books questioning the idea that there could ever be a firm
> definition of crime, that it is all to do with the defined and the definers.
> *And that led to the idea that it was impossible to make any truth claims at all.* This
> is exactly what happened when my report on torture came out in Israel
> [emphasis added].[47]

A few years earlier, in his book *States of Denial*, Cohen made this related and
relevant point:

> The most pernicious element [...] [of] what is variously called 'positivism',
> 'rationality', 'science' or 'the Enlightenment', is the idea that there can be no

access to current or historical reality from outside a vantage point of power. *Ultimately there is no way of determining that one version of reality is more valid than any other.* All of us who carried the anti-positivist banners of the sixties are responsible for these philosophical high jinks. When contemplating the versions of epistemic relativism favoured by the cultural Left, we should at the very least have the grace to say, *'That's not what we meant'* [emphasis added].[48]

These frank statements are particularly relevant in relation to Cohen's ambivalence about CSA as a putative moral panic, which I noted in the previous chapter. The recent trivialisation from some academics of the scale and harmfulness of CSA, when they reassert confidently that it is a moral panic, fits poorly with these wise cautions from Cohen. CSA, like torture, should not be trivialised, as Cohen was keen to emphasise.

Here he leaves us in no doubt about this concern about the moral panic thesis being misused: 'Intellectuals who keep silent about what they know, who ignore the crimes that matter by moral standards, are even more culpable when their society is free and open. They can speak freely but choose not to'.[49] Surely, adults seeking and acquiring sexual gratification from children *are* committing 'crimes that matter by moral standards'. The only way that Cohen's statement can be challenged is by arguing that adult–child sexual contact is *not* inherently immoral; and so its criminalisation is thereby irrational and unjust. (This retort was indeed present in the French lobby in 1977 led by Foucault.) Cohen invented a term for mundane complicity from third parties knowing about events, such as child abuse: he calls it the 'passive bystander effect'. In the range of case studies I have summarised in earlier chapters, we find that effect recurring repeatedly. That inactivity is then a precursor to the inner experience of 'moral stupor' or 'chilling denial'. The everyday effect is joined then by smug intellectual arguments from those who 'ignore the crimes that matter by moral standards'.

The first wave of libertarian reasoning from self-interested members of PIE or NAMBLA relied on two core and yoked arguments: the self-evident status of CSA as a moral panic and the right of children and adults to have unconstrained sexual intimacy. The second wave (if we exclude Yuill's work) has tended to limit itself to the moral panic point alone. We can only speculate what Cohen might have made of the focus of this chapter, were he still alive today, but the citations I offer above give us some clue.[50]

Conclusion

There are three pertinent motives of academic researchers for us to consider in relation to those choosing to focus on moral panics and sexual citizenship implicating children. First, some are sexually interested in children and they are using their role to offer justifications for adult–child sexual contact, or to undermine the evidence that CSA is a warranted public policy concern, rather than it being merely a moral panic. Second, some are not sexually interested in children but they are keen to defend a strong social constructivist position in social science (particularly in relation to moral panic theory). Third, some are offering a re-professionalisation strategy for social work in the wake of attacks upon it for its child protection failures. These motives may exist separately or together, case by case.

Some casual libertarianism and moral relativism in academic culture still persists about enacted paedophilia, even if this position's more self-righteous aspirations are no longer as confident as in the halcyon days of PIE and NAMBLA in the 1970s. Today, most academic health and social care professionals address seriously CSA as a matter of gross immorality and criminality. Many of those editing or contributing to journals, such as *Child Neglect & Abuse* or *Child Abuse Review*, are those academics. However, the contrarian minority position has echoed recurrently in the past 40 years.

Pro-paedophile organisations and those researching them sympathetically, as well as those stretching the moral panic thesis to CSA, between them come up with six recurring arguments. First, the crime of CSA could be eliminated by lowering or abandoning the age of consent. Second, children are not victims of adult–child sexual contact but participants. Third, we confuse our current norms of sexual abuse and definitions of childhood with a permanent societal state. Fourth, the prevalence of CSA is exaggerated and, anyway, it is rarely coercive in character. Fifth, there is no evidence that 'consensual' sexual contact harms children and what harm is done is an artefact of social censorship and legal proceedings. Sixth, adults have a civil right to express their sexual interest in children and that sexual interest is not psychologically abnormal.[51] My immanent critique of these claims was set out in the previous chapter, I hope persuasively.

As I noted at the beginning of that chapter, the academic community is divided on this topic. There are two moral positions. One emphasises the underestimation of CSA and an associated 'moral stupor' in society with a web of factors reflecting deceit and complicity. The other argues that we are in the grip of a needless moral panic, promoted by self-interested moral crusaders and child protection experts. Both take the moral high ground and they cannot both be right.

The reader can decide which camp they prefer. For those of us seeking to find effective ways to protect children from the sexual interest of adults, we need to address a substantial challenge which has been fed by the sorts of rhetorical objections, often in an evidence-free zone, discussed in this chapter from libertarian social constructionists. That wider challenge is the focus of the next and final chapter.

Notes

1 Krizman, D. (ed.). (1990). *Politics, Philosophy, Culture: Interviews and Other Writings, 1977–1984.* London: Routledge. See also Henley, J. (2001). Calls for legal child sex rebound on luminaries of May 68. February 24. *The Guardian.* Available at www.theguardian.com/world/2001/feb/24/jonhenley.

2 PIE was affiliated to the National Council for Civil Liberties in the 1970s. Liberty (the changed name of NCCL) now firmly rejects any assumed legacy of support for adult–child sexual contact.

3 Taylor, B. (ed.). (1981). *Perspectives on Paedophilia*. London: Batsford.

4 Barton, H. (1976). Paedophile politics. *Kalos, on Greek Love* 1(1), Spring.

5 Taylor, B. (1976). Motives for guilt-free pederasty: some literary considerations. *Sociological Review* 24(1), 97–114. Taylor left his employment at the University of Sussex in the early 1990s to live in France. He died in 2016. Protests about the hagiographic obituary of him in *The Guardian* eventually led to the newspaper removing it from its website.

6 Taylor, B. (1981). *Perspectives on Paedophilia*, p. vii.

7 I could only trace a detailed PIE membership list for 1984–1985 (the year the organisation collapsed) by which time, of the four authors, three remained on record. Fraser's name was now missing, which may have been because of the scrutiny of the press about his offending after the GMC had failed to ban him from practice, pushing him beyond even the planned secrecy of PIE (see Chapter 5).

8 Plummer, K. (1981). Paedophilia: constructing a sociological baseline. In M. Cook & K. Howells (eds), *Adult Sexual Interest in Children* (p. 244). London: Academic Press.

9 Meehan, N. (2016). Morris Fraser, child abuse, corruption and collusion in Britain & Northern Ireland. Spinwatch. See www.academia.edu/23870062/.

10 In UK law, this was codified in the 2003 Sexual Offences Act.

11 It is possible but barely conceivable that Taylor, as a fellow PIE member, was unaware of Fraser's record of offending going back to the early 1970s, when inviting him to write his chapter on 'The Child'.

12 *Magpie*, May 11, 1978, 'Member 324'.

13 Ibid., 'Member 214'.

14 The sexual exploitation of children in music education was noted in Chapter 5. A member of PIE, Alan Doggett, who taught music at St Paul's public school, committed suicide in 1978 after being charged with molesting a 10-year-old boy. Subsequently, other ex-pupils came forward to report being sexually assaulted by him. See also Bracchi, P. (2014). How a paedophile scandal was hushed up at George Osborne's old school. March 29. *Mail Online*. Available at www.dailymail.co.uk/news/article-2592068/How-paedophile-scandal-hushed-George-Osbournes-old-school.html.

15 See Paedophile campaigner is jailed. www.youtube.com/watch?v=XM_se7pb8t8. The two PIE members interviewed (very firmly) by John Tusa for BBC's *Newsnight* were Steven Adrian Freeman (a.k.a. Steven Smith) and Peter Bremner (a.k.a. Roger Nash). Both were subsequently convicted of sexual crimes against children. See Ex-paedophile group leader Freeman jailed over child rape drawings. (2011). July 15. BBC News, London. Available at www.bbc.co.uk/news/uk-england-london-14169406; Child sex men found guilty. (1984). November 14. *The Herald*. Available at https://news.google.com/newspapers?nid=2507&dat=19841114&id=mcBAAAAAIBAJ&sjid=0KUMAAAAIBAJ&pg=3818,2889704&hl=en. These publicly recorded news items gave confidence to those like the campaigning MP Geoffrey Dickens to make his claims in Parliament about a well-organised paedophile ring. The public advocates of 'consensual' paedophilia were drawn from the PIE executive and most were subsequently prosecuted for sexual offences against children or the possession of indecent images of children. These offenders and PIE leaders included David Joy, Charles Napier and Tom O'Carroll (see next footnote). For respective news items on each, see Paedophile campaigner jailed over child images. (2007). August 13. *The Guardian*. Available at www.theguardian.com/uk/2007/aug/13/ukcrime; Peachey, P. (2014). Tory MP's half-brother Charles Napier sentenced to 13 years over 'prolific' child sex abuse. December 23. *The Independent*. Available at www.independent.co.uk/news/uk/crime/tory-mps-half-brother-charles-napier-sentenced-to-13-years-over-prolific-child-sex-abuse-9942651.html.

16 In 2006, O'Carroll was jailed for 30 months for conspiring to distribute indecent images of children, with his co-defendant Michael John De Clare Studdert, who had a collection of over 50,000 indecent images of children (the largest on record for one offender, according to the Metropolitan Police). Subsequently, in 2015, O'Carroll pleaded guilty to one count of indecently assaulting a boy and one count of gross indecency with another. His prison sentence of two years was suspended for the same period, though he was placed on the Sex Offenders Register and made the subject of an indefinite sexual harm prevention order. (See, for example, Two jailed for child porn library. (2006). December 20. BBC News. Available at http://news.bbc.co.uk/2/hi/uk_news/england/coventry_warwickshire/6196811.stm.) O'Carroll is a rare 'political' paedophile. He is habitually unrepentant, despite his repeated convictions. He keeps the spirit of PIE alive and reminds us of its original and unaltered political ideology about 'normalising' adult–child sexual contact.

17 For emphasis, this point is strictly correct – paedophilia is a *sexual orientation*. What is morally and politically contentious is whether the *enactment* of those desires should be defended as a matter of sexual citizenship.

18 The opening sentence from Hartley, L. (1953). *The Go Between*. Harmondsworth: Penguin. Markers of a change in British norms about paedophilia in the past 40 years include the controversy over the satirical support for a moral panic position in the *Brass Eye* episode of July 28, 2001. (The political paedophile Tom O'Carroll noted above boasts that he gave advice to the *Brass Eye* production. See Tom O'Carroll Bibliography at www.williamapercy.com/wiki/index.php?title=Tom_O%27Carroll Biography.) More recently, (February 2017) the right-wing libertarian position of Brietbart in the USA reached its own limits on attacking 'political correctness', when one of its leading writers, Milo Yiannopoulos, resigned (and lost a book contract) for defending some forms of pederasty. See Sinclair, H. (2017). Milo Yiannopoulos resigns from Breitbart amid paedophilia controversy. February 22. *International Business Times*, UK. Available at www.ibtimes.co.uk/milo-yiannopoulos-resigns-breitbart-amid-paedophilia-controversy-1607842.

19 See, for example, Frits, B. (1985). *Paedophilia: A Factual Report*. Rotterdam: Enclave; Brongersma, E. (1986). *Loving Boys*. Amsterdam: Global Academic Publishers; Constantine, L. & Martinson, F. (1981). *Children and Sex: New Findings, New Perspectives*. Boston: Little, Brown and Company; Cook, M. & Howells, K. (eds). (1981). *Adult Sexual Interest in Children*. London: Academic Press; Rossman, G. (1985). *Sexual Experience Between Men and Boys*. Middlesex: Temple Smith; Sandfort, T. (1987). *Boys on their Contacts with Men*. Amsterdam: Global Academic Publishers; Wilson, G. & Cox, D. (1983). *The Child-Lovers*. London: Peter Owen Publishers; West, D. & Woodhouse, T. (1990). Sexual encounters between boys and adults. In C. Li, D. West & T. Woodhouse (eds), *Children's Sexual Encounters with Adults*. London: Duckworth.

20 See Davis, L. (1983). *Sex and the Social Worker*. London: Heinemann Educational Books, and West, D. (1981). Adult sexual interest in children: implications for social control. In M. Cook & K. Howells (eds), *Adult Sexual Interest In Children*. New York: Academic Press.

21 Wilson, P. (1981). *The Man They Called a Monster*. North Melbourne: Cassell. As with many PIE intellectuals in Britain, Wilson was subsequently prosecuted for sexual offences against boys in Australia. See Condon, M. (2016). Criminologist Paul Wilson wrote controversial book on pedophile Howard-Osborne and 'man-boy love'. November 25. *The Courier Mail*. Available at http://www.couriermail.com.au/news/queensland/crime-and-justice/criminologist-paul-wilson-wrote-controversial-book-on-pedophile-howardosborne-and-manboy-love/news-story/e6dfb85456137287b5fcad047f2e3c88.

22 Gilligan, A. (2014). 'Paedophilia is natural and normal for males'. July 5. *The Telegraph*. Available at www.telegraph.co.uk/comment/10948796/Paedophilia-is-natural-and-normal-for-males.html.

23 Plummer, K. (2014). Child abuse and paedophilia: An open letter. July 26. Available at https://kenplummer.com/2014/07/27/child-abuse-and-paedophilia-an-open-letter/. Plummer announces the removal of his earlier research from the Internet and apologises for its possible misuse 'as a rationale for doing "bad things" – and I regard all coercive, abusive, violent and exploitative sexuality as a "bad thing"'. He goes on:

> These early papers from the 1970s are of some historical interest, but given the changes in the wider world, I believe their conclusions are no longer tenable. I am saddened to think they might have been used to justify child abuse.

Indeed, on his website, the list of pre-2000 publications no longer contains Plummer's work on paedophilia. This is ironical – paedophilia is a real sexual orientation, acted out or not, explored by him extensively and usefully in the past. The fact of both its existence, and his research about it, is removed from scrutiny by Plummer opting for a form of self-censorship. He might instead have left them intact but offered empirical or ethical hindsight criticisms of the material he authored. The socio-political process of 'drawing a line under the past' is discussed in relation to both arguments for a statute of limitation for offenders (see Chapter 10) and institutional denial in the BBC about Jimmy Savile and others (see Chapter 2).

24 See Woodiwiss, J. (2014). Beyond a single story: The importance of separating 'harm' from 'wrongfulness' and 'sexual innocence' from 'childhood' in contemporary narratives of childhood sexual abuse. *Sexualities* 17(1), 139–158.

25 Plummer, K. (1991). Understanding childhood sexualities. In T. Sandfort, E. Brongersma & A. Van Naerssen (eds), *Male Intergenerational Intimacy: Historical, Socio-Psychological and Legal Perspectives*. London: Haworth Press.

26 Masson, J. (1998). *The Assault on Truth: Freud's Suppression of the Seduction Theory*. New York: Pocket Books.

27 This term, like 'participant', in itself strips away the negative connotation of 'child sexual abuse' or 'child molestation'. The words used in this field of inquiry inherently point to differing ideological positions.

28 Smith, H., Fromuth, M. & Morris, C. (1998). Effects of gender on perceptions of child sexual abuse. *Journal of Child Sexual Abuse* 6(4), 51–63.

29 Some feminists have retained a loyalty to Foucault's poststructuralist libertarianism. Others have attacked radical social constructionism for its gender-neutral approach to power and its lack of recognition that the sexual exploitation of children is part of a set of patriarchal capitalist relations in which men routinely dominate women and children. This is not just about the micro-politics of domination and transient sexual pleasure but also the macro-politics of organised profit seeking from the sex trade. See Haug, F. (2001). Sexual deregulation or the child abuser as hero in neoliberalism. *Feminist Theory* 2(1), 55–78; Bray, A. (2009). Governing the gaze: child sexual abuse, moral panics and the post-feminist blind spot. *Feminist Media Studies* 9(2), 173–191.

30 My appraisal here of Weeks is sympathetic to his early cautions about paedophilia and his later deletion of PIE-inspired rhetoric. A less sympathetic reading of Weeks is offered by Ian Pace, the blogger on child sexual abuse, in his Academia and Paedophilia 1: The Case of Jeffrey Weeks and Indifference to Boy-Rape (2014). September 29. Available at https://ianpace.wordpress.com/2014/09/29/academia-and-paedophilia-1-the-case-of-jeffrey-weeks-and-indifference-to-boy-rape/.

31 Kitzinger, J. (2002). The ultimate neighbour from hell? Stranger danger and the media framing of paedophiles. In Y. Jewkes & G. Letherby (eds), *Criminology: A Reader*. London: Sage.

32 Kitzinger, J. (2004). *Framing abuse: Media Influence and Public Understanding of Sexual Violence Against Children*. London: Pluto Press; Cheit, R. (2014). *The Witch-Hunt Narrative: Politics, Psychology and the Sexual Abuse of Children*. Oxford: Oxford University Press; Salter, M. (2017). Child sexual abuse. In W. Dekeseredy & M. Dragiewicz (eds), *Routledge Handbook of Critical Criminology*. London: Routledge.

33 Cree, V. (ed.). (2015). *Gender and the Family*. Bristol: Policy Press; Clapton, G. (ed.). (2015). *Childhood and Youth*. Bristol: Policy Press; Cree, V. (2015). *The State*. Bristol: Policy Press; Clapton, G., Cree, V. & Smith, M. (2012). Moral panics and social work: towards a sceptical view of UK child protection. *Critical Social Policy* 33(2), 197–217.

34 ESRC seminar series 2012–14 (ES/J021725/1). Revisiting Moral Panics: A Critical Examination of 21st Century Social Issues and Anxieties.

35 In Smith, M. (ed.). (2015). *Moral Regulation*. Bristol: Policy Press.

36 See Beck, R. (2015). *We Believe the Children: A Moral Panic in the 1980s*. New York: Public Affairs.

37 In series preface of Cree, V., Clapton, G & Smith, M. (eds). (2015). *Moral Panics in Theory and Practice*. Bristol: Policy Press.

38 This tendency towards rhetoric, and an avoidance of detailed evidence, is in part a function of the idealist tradition in social science, which culminates in an overstatement of the social construction of reality and a lop-sided methodological preference for qualitative inquiry (thus avoiding quantitative evidence about anything). For strong constructionists, evidence becomes irrelevant, vague, selective, or it is replaced by assertion. In formal philosophical terms, this tradition is preoccupied with epistemology and has little interest in, or respect for, ontology (except for its selective rhetorical utility). See Pilgrim, D. (2017). The perils of strong social constructivism: The case of child sexual abuse. *Journal of Critical Realism* 16(3), 268–283.

39 See, for example, the type of social justice being demanded by napac.org.uk and clearlines.org.uk.

40 Pilgrim, D. (2017). Child sexual abuse, moral panics and emancipatory practice. *Critical and Radical Social Work* 5(1), 7–22.

41 Taylor, M. (2004). Paedophilia thesis comes under fire. December 2. *The Guardian*. Available at www.theguardian.com/uk/2004/dec/02/research.children. This report from *The Guardian* notes that the University of Glasgow did not endorse the views on the thesis but affirmed its legitimacy as a piece of academic work. Strathclyde Police looked at it and announced that there was no illegality. Concerns had been expressed to both the university and the police in 2001; these were reported at the time by the freelance Edinburgh journalist Marcello Mega in the *Times Higher Education Supplement*. See Mega, M. (2001). If no rules have been broken, perhaps the rulebook requires some attention? November 23. *Times Higher Education Supplement*. Available at www.timeshighereducation.com/features/if-no-rules-have-been-broken-perhaps-the-rulebook-requires-some-attention/165893.article.

42 The Yuill thesis is available in full online at theses.gla.ac.uk.

43 Mega, M. (2001). If no rules have been broken.

44 This was history repeating itself: Ken Plummer played an analogous role in PIE at the end of the 1970s.

45 This term refers to a view and/or a social group in society that dominates others. It is sometimes used in relation to 'doxa', which refers to the main views prevalent in a

culture at a point in time (hence 'orthodoxy' and 'heterodoxy'). 'Hegemony' can refer to a dynamic process of domination or to a description of its outcome.

46 Even more recently than this PhD we find similar arguments to those of Yuill being repeated by academic defenders of a more politically tolerant and legally lax attitude to paedophilia. Presentations included at a conference at the University of Cambridge in 2013 were "Liberating the paedophile: a discursive analysis", and "Danger and difference: the stakes of hebephilia". See Gilligan, A. (2014). 'Paedophilia is natural and normal for males'.

47 Taylor, L. (2007). The other side of the street: An interview with Stan Cohen. In D. Downes, P. Rock, C. Chinkin & C. Gearty (eds), *Crime, Social Control and Human Rights: From Moral Panics to States of Denial; Essays in Honour of Stanley Cohen*. London: Willan. In the same volume, Ken Plummer wrote a chapter on 'intimate citizenships' without a single mention of paedophilia. However, in another chapter by Andrew Rutherford entitled 'Sexual offenders and the path to a purified domain', the author draws on the authority of Michel Foucault to query the emergence of 'the punitive city'. Foucault's role in the 1977 lobbying was not mentioned. Those honouring Cohen were still not reflecting his strong personal ambivalence about the moral status of CSA. This may reflect a legacy in critical criminology of naïve leftism, in which criminals are seen as expressing resistance to current power relations: they are unrecognised folk heroes, not folk devils. A critique of this naïvety in his subdiscipline is well argued by Michael Salter (Salter, M. (2017). Child sexual abuse. In W. Dekeseredy & M. Dragiewicz (eds), *Routledge Handbook of Critical Criminology*. London: Routledge).

48 Cohen, S. (2001). *States of Denial: Knowing About Atrocities and Suffering* (p. 281). Cambridge: Polity.

49 Ibid., p. 286.

50 Cohen died in 2013.

51 The conference noted in endnote 46 was aimed in large part at challenging the inclusion of paedophilia and hebephilia in the incipient revised edition of the Diagnostic and Statistical Manual of the American Psychiatric Association (DSM-5). Pro-paedophile ideologues are always keen to argue that the sexual desire for children is normal and not pathological. They have no interest in a *general* critique of psychiatric diagnosis but only on their perception that a diagnosis is inappropriate in *their own case*. Thus, we can make a distinction between a legitimate critique of psychiatric diagnosis in the wake of DSM-5 and the special pleading of pro-paedophile advocates. See Pilgrim, D. (2015). Influencing mental health policy: DSM-5 as a disciplinary challenge for psychology. *Review of General Psychology* 18(4), 293–301. Note that if we naïvely accept that paedophilia is a minority form of sexual pathology then this limits our understanding of the full scale of CSA. Many adults offending against children do not fulfil DSM criteria for paedophilia, reminding us that the latter narrow category should not be conflated with child sexual offending. Not only do a small minority of paedophiles not offend, but some offenders also are not paedophiles by psychiatric criteria. See Cossins, A. (2000). *Masculinities, Sexualities and Child Sexual Abuse*. The Hague: Kluwer Law International.

10

PROTECTING CHILDREN FROM SEXUAL VICTIMISATION

Introduction

If we are unconvinced by moral panic arguments and libertarian special pleading for unbounded 'intimate citizenship', then we have to face the challenge of protecting individual children from the sexual advances of adults. This chapter considers the practical aspects of that broad task. One starting point for this discussion is the overarching policy intention of the European Council Treaty (201) issued in 2007.

> This Convention [Treaty 201] is the first instrument to establish the various forms of sexual abuse of children as criminal offences, including such abuse committed in the home or family, with the use of force, coercion or threats. Preventive measures outlined in the Convention include the screening, recruitment and training of people working in contact with children, making children aware of the risks and teaching them to protect themselves, as well as monitoring measures for offenders and potential offenders. The Convention also establishes programmes to support victims, encourages people to report suspected sexual exploitation and abuse, and sets up telephone and internet helplines for children. It also ensures that certain types of conduct are classified as criminal offences, such as engaging in sexual activities with a child below the legal age and child prostitution and pornography. The Convention also criminalises the solicitation of children for sexual purposes ("grooming") and "sex tourism". With the aim of combating child sex tourism, the Convention establishes that individuals can be prosecuted for some offences even when the act is committed abroad. The new legal tool also ensures that child victims are protected during judicial proceedings, for example with regard to their identity and privacy.

This statement sets out the agenda of improving child protection. If we consider the devil in the detail of it and its practical implications, we must start with the methodological challenge of estimating the scale of the problem, which in turn has implications for its definition (I discussed this in Chapter 3).

Estimates are inflected by the definitions we use. If a very wide definition of CSA is used to include, for example, kissing a child on the lips or stroking their arm sensually, then this will generate markedly different rates of prevalence than one limited only to coerced penetrative sexual activity. Similarly, if we only focus on true active paedophilia, then it will only address pre-pubescent victims and not take into account hebephilia. Also, CSA can occur at the hands of other children and can be situational: some adults only act out against children in specific circumstances, as in incestuous contact, which itself may range from being persistent over years to a one-off occurrence.

These situated events can be distinguished from those particular perpetrators who have clear prone disposition to target children in a specified age range recurrently for sexual gratification. Typically, that type of offender starts young and then can accumulate hundreds of victims during their lifetime. They develop a preoccupation about children in the way that drug addicts are obsessed by drugs in their lives or gamblers persist in the financial ruin of their family. Some (but not all) have no interest in having sex with adult partners at all. Those who can perform sexually with adults may use the latter to access child victims. In turn, these core prototypical sex offenders can be distinguished from those who desire children but desist for moral reasons (i.e. the celibate, 'virtuous' or 'moral' paedophile or hebephile).[1]

To complicate matters, when we are estimating risk to children, other factors than sexual interest are relevant. For example, core recidivist sexual abusers of children are more likely than the general population to display other criminal tendencies. This linkage probably reflects a pervasive lack of conscience more typical in offender populations than in the general population. Comparing the 'moral' paedophile with the 'amoral' paedophile is instructive for this reason.

One explanation for this is the well-known cycle of abuse (i.e. brutal adults were often brutalised as children). While this explanation could fit well with physical and emotional abuse, it works very poorly for CSA. Some, but not all, of those who sexually abuse children were abused themselves and most children abused do not go on to abuse others. Many perpetrators (abused or not themselves) simply deny that abuse is the matter at hand. For example, the unrepentant 'political paedophile' Tom O'Carroll, discussed in Chapter 8, boasts of his loving upbringing and deals with his desire by re-casting it as a civil right not an immoral impulse.

Most victims of CSA are girls (by a ratio of 3:1)[2] but women only constitute a minority of offenders. It seems that being a victim inflects the chances of abusing others, but it is neither a necessary nor a sufficient condition. Those survivors of abuse who victimise others do not feel compassion for new victims. Instead of seeking justice for themselves and fellow victims, they simply impose further injustice on newcomers. They re-enact their own abuse but now as perpetrator. This all suggests that a mechanistic formulation of a 'cycle of abuse' is not fit for purpose in this field, though it may apply in some individual cases and so warrants some reflection.

The recidivist sex offender has to learn a moral position (or feign doing so) for the very reason that they did not adopt that moral position already. In other words, there was a failure of primary socialisation from their culture, in relation to adult–child sexual contact.[3] In a sense, this is no different to other forms of criminal action: typically, criminals understand the literal *meaning* of illegality but they have no moral sympathy for it. If they did not understand that, in principle, what they were doing was wrong, then they would make few efforts to evade detection or make excuses for themselves or lie assuredly when they are detected. The detected offender against children behaves with the very same range of evasions, deceit and excuse-making of any other criminal.

Also, they have an impaired inner control on transgression. They experience less guilt, shame and anxiety typically experienced by the non-offender. Instead, their anxiety is not about transgression in itself but about being *detected and punished*. Indeed, other emotions, such as the thrill of transgression, may come into play instead. The furtive scheming of PIE members, discussed in the previous chapter, highlights this point about evasion of detection and thrill seeking. By contrast, the virtuous or moral paedophile *does* have the inner inhibitions of shame and guilt, not just anticipatory anxiety about being caught (see below).

These definitional matters are noted here because they are important. They point to the complex picture about those who sexually offend against children, in terms of their motives and conscience, their offending profile and their preferred forms of sexual activity. However, it is *because* there is a definitional challenge, then sometimes those who crave sexual intimacy with children can slide around in their self-justifications. Once they claim to reject only the explosive rape of a child, then everything else can be made into a matter of harmless fun, a social construction or even a reasonable civil right. Individual offenders and the academics I critiqued in the two previous chapters go through the same contortions of reasoning, which leaves most of us unconvinced. However, the challenge of defining CSA can play into the interests of that contorted world.

Features of the offender population

I mentioned in the introduction to the book a conservative estimate of 1–2% of adults, most of whom are men, being a core group of those with a lifelong and recurrent sexual interest in children. Another figure of 5% has been estimated by the Canadian psychologist James Cantor, but this would include the prevalence of less coercive acts and those that could be classified as 'situational' rather than 'dispositional' (see above). Cantor also offers a biopsychosocial account of offenders he has studied. A picture of lower IQ and raised levels of childhood head injury emerges from this as relevant factors. The head injury tendency might also explain sex offending being embedded often within general antisocial activity and criminality.[4] Indeed, with incorrigible sex offenders, it may be their general antisocial outlook is as important to consider as their sexual preferences *per se*, when we try to predict reoffending.[5]

In a recent review of the evidence on adult male interest in pre-pubescent children, we find the following picture from community samples (i.e. not prisoners or forensic patients who are sex offenders). Around 9% reported that they would use 'child pornography' or actually have sex with a child if they would not get caught.[6] Around 1% reported that they currently enjoyed sexual activity with children in practice.[7] In studies of internet use, the term 'preteen' was the third commonest search term and around 20% of internet porn use entails images of children.[8] The regular use of these images is a better predictor of offending than even the presence of a previous offence against a child. That three-way link between the Internet, sexual fantasies and predation against children is made strongly by the authors overviewing this literature.[9]

Finally, in this section, it is worth noting that although risk factors (beyond being male) must involve dynamic factors (such as place of the offender and their emotional state), there are certain personal features that seem to increase the probability of sexual offending against children. Perpetrator characteristics of contact offending include: younger offender age; never been married; poor educational achievement; prior criminal activity (especially violent and sexual offending); conditional release failure in the past; substance misuse; collection of non-internet pornography; and sexual interest in young adolescents. The list is slightly different for internet offenders, where higher intelligence and educational level than the average are noted.[10] What dominates the lists of risk factors are three features: the regular masturbatory use of indecent images of children; prior criminality involving coercion; and a persistent and focused sexual interest in children.

When we consider perpetrators under regimes where adult–child sexual contact is roundly condemned and criminalised, those trends of antisocial conduct and sexual interest draw us into pathologising (with fair cause) those who sexually offend against children. But this is a first-world discourse. In some parts of the world, such contact is normalised. Figure 10.1 shows a recent bar chart summary from UNICEF about the scale of child brides in the early twentieth century, which illuminates this point.

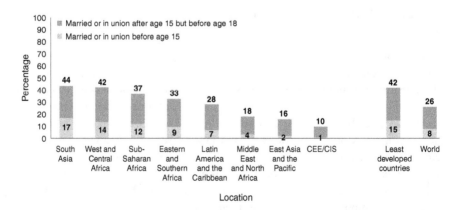

FIGURE 10.1 Global frequency of child brides

If the policy advice of libertarians discussed in the previous two chapters were followed, the above bar chart would be rendered irrelevant. The argument goes that our concern, especially in relation to the grey band referring to under-15-year-olds, is simply an artefact of cultural and legal definitions of the appropriate age to offer sexual consent. My counter-argument to this is that the harm done to child brides is evident: they are denied a period of personal development ('lost childhood') in which they form peer relationships; their schooling period is curtailed as they are subjugated in a domestic role from a young age; and they are exposed to genital injury and the health risks associated with early teenage pregnancies entailing immature pelvic development (including death in labour and vesico-vaginal fistulas). Thus, what we call a 'civilising process', for the libertarians might include the right of children to have sex with adults. I would argue instead that such a suggestion reflects a de-civilising tendency; the reader will make their own judgement at this point.

What is to be done with perpetrators?

Some criminologists have expressed an understandable concern that some forms of criminal activity have invoked a primitive and regressive impulse for forms of punishment that were linked to pre-Enlightenment times. An example could then be of the retention of the death penalty for proven perpetrators of CSA. In January 2017, Donald Trump announced that he would introduce the death penalty for sexual offences against children, in response to this trend of punitive or retributive populist demand.

If state execution is not to be the default position at present, then what is the alternative? One is to permanently segregate offenders from new victims and this has two versions: 'life means life' imprisonment or a *cordon sanitaire*. The latter could involve sending child sex offenders to islands without escape and with no access to children or the Internet to obtain indecent images.

In the meantime, most countries do not have capital punishment for non-homicide offending. Moreover, permanent segregation of some sort is rarely evident about offences against children, though there may be a health-economic case for its warranted costs to the public purse. For example, sentencing policy is very flexible, with some repeat offenders routinely being jailed for periods of a couple of years and some being given much longer periods (see examples given in earlier chapters). Often, the non-offending general public may be unaware of this variation and naïvely expect lengthy sentencing to be the norm.

The cost of permanent imprisonment (say a 'three strikes and out' policy for habitual offenders) would offset the costs currently incurred by treating offenders, which I am now about to address. The policy would pre-empt the distress and dysfunction created in potential victims. Substance misuse, self-harm and a range of post-traumatic states presenting to mental health services by distressed victims would be prevented if that permanent incarceration policy were to be implemented efficiently.

Given the prevalence of sexual offences against children (if we include the downloading of indecent images), permanent segregation would be extensive in its scale. If we add together a 1–2% estimate of persistent sexual interest in pre-pubescent children to some portion of the 20% of men who find children sexually arousing and access online indecent images, then the scale of offending becomes obvious. Take the example of the UK. Currently, it contains just over 20 million males between the ages of 16 and 64. Focusing on a conservative estimate of offenders of 1% in the first ('persistent interest') group, then that would translate into at least 200,000 child sex offenders. (This sort of estimate can be calculated approximately for other countries where the adult male population is known.)

This figure does not include any estimate of the actions of a larger 20% group potentially sexually aroused by children, nor of male offenders over 64. It is true that a small minority of paedophiles are celibate,[11] but my conservative estimate (of 1% not 2%) readily eliminates that caution. Also, using the 200,000 calculation for a further estimate, if each of them had only *one* victim, then it would imply that 200,000 children in the UK would be sexually victimised by men. This life prevalence estimate of one victim per perpetrator is highly conservative because it does not take into consideration multiple victimisation, nor the victims of female offenders. A core group of recidivist offenders against children have multiple victims.[12]

Thus, the option preferred by those favouring capital punishment has an economic, not just punitive, dimension to its case. Its scale would also be significant. Apart from the large number of state executions the policy would spawn, a steady flow of guilty prisoners on death row would continue. CSA and those adults who sustain an unshakeable sexual desire for children are not like, say, smallpox that could be eliminated permanently by a known policy for eradication. They will always be with us to some extent and killing detected perpetrators would create costs (of judicial process and criminal investigation). Thus, if we support capital punishment for incorrigible child sex offenders, as some countries do at present and so could in the future, then we need to be clear about our motives and be prepared to use state execution on a very large scale. The moral case is largely vengeful, and so to my mind dubious. An economic case could be made, but it would have some costs not just benefits, which would need to be expressed honestly.

For those of us opposed to capital punishment in principle, the extensive challenge of containing child sexual offending is now laid bare. It has been added to by the ready availability of online offending. The commercialisation of the production and distribution of online indecent images of children, involving sexual acts with adults, not just nudity, has been a 'game changer' in the past 20 years.

In the USA, the National Crimes Against Children Research Center reported a growth in arrests for possession of online indecent images of children. For example, in 2006, there were 3,672 such arrests, whereas in 2009 it was 4,901. The upward trend is indicated by the comparable figure for arrests in 2001, which was 1,713. The arrests were in diverse locations and predominantly of white offenders, though the profile of the group became more ethnically diverse as the decade progressed. Two-thirds of the offenders were single, but about a quarter lived with someone under the age of 18. A methodological conundrum here is about the meaning of this trend. It might be a reflection of more efficient police detection and resource levels or an actual measure of increased offending (or, more likely, a combination, in some ratio).

More recent British data confirms this picture of rising levels of online offending. In June 2016, a Freedom of Information request from the NSPCC about offending data held by the police found that, in the previous year, there were 100 children raped on the images detected being used online.[13] One of these was of a child under the age of one. Moreover, this data trawl was very limited. It did not include information from six local police forces. Even with this restricted sample of police data, 3,000 offences were on record between April 2015 and March 2016. Of these, 270 children below the age of ten were victimised.

A statement from the National Police Chiefs' Council said that internet-related abuse was one factor underpinning an estimated 80% increase in the reporting of child sex offences in the previous four years. The statement also noted the methodological challenge of discerning the source of this increased reporting (better identification methods and/or actual rises in offending rates?). The police and NSPCC agreed that this picture revealed the 'tip of the iceberg' of online offending. The sheer volume of offending online now means that a full investigation of all cases is beyond the capacity of the police. However, some offenders are caught and many are put on sex offender treatment programmes, the focus of the next section.

The role of detection and treatment programmes

Turning, then, to the commonest current policy option, which is the detection and episodic detention[14] of child sex offenders, along with treatment interventions, how do they operate and are they effective? This question refers to what in public health is called 'tertiary prevention'.[15] That is, can we identify, and intervene in, the actions of those who have already sexually abused children in order to lessen the probability of that happening more? In answering this question, the first element is detection, and this has two policy elements. The first relates to the ability of the police to detect offenders in any setting accurately, with that word referring to both the 'true positives' I discussed in Chapter 2 and the scale of the offending. In other words, 'accurately' here refers to both identifying and accusing offenders fairly *and* it refers to ensuring that cases of abuse do not go *undetected*. Libertarians (such as Frank Furedi and Barbara Hewson, see below) tend to emphasise justice for adults accused[16] and the perverse motives of accusers. Child protection lobbyists focus instead on justice for victims. 'Innocence' has a different connotation and emphasis across this divide.

The second element to tertiary prevention relates to the effectiveness of interventions. Preventative detention is only fail-safe if it is permanent (e.g. the notion noted above of a lifelong *cordon sanitaire*, which debars sex offenders from ever being in contact with children). Even if that policy were deployed, then if that segregated population of offenders retained access to the Internet then they could continue to offend online. Moreover, given that, for now, in many countries, such as the UK, sexual offences against children rarely entail lifelong segregation, then the development of interventions which succeed in reducing the probability of offending is extremely important and, likewise in its wake, methods of research which demonstrate that success.

No matter how much 'treatment' for child sexual offenders is available, it will not prevent offending at the outset[17] and, even when offered, it only reduces reoffending in some individuals, some of the time. Most seem to be impervious to intervention. Indeed, reviews of sex offender programmes have suggested that treatment has a very weak impact on reoffending levels. For example, in one well-controlled study which compared rapists and child sex offenders treated with cognitive-behaviour therapy and those simply imprisoned, there was no difference in relapse rates.[18]

This might suggest that the fear of re-arrest and detention might be a deterrent for some offenders, rather than treatment programmes *per se*. There was a subgroup of offenders who were 'better bets'. In their case, the intervention was well carried out ('treatment fidelity') and the offenders adhered well to the treatment contract. However, overall, treatment effects (compared to the deprivations and personal learning during mere incarceration) were not well demonstrated. Thus, we would be unwise to rely on sex offender treatment programmes as *the core feature* of a policy to reduce risk to children. What marginal impact they have is at the aggregate level of risk reduction, i.e. they do not predict *individual risk*, which of course is the very concern that those around released sex offenders focus upon, quite understandably.

This outcome of poor treatment efficacy is not that surprising. Just as pro-social behaviour tends to be a lifelong habit, so too with antisocial behaviour, such as sexual offending; old habits die hard for all of us. What research on incorrigibility in this field shows us is that general antisociality seems to increase the risk to children; maybe the virtuous paedophiles represent the opposite end of the spectrum to this group. A review of studies of recidivism in nearly 30,000 child sex offenders indicate that it is a combination of a primary sexual interest in children alongside general antisocial habits that predict a high risk of reoffending.[19] The genuinely celibate paedophile desists from acting on their desires for the very reason that they are people with a conscience and know that sexual contact with children is wrong and potentially harmful to individual victims.[20]

The perpetrator-setting context of CSA

It has been clear in most of the case studies given in this book that sexual offending against children, though underestimated in its scale and emotive in its character, is no different in one sense to any other sort of conduct. If we want to understand human conduct we need to be inclusive in our formulations about the agent of the actions, on the one hand, and their situating context, which includes opportunities to offend and the non-intervention of third parties, on the other. The models of child sexual offender available to us vary in their consideration of these two core factors; these can be seen in Table 10.1.

TABLE 10.1 Theories of sexual offending against children

Model/theory[21]	Source	Perpetrator factors	Contextual factors	Comments
Four preconditions model	Finkelhor (1984)[22]	1. Motivation 2. Overcoming inner inhibitions of guilt or shame 3. Overcoming external inhibition from others 4. Manipulation of the child	Opportunities to act in relation to four perpetrator factors	Focus on perpetrator action and motivation. A psychological model but with context being left vague
Quadripartite model	Hall and Hirschamn (1992)[23]	1. Sexual attraction to children 2. Assume children are participants 3. Poor impulse control 4. Personality disturbance	As above	As above
Pathways model	Ward and Seighart (2002)[24]	Combination of two models above leads to pathways of offending in particular individuals	As above, but focuses on contextual factors in shaping a pathway of offending	Inclusive model to encourage multi-factorial formulations. Context is foregrounded
Confluence model of sexual aggression	Malamuth (1998)[25]	Two main factors (hostile masculinity and sexual promiscuity) merge to create rapists	Wholly focused on predatory implications of two factors across but does make link with general antisociality	Mainly applicable to those who rape adults but has elements that can transfer across to children in some cases
Integrated theory of sexual offending	Marshall and Barbaree (1990)[26]	Emphasises the biography of offenders and the factors that lead to their sense of poor self-worth and nurturing attachments	The context of the perpetrator's development is the focus but it is individualistic	Psychological focus on the perpetrator, not their offending context
Evolutionary theory of sexual offending	Thornhill and Palmer (2000)[27]	Evolutionary theory to explain male sexual aggression required to pass on genes	Context is irrelevant as sexual offending is genetically driven	Reductionist and fails to address non-genetic factors to explain why most men are not sexually aggressive

Thus, with the exception of the 'pathways model' in Table 10.1, the others show the limitations of a perpetrator-focused approach to protecting children. Those limitations arise from forms of individualism which psychological models are prone to. That is what psychologists do: they tend to focus on the relationship between experience and behaviour within individuals (in this case the perpetrators of CSA).

For psychology (and psychiatry), typically, the 'environment' is always a given, but vague, backdrop to any form of conduct. However, we need a more elaborate version, which offers a rich and dynamic picture of *context*. I introduced one version of context ('field') from Pierre Bourdieu in Chapter 6. Any particular field will be open, in flux, involve past, present and future aspects and is always multi-factorial in character. Complexity is inevitable in open systems. All of these field features need detailed consideration, case by case, not bundled up simplistically as 'the environment'. In this case, ecological complexity needs to take into account places such as:

1. The home
2. Social media
3. The school
4. Private places of tuition
5. Sports clubs
6. Scouting
7. Youth groups
8. Nurseries
9. Entertainment venues for children
10. Parks and other play areas
11. Residential childcare facilities.

Where children are then needs to be a policy focus for all responsible adults in those settings. Much has been achieved already in this regard but that trend needs to continue and not be diverted by the singular focus on perpetrators. In particular, the forms of isolation that come with each of these places and the degree of scrutiny from those with a protective rather than predatory orientation to children are important; this matter of varieties of systemic isolation was discussed in Chapter 4.

Desistance as a connecting theme across forms of prevention

A bridge between all forms of prevention in relation to perpetrators is the matter of desistance. That is, how do some adults who are sexually attracted to children resist putting their desire into practice? At present, schemes that allow men (it is usually men) who have such urges to seek early help are less readily available than sex offender treatment programmes for proven offenders. Lessons from research on primary or original desistance (i.e. the genuinely permanent inaction of the truly celibate paedophile) and subsequent desistance (i.e. from ex-prisoners who truly do not reoffend, rather than those who offend but avoid detection) are also very important for child protection policy.

This matter of desistance connects to a psychological process we can all understand. All of us at times have the impulse to act in a way that might offend or harm others; as we develop, we learn to control our aggressive impulses and sexual desires in the world. Most of us, most of the time, succeed in this task, but this general trend signals that what makes those who offend against children different is not that they are special in relation to having sexual and aggressive impulses. What makes them different is that their impulses involve objects of desire, which are disallowed according to social norms (and will be for the foreseeable future). The celibate paedophile in good conscience and out of guilt, shame or both then desists from acting on his desire. By contrast, the non-celibate paedophile or the intra-familial offender simply acts out his desire and then seeks to avoid detection.

For this reason, research on how we resist acting in an antisocial manner is important in this field. Also, research on how individual offenders rationalise and deny the antisocial aspects of their sexual contact with children complements this point. A recurring finding in the 'treatment' of sex offenders is that they think about their action differently from non-offenders ('cognitive distortions'). These justifications include the belief that the victim was a willing participant, with the full capacity to reflect on his or her actions, as well as the belief that they enjoyed the activity and that it was harmless to them in the short and long term. This complex of convenient assumptions recurs in those who offend against children.

The academic justifications I criticised in the previous two chapters provide a ready-made rationalisation for child sex offenders, deleting the need to consider the importance of desistance. The latter might also be comforted by political libertarians such as Barbara Hewson, who selectively focus on the *assumed* financial gain of victims, rather than the harm done to them:

> One of the driving factors behind this hysteria is the compensation industry. This plays a key role in the explosive amplification of claims of abuse. It began in the US, with the upsurge in litigation about clerical-abuse scandals in the 1980s. As Philip Jenkins noted in *Pedophiles and Priests: Anatomy of a Contemporary Crisis* (1996): 'Intensive litigation and high-damages awards effectively create a range of interest groups with a powerful interest in discovering and exposing new clerical-abuse cases, and in the most visible public forum.'[28]

In contrast to this cynical approach to child sex offending, the pro-social position adopted by celibate paedophiles and expressed in the work of the online group Virtuous Paedophiles contains lessons about keeping the agency of those who sexually desire children in clear focus. A positive dialogue with that group is implied. That dialogue does not come easy within a general population in which there is a mixture of collective denial and episodic explosive anger about the topic of adult–child sexual contact.

Finally, in this section, we can note that we need to bring the complicity of others, as well as ecological risk factors, into the picture, and not limit our attention to the psychopathology of perpetrators alone. Perpetrators are fascinating and the judicial system tends to focus on their moral autonomy and individual culpability, but this leads us to focus overly on the responsibilities or compulsions of only *one party* within a complex picture. As the earlier chapters in this book pointed up, what we see recurrently and sadly[29] is that good men and women stand by and do nothing when faced with the evidence, or strong suspicion, that CSA is happening in their presence. Currently, an unhelpful expression of interventionism from the general public is vigilantism, which the police co-opt at times but with some reservations (see Box 10.1).

BOX 10.1 CITIZENS' ACTION ABOUT CHILD SEX OFFENDERS

Vigilantism tends to emerge in any society when law enforcement is either absent or is perceived to be ineffectual by ordinary citizens. In its most passive form, it entails ordinary people acting as agents of surveillance for the police (such as 'Neighbourhood Watch' schemes). The co-option by the state of lay involvement in public services is now common (called 'co-production') and began its life in community policing initiatives.[30]

As far as organised anti-paedophile vigilante activity is concerned, this has focused on the detection of strangers online planning to meet up with those they believe to be children, after indulging in sexualised conversations with them. On April 27, 2016, in the UK, Channel 4 screened an episode of their series *24 Hours in Police Custody*.[31] It involved a group called 'Paedo Hunters' led by a man calling himself 'Chris Fear'. The latter's girlfriend engaged in online chats with likely offenders, leading them to believe that she was a 12-year-old girl. A first meeting would then be arranged and a group of men would pitch up to confront the bemused (and frightened) offender.[32] In the case of the screened programme, the vigilantes caught two offenders, both of whom were prosecuted successfully and received prison sentences (of 28 months and 15 months).

In both of the cases reported, they were indignant about being caught (seeing themselves as victims of unwarranted harassment) and showed no immediate signs of either shame or guilt about their sexual intentions. They did show signs of fear and desperation, though, about the personal and social consequences of their *detection*. They had a twin narrative for themselves. On the one hand they argued, and maybe believed, that they had done nothing wrong. On the other hand, they were more than aware of the social censorship and rejection that may well ensue with their exposure.

A grey area is exposed by these cases, in relation to the notion of 'entrapment'. In the programme, the police were worried that the Crown Prosecution Service would refuse to endorse charges being made because of the fake identity of the victim and the luring of the offenders. Usually, the term 'entrapment' refers to *police* (i.e. not citizen) activity of this sort, which might jeopardise a successful prosecution. Strictly, then, entrapment is used to describe police subterfuge but its meaning seems to generalise at times to investigative journalists and vigilantes. Because it involves deceit and the encouragement of crime (not merely its *post hoc* detection) then it is ethically dubious, even if, at times, it is effective in practice.

Another problem the police faced in the Channel 4 screening was that the mobile phone recording of the apprehension of the accused by the vigilantes was posted online directly after the arrest but prior to a decision to formally charge. The vigilantes were only prepared to remove the 'viral' sharing online of the public encounter with the accused once a charge was made. This aspect of the case (more than that of the legal or semantic technicalities of 'entrapment') seemed to threaten the prospect of a successful prosecution. What the vigilantes were doing was jeopardising a fair trial by placing evidence in the public domain in advance of court proceedings.[33] They were also using a bullying tactic against the police, thereby undermining the rule of law.

In light of the need to encourage pro-social (i.e. truly celibate) paedophiles to come out and seek support, acts of contrived entrapment and vigilantism, with violence always hovering menacingly, may be counter-productive. Adults sexually attracted to children are human beings who do things, or want to do things, that are morally condemned. Vigilantism is a crude response to resolve that tension. It largely boosts the egos of 'paedo hunters' and provides them with the temporary satisfaction of enacting rough justice or the release of revenge if they are survivors of CSA. The evident risks and benefits of vigilantism pose a serious challenge for all citizens about what an appropriate response should be as a middle way between indifference, moral stupor or being a passive bystander on the one hand, and being a risk-taking vigilante on the other.

A different form of citizens' action than the contrived vigilantism just discussed is when (non-abusing) parents seek to protect their children from risk. Parents may actively monitor the circumstances under which their children may be at risk and act in response to that perceived risk.

In April 2016, the *Sunday Mirror* reported a case that resembled that of 'Chris Fear' and his girlfriend, noted above. It involved an adult meeting up with a man in a park who believed that he was about to see a 12-year-old girl that he had groomed online: on this occasion, though, the adult woman confronting him was a mother, not a vigilante displaying their power. She had come across the online grooming of her daughter and then taken over the conversation in order to lure the man into public view. She informed the police and coordinated their attendance at the point of meeting to make an arrest.

Given the rise in internet grooming, parental protection does have a role to play. Indeed, any party relevant to disruption of the use of the Internet by offenders may in the future be important. This also points up that when we consider the ecology of risk, then the Internet is important now as a field of opportunity for offenders, both as groomers and consumers of indecent images, created by the abuse of children in the recent past (or even in vivo). Parents and those acting in *loco parentis* can hereon play a protective role by disrupting the impact of the Internet.

Advice from child protection experts

Those charged with investigating wrongdoing, such as Alex Jay, reported in Chapter 4, tend to focus on social administrative recommendations aimed at minimising the chances of mistakes being made in the local state apparatus. Policies, procedures and protocols are examined and managerial responsibilities in the police and social services are of most salience in such reports. Similarly, those charged with the forensic investigation of alleged cases of CSA share their view of priorities. For example, from the USA, Colleen Friend and Susan Snyder discussing Ross Cheit's book *The Witch-Hunt Narrative: Politics, Psychology and the Sexual Abuse of Children* (noted in the previous chapter), argue that we need to focus on six priorities:[34]

1. Enhancing the training of teachers in CSA.
2. Improving court processes in relation to the needs of victims.
3. Applying best practice forensic interview protocols to improve efficiency in complex cases of vulnerable children in 'multi-problem families' and those with disabilities.
4. Broadening our consideration of CSA to include prevention and recovery for victims.
5. Using multistate (this was a US study) research on allegations of CSA in day care settings.
6. Educating juries and the general public about the complexities of CSA prosecutions and 'the illusion of toughness in how we respond to convicted offenders'.

This checklist is another reminder about CSA being everyone's business. The final point reflects a frustration of some working in the field of child protection that the public may not appreciate the relatively weak and inconsistent measures currently deployed by the criminal justice system to reduce reoffending. Prevention is mentioned in the checklist and, for some policy researchers, this is the highest priority.

Stephen Smallbone and his colleagues[35] have been prominent in this preventative approach. Much is known about perpetrators, especially about the success of treatment or tertiary prevention, which has been fairly poor to date (see above). What we have a less clear research base about is *primary* prevention. As they point out, if we for now 'park' our concern with existing offenders in favour of other parties and settings, then we are beginning to map out a belt-and-braces, or multi-factorial, approach to protect children from sexual victimisation. These primary prevention initiatives (many of which have now been triggered but await full expression in practice and repeated evaluations) include:

1. Personal safety programmes for children.
2. Resilience building in children.
3. Enlargement of guardianship (i.e. all adults should shift from passive bystander to guardian mode).
4. Identifying and then minimising situational risks in organisational and public settings (the conditions of ecological isolation that increase risk).
5. Improving public education about the complexities and scale of CSA.
6. Community services and community capacity building.

This list fits with the lessons learned across the earlier chapters. Although we should not overload children with the responsibility for self-protection, they do have a role to play. Likewise, all adults do have a responsibility to protect children and deal with evidence they have about those at risk or the conduct of offenders. The ecological aspects of risk are vital to map in every organisation and public setting where children and adults interact. The public do need to understand more about CSA. Much of the content of this book has been about exploring that complexity. This is a different exercise to the one offered by pro-paedophile groups and their academic apologists, and so a public understanding should also include an awareness of the *existence* of that tension or ideological struggle.

Community engagement is an extension of that opening up of the specialist arena of child protection. Leaving CSA to agents of the local state is simply not enough. Moreover, child protection experts, in the main, become involved when the dreadful has already happened. This means that they are wedded to identifying adult wrongdoing and preventing harm to children who have *already* been abused. That role is very important and highly necessary, but it is not primary prevention. This is also true of offering therapeutic help for survivors.[36]

Sarah Nelson[37] has recently offered her account of a prevention strategy and child protection priorities. Echoing the work of Ross Cheit, she emphasises that a range of social forces have created a backlash against taking the scale of CSA seriously. These include a tendency to use numbers of convictions and children placed on child protection registers as a valid measure for *actual* levels of risk in society. (In Chapter 8, I discussed the naïvety of confusing the empirical with the actual and thus ignoring the iceberg of offending.) For more accurate measures of offending to be recognised accurately, Nelson notes that more information flows about abuse need to be set up and adult culture needs to move more confidently from being atomised passive bystanders to a position of collective active guardianship. Professionals need to work consistently across agencies (health and social services, policing and education) to protect children. She endorses community-based initiatives, suggested by those like Smallbone et al. above, and she argues that governments should now make internet offending a top priority. The tendency of state agencies to forget lessons from the past and not even put into practice what is well known, is highlighted here by Nelson:

> why does the criminal justice system still rely heavily on children disclosing sexual abuse, when we know most children do not? Why have possible indicators of sexual abuse long been written into child protection guidelines if hardly anyone acts on them? Why does the medical model still dominate in mental health when psychiatric wards have always been filled with the victims of child sexual abuse?[38]

Those involved specifically in social-work interventions also offer practitioners advice. A fuller account of this can be found in Davies and Duckett.[39] In summary, they advise practitioners about the following. First, appraisals of power discrepancies in relationships are needed at all times and judgements about when these become abusive need to be made. Second, a detailed collation and appraisal of information is required. This means that the fuller the formulation of risk, the better chances that a child will be protected. Third, typically, social workers are more confident in attending to the first two points in family work, with male perpetrators, but may be less sure of making formulations about female offending or historical reporting or non-familial abuse (for example, at the hands of criminal gangs). Fourth, some types of children are more at risk but they are also harder to assess; this is one reason why they are targeted by perpetrators. Younger children may not be aware they are being abused and subjectively and objectively they have less autonomy to report what is happening to them. This extra vulnerability is also true of children with disabilities, a point emphasised by Friend and Snyder above.

This advice from policy researchers is all underpinned by the striking lesson, reflected throughout this book, that we are collectively responsible for either being complicit in, or in challenging, CSA in our midst. The conundrum about vigilantism, noted in Box 10.1, points to the need for greater clarity in localities about what citizens *should* do optimally to protect children at risk, with the agreement and routine support of the police. Citizen–police synergy could still be improved about detection of imminent offending. That secondary prevention approach is important, but we need to remember it is still offender focused. The primary prevention list noted above from Smallbone and backed up by others remains the most important policy priority.

Conclusion

We all need to be aware of our contribution to the collective denial about the presence and scale of CSA. That moral stupor involves non-offenders acting with complicity and it allows perpetrators to go unchallenged. Also, we need to be aware that child sex offenders' own accounts reflect that wider process of denial (from lying about offending, to arguing that the child was not harmed or exploited, to arguing that 'non-contact' offending is a trivial matter).

The relationship between the self-deceptions of offenders, and similar intellectual arguments in social science, bears particular critical scrutiny. Some social constructivist arguments from contrarian academics provide us with a lot of words but little substantive evidence. However, they may still give comfort and legitimacy to perpetrators. The academic community is now a site of ideological struggle about child protection. The continued, and I think perverse, insistence by some academics that CSA is merely a moral panic is the focus of that struggle. Behind that, there are still residual traces of a libertarian intellectual defence, found across many disciplines, about adult–child sexual contact.

We are facing a major public policy challenge about adults who sexually abuse children. 'Treatment' programmes are needed but they are only marginally effective and so other means to keep children safe are required, including a sensibility about the ecology of risk. The successful disruption of online offending now presents the largest problem for law enforcement agencies. A range of primary prevention measures are now available to us but they need to be systematically appraised, and what we already know works should be put into routine practice; this is not currently the case. This would be a separate exercise from researching offender treatment programmes and implementing best practice. There may be grounds, though, to focus on researching primary prevention via the ongoing desistance of celibate paedophiles.

Another aspect of poor application of evidence is the failure of the psychiatric system to recognise the high proportion of survivors of CSA in its care and control. Rather than merely diagnosing what is wrong with patients[40] they should shift instead to formulating routinely what has happened to them in their lives. A history of childhood adversity is very common in adults with mental health problems and, within that, sexual abuse creates a particular personal toll. It is only possible to help a person who has survived CSA if its occurrence is acknowledged honestly by professionals. If the *current* distress and dysfunction of the patient is the only focus then crimes from the *past* are being ignored. Psychiatric service norms thereby are part of a wider picture of complicity about sexual crimes against children.

CSA is a global problem and boys and girls from poorer nations are at greater risk of sexual exploitation. Sex tourism in developing countries, the making there of indecent images and child brides are all reminders to those of us in the developed world about the international dimension to CSA. The Internet now beams into the homes of sex offenders the abuse of children far away. This is not 'child pornography' but recordable evidence of sex crimes. Interactive sites allow offenders to give moment-to-moment instructions about the *in vivo* abuse of children.[41] The thrill of present involvement shows that offenders online are direct perpetrators, not merely the passive users of masturbatory material already produced. The Internet has now ensured that the boundary between sexual voyeurism and rape has been broken. There is no turning back to the 1970s, when rationalisations from PIE or NAMBLA celebrated the existence of 'kiddie porn' or, hypocritically, offered their members images with more artistic pretensions (see Chapter 9).

Children have a right to grow up without the predatory sexual attention of adults, whether this emerges by cunning stealth or by crude force. Those adults have no right to put their desire and curiosity into practice. This is indeed a human rights issue but not in relation to the 'democratic' right of adults to express their sexual needs in any circumstances. Children cannot be 'participants' in 'intergenerational sex' because of their underdeveloped mental capacity and their lack of power, compared to adults. 'Intimate citizenship' has had long-standing and important moral limits; it should not include adults having sex with children, animals[42] or corpses. I cannot envisage any society in the future 'normalising' such practices.

For both moral and public health reasons, CSA should not be tolerated. This book has set out the case for that conclusion. It has drawn particular attention to the interest groups in political, professional, religious, criminal and academic life, which have obstructed progress about our honest and realistic understanding of an under-reported, and often underestimated, public policy challenge. As a clinical academic, I have focused my main attention in the closing chapters of this book on how, troublingly, some sections of the academic community have been part of this wider web of complicity. Intellectual competence has been co-opted for a questionable cause and rhetoric has been preferred to evidence.

To finish, and for emphasis, we might recall the quote I used in the previous chapter from Stanley Cohen:

> Intellectuals who keep silent about what they know, who ignore the crimes that matter by moral standards, are even more culpable when their society is free and open. They can speak freely but choose not to.[43]

This exhortation from a key figure within moral panic theory should be well heeded by those allegedly celebrating his legacy, as well as those of us who are less in its thrall.

Notes

1 The online group 'Virtuous Paedophiles' is an important example of this. It is a group of people who admit to desiring children but consider it immoral if that desire was turned into action. They support one another to live with the tensions created by desistance. For an illuminating study of celibate paedophiles, see Goode, S. (2011). *Paedophiles in Society: Reflecting on Sexuality, Abuse and Hope*. Basingstoke: Palgrave.

2 Pereda, N., Guilera, G., Forns, M. & Gomez-Benito, J. (2009). The prevalence of child sexual abuse in community and student samples: A meta-analysis. *Clinical Psychology Review* 29(4), 328–338.

3 This is why the ideological support that offenders gain from academic arguments I criticised in the previous two chapters is important. Those arguments tend to be similar or identical self-justifications offered by individual offenders, but now writ large. See Mihailides, S., Devilly, G. & Ward, T. (2004). Implicit cognitive distortions and sexual offending. *Sexual Abuse: A Journal of Research and Treatment* 16, 333–350.

4 Damage to the frontal lobes of the brain, for example, creates social disinhibition. The retrospective speculations about the unending hyper-sexuality of Jimmy Savile include

his personality change after being caught in a mining explosion when he was a teenager that may have left him minimally brain damaged.

5 Hanson, R. & Morton-Bourgon, K. (2005). The characteristics of persistent sexual offenders: A meta-analysis of recidivism studies. *Journal of Consulting and Clinical Psychology* 73, 1154–1163.

6 Wurtele, S., Simons, D. & Moreno, T. (2014). Sexual interest in children among an online sample of men and women. *Annals of Sex Research* 26(6), 12–20.

7 Dawson, J., Bannerman, B. & Lalumière, M. (2014). Paraphilic interests: An examination of sex differences in a nonclinical sample. *Sexual Abuse: A Journal of Research and Treatment* 28(1), 20–45.

8 Ogas, O. & Gaddam, S. (2012). *A Billion Wicked Thoughts.* New York: Penguin/Random House; Ray, J., Kimonis, E. & Seto, M. (2014). Correlates and moderators of child pornography consumption in a community sample. *Sexual Abuse: A Journal of Research and Treatment* 26(6), 523–545.

9 Dombert, B., Schmidt, A., Banse, R., Briken, P., Hoyer, J., Neutze, J., et al. (2016). How common is males' self-reported sexual interest in prepubescent children? *Journal of Sex Research* 53(2), 214–223.

10 Seto, M. (2012). Presentation to the US Government Sentencing Commission. Presentation: Possible Relationship Between Sexually Dangerous Behavior and Child Pornography. Child pornography offenders: characteristics and risk to reoffend. See www.ussc.gov/policymaking/meetings-hearings/february-15-2012.

11 Confidence in this assumption comes from the data gathered by the StopSO organisation, which offers help to sex offenders and those yet to offend, but troubled by their sexual attraction to children. The data suggests that only 8% have never offended (www.stopso.org.uk/statistics/).

12 Estimates of extra-familial offending vary from 8 to 150 victims per perpetrator. Examples of this range can be found in Lockhart, L., Saunders, B. & Cleveland, P. (1989). Adult male sexual offenders: An overview of treatment techniques. *Journal of Social Work & Human Sexuality* 7(2), 1–32; Beckett, R. (1994). *Community-Based Treatment for Sex Offenders: An Evaluation of Seven Treatment Programmes.* London: Home Office.

13 Child sex abuse: More than 100 rapes with online link in past year. (2016). June 21. BBC News, UK. Available at www.bbc.co.uk/news/uk-36578945. Note that the police and NSPCC agreed on a 'tip of the iceberg' picture about offending.

14 In some cases, child sex offenders deemed to be mentally disordered are detained in secure psychiatric facilities, not prisons.

15 Primary prevention refers to the full prevention of an occurrence. Secondary prevention includes 'nipping problems in the bud' at an early stage. In this case, it might mean dealing early on with an adolescent offender before he progresses to a lifetime sexual interest in children. Tertiary prevention is basically the treatment or mitigation of a problem that is already well established.

16 Another example of libertarianism in legal reasoning, is that sex offenders released from prison should have the same right as another offender to foster or adopt children. See Reece, H. (2010). Bright line rules may be appropriate in some cases, but not where the object is to promote the welfare of the child: Barring in the best interests of the child? *Family Law Quarterly* 22(4), 422–448. The controversy this article provoked pointed up a dilemma about risk management. Prisoners are discharged and re-installed as full citizens once their sentence is served. In the case of child sex offenders, there are high rates of recidivism. *Ipso facto* there is a real albeit aggregate risk to potential victims. Because libertarian arguments are narrowly preoccupied with one set of individual rights (in this case offenders), the rights of others (in this case children) are set aside.

17 The experimental alternative though to treating offenders is to offer support to desisting or celibate paedophiles. An example of this innovation from Germany is Prevention Project Dunkelfeld, at present still being evaluated. See Beier, K., Neutze, J., Mundt, I., Ahlers, C., Goecker, D., Konrad, A., et al. (2009). Encouraging self-identified pedophiles and hebephiles to seek professional help: First results of the Prevention Project Dunkelfeld. *Child Abuse & Neglect* 33, 545–549.

18 Marques, J., Wiederanders, M., Day D., Nelson, C. & van Ommeren, A. (2005). Effects of a relapse prevention program on sexual recidivism: final results from California's Sex Offender Treatment and Evaluation Project (SOTEP). *Sexual Abuse: A Journal of Research and Treatment* 17(1), 79–107.

19 Hanson, R. & Morton-Bourgon, K. (2005). The characteristics of persistent sexual offenders: A meta-analysis of recidivism studies. *Journal of Consulting and Clinical Psychology* 73(6), 1154–1163.

20 Those struggling to desist might be helped if those who self-identify as being sexually attracted to children could come forward to be helped by the state. See Beier, K., Neutze, J., Mundt, I., Ahlers, C., Goecker, D., Konrad, A., et al. (2009). Encouraging self-identified pedophiles and hebephiles to seek professional help: First results of the Prevention Project Dunkelfeld. *Child Abuse & Neglect* 33, 545–549.

21 Strictly, a theory is a wide and abstract framework to account for a set of phenomena, and a model refers to a narrower practical application. However, it is common in human science for the terms to be used interchangeably.

22 Finkelhor, D. (1984). *Child Sexual Abuse: New Theory and Research.* New York: Free Press.

23 Hall, G. & Hirschamn, J. (1992). Sexual aggression against children: A conceptual perspective of etiology. *Criminal Justice and Behavior* 19, 8–23.

24 Ward, T. & Seighart, R. (2002). Toward a comprehensive theory of child sexual abuse. *Psychology, Crime and the Law* 9, 319–353.

25 Malamuth, N. (1998). The confluence model as an organizing framework for research on sexually aggressive men: Risk moderators, imagined aggression, and pornography consumption. In R. Green & E. Donnerstein (eds), *Human Aggression: Theories, Research, and Implications for Social Policy* (pp. 229–245). San Diego, CA: Academic Press.

26 Marshall, W. & Barbaree, H. (1990). An integrated theory of the etiology of sexual offending. In W. Marshall, D. Laws & H. Barbaree (eds), *Handbook of Sexual Assault: Issues, Theories, and Treatment of the Offender* (pp. 257–275). New York: Plenum Press.

27 Thornhill, R. & Palmer, C. (2000). *A Natural History of Rape: Biological Bases of Sexual Coercion.* Cambridge, MA: MIT Press.

28 Hewson, B. (2015). Compo culture and the child abuse panic: Historic sex abuse claims have fuelled the UK's compensation industry. *Spiked!* Available at www.spiked-online.com/newsite/article/compo-culture-and-the-child-abuse-panic/17145#.We-F_o-cEcA.

29 Smallbone, S., Marshall, W. & Wortley, R. (2008). *Preventing Child Sexual Abuse: Evidence, Policy and Practice.* Portland, OR: Willan Publishing.

30 Ostrom, V. & Ostrom, E. (1977). Public goods and public choices. In E. Savas (ed.), *Alternatives for Delivering Public Services: Toward Improved Performance.* Boulder, CO: Westview Press.

31 24 Hours in Police Custody. Channel 4, All 4, Programmes. Available at www.channel4.com/programmes/24-hours-in-police-custody/on-demand/61751-007 (also, see ★ in endnote 33).

32 In the UK and other countries, vigilante groups have sprung up to entrap would-be child sex offenders with decoy social media messages. Some are led by men who make it explicit, in the clips of their citizen's arrests posted online, that they are motivated by

their own victimisation as children. The targets are usually terrified and plead pathetically to no avail, though some show pompous indignation about their entrapment. The vigilantes might spend long periods, prior to an eventual police presence, of rehearsing the warranted dark fate that awaits their target in prison. Some onlookers to the exciting drama bay for the blood of the targets, try to assault them and some succeed. See Booth, R. (2013). Vigilante paedophile hunters ruining lives with internet stings. October 25. *The Guardian*. Available at www.theguardian.com/uk-news/2013/oct/25/vigilante-paedophile-hunters-online-police; The Paedophile Hunter. Channel 4, All 4, Programmes. Available at www.channel4.com/programmes/the-paedophile-hunter.

33 This documentary illuminated the concern about rough retributive justice in principle but also the practical challenges that vigilantism creates for the police. See Trott, F. (2015). Are 'paedophile hunters' hindering police? June 4. BBC News, UK. Available at www.bbc.co.uk/news/uk-32975562; *note that a second programme in the Channel 4 series (screened June 12, 2017) dealt with two successful prosecutions of child sex offenders, which did not rely upon the precarious entrapment tactics of vigilantes.

34 Friend, C. & Snyder, S. (2017). A response to "The Legacy of the Witch-Hunt Narrative". *Journal of Interpersonal Violence* 32(6), 979–1001.

35 Smallbone, S., Marshall, W. & Wortley, R. (2008). *Preventing Child Sexual Abuse*.

36 Therapy for victims risks individualising social problems and encourages a de-politicised culture of 'healing and reconciliation'. This might defuse the legitimate anger needed to maintain collective campaigns for justice. See Armstrong, L. (1990). Making an issue of incest. In D. Leidholt & J. Raymond (eds), *The Sexual Liberals and the Attack on Feminism*. Oxford: Pergamon.

37 Nelson, S. (2016). *Tackling Child Abuse: Radical Approaches to Prevention, Protection and Support*. Bristol: Policy Press.

38 Ibid., pp. 373–374.

39 Davies, L. & Duckett, N. (2016). *Proactive Child Protection and Social Work*. London: Sage.

40 What is wrong is relevant, but it is about rule transgressions and role failures. Psychiatric diagnoses rubber stamp ordinary normative judgements about these social processes. This begs a recurring question, then, about why some of us some of the time are distressed or alienated from others. Tracing biographical events is a window into distress and alienation. Point diagnoses derived from a 'present mental state examination' simply miss this point.

41 See National Crime Agency report on serious and organised abuse discussed at http://cdn.basw.co.uk/upload/basw_14328-9.pdf. A recent example is the case of Darren Williams in South Wales. In July 2017, the former youth worker was jailed for 11 years after abusing a child in an *in vivo* rape 3,500 miles away in the USA. During the live stream, his instructions included: 'Prove the video is live and smack him.' The Williams' case also highlighted that sentencing norms vary widely from court to court in a shared culture. Within two weeks of this UK case, another was reported with similar features. A Somerset primary-school teacher, Wayne Brooks, was only jailed for 20 months after joining 45 other paedophiles online to watch four cases of children abused, streamed live from America. He looked at the live rape of children and a recording on the same site of a six-month-old baby being abused. See Teacher jailed for watching live stream of child rape. (2017). August 1. BBC News, Somerset. Available at www.bbc.co.uk/news/uk-england-somerset-40796362. The sentencing contrast between these cases is bemusing.

42 Given that animals do not give their consent to being killed, milked or reared as beasts of burden, this is a wider inter-specific moral question than sexual contact alone.

43 Cohen, S. (2001). *States of Denial: Knowing About Atrocities and Suffering* (p. 286). Cambridge: Polity.

INDEX